MARRIAGE
and the IRISH:
a miscellany

D1342286

MARRIAGE
and the IRISH:
a miscellany

Salvador Ryan (ed.)

Wordwell

First published 2019
Wordwell Ltd
Unit 9
78 Furze Road
Sandyford Industrial Estate
Dublin 18
www.wordwellbooks.com

Copyright © The authors
Editing, design, typesetting and layout © Wordwell Ltd

Vol. 2 in the series entitled: Birth, Marriage and Death Among the Irish.

All rights reserved. No part of this book may be reprinted or reproduced or utilised in any electronic, mechanical or other means, now known or hereafter invented, including photocopying and recording, or otherwise without either the prior written consent of the publishers or a licence permitting restricted copying in Ireland issued by the Irish Copyright Licensing Agency Ltd, 25 Denzille Lane, Dublin 2.

ISBN: 978-1-9164922-2-6

British Library Cataloguing-in-Publication Data.
A catalogue record for this book is available from the British Library.

This publication has received support from the Scholastic Trust, St Patrick's College, Maynooth.

Typeset by Sophie Holford.

Copy-editor: Emer Condit.

Book design: Nick Maxwell.

Cover design: Ger Garland.

Front cover image: *The Old Grass Road*, Jack B. Yeats, courtesy of the Merrion Hotel, Dublin 2. Photograph by Hugh MacConville.

Printed by Digital Print Dynamics, Dublin.

Contents

Acknowledgements

In 2016 *Death and the Irish: a miscellany* was published by Wordwell Press. This present volume is the second in the series 'Birth, Marriage and Death among the Irish'.

My thanks to all who have made this volume possible since work first began on it over two years ago. I would first like to acknowledge the generosity of a number of institutions and individuals who have assisted in providing images for this collection, and also for the permission to use them: the National Gallery of Ireland; Triarc, Irish Art Research Centre, Trinity College Dublin, and in particular Prof. Rachel Moss; Castle Leslie Estate, and especially Sammy Leslie, Trustee, and Yvonne Murphy, Cultural Heritage Manager; Crawford Art Gallery, Cork, and Anne Boddaert; the National Museums of Northern Ireland and Stephen Weir, Picture Library Executive; Georgetown University Library and LuLen Walker; and the National Library of Ireland.

This project has received a grant from the Maynooth Scholastic Trust, and the D'Alton Fund, Maynooth for which I am most grateful.

I would also like to pay tribute to a number of people who have provided both practical assistance and moral support at various stages of the project, and in particular to Sharon Walsh, Jessie Rogers and Aoife McGrath.

To my own family in Thurles—Michelle, Michael, John Joe, Martin and Kieran—for the times when work on this book kept me away from home for longer than I would have wished, I will always be grateful for your forbearance.

I would also like to express my deep appreciation to Nick Maxwell and the staff at Wordwell Ltd for seeing this volume to print with their customary courtesy and efficiency.

Finally, this project could not have come to pass without the generous collaboration of a large number of contributors whose collective work makes this volume what it is, and it is to them that I owe the deepest gratitude. Sadly, one of the volume's contributors, John Glynn Douglas, passed away in February 2018, while the book was still in preparation. I can only hope that he would have been pleased with the collection that has emerged.

Salvador Ryan
10 September 2018

Foreword

Art Cosgrove

There is an abiding interest in the subject of marriage. Popular curiosity about how and why couples get together, and the ritual and customs surrounding their unions, is matched by the interest of legal, ecclesiastical, social and cultural historians in an institution which has a profound influence on the structure of society. This collection of essays ranges over the centuries, from the concept of marriage in early Irish law to its place in today's society, and provides evidence of the changes that took place in attitudes and practices as marriage evolved to match different social expectations.

One important constant was the acceptance of the principle that the consent of the two parties, freely given, was necessary for the validity of the union. Though often compromised in practice, it has survived as an essential element of what constitutes a marriage today. In earlier times it provided an opportunity, especially for women, to defy parents in the choice of a partner, though it was rare for a young woman of property to successfully challenge such a parental decision. Parental wishes could be frustrated, however, by the 'runaway match' or, more shockingly, by violent abduction.

Attempts to make marriage practices conform to the rules laid down by church or state often encountered opposition. The canon law of the church could not eliminate older attitudes based on early Irish law. The ideal that weddings be solemnised publicly in church was ignored by many who could validly exchange consent without recourse to the church in what were condemned as 'clandestine' unions, while the attempt at reform by the Council of Trent in 1563 in insisting that marriages were valid only if celebrated before a priest and at least two witnesses was frustrated by the failure to implement this ruling in Ireland until 1827. The divisions introduced by the Reformation in Ireland provided a further complication, and the dominance of the Established Church provided problems not only for Catholics and Presbyterians but also for other Protestant denominations. And Catholic dominance subsequently produced the infamous *Ne Temere* decree of 1907.

Ultimately regulation had to conform to the popular will. The legalisation of divorce in 1996 and of same-sex marriage in 2015 demonstrated the changes in attitudes and the power to enforce them. The growing number of people living together in partnership without civil or religious endorsement also reflects a view that relationships between couples are matters of private rather than public concern and, in some ways, are similar to the participants in 'clandestine' unions of earlier times.

These short essays (almost 80 of them) are a very welcome contribution to the story of marriage in Ireland and a stimulus to further research. This is a treasure trove to be explored not only by historians, anthropologists, sociologists and folklorists but also by anyone curious to discover how marriage has evolved in Ireland over the centuries.

1

The language of marriage

Sharon Arbuthnot

The Marriage Act of 2015, which gave full marriage rights to same-sex couples, is known in Irish as *An tAcht um Pósadh*. The term used here for 'marriage', *pósadh*, derives ultimately from Latin *sponsare*, the same verb that gave us English 'espouse'. The earliest surviving examples of *pósadh* and related words seem to be from the eleventh or twelfth century, however, and within the Gaelic legal system the union of marriage came under the broad category of *lánamnas*.

The word *lánamnas* actually appears in some of our earliest sources of evidence for Irish, in glosses on Latin thought to have been written around the year 800, and it is still current in the modern language in the revised spelling *lánúnas*. In Modern Irish legal terminology *lánúnas* is sometimes set against *pósadh*, so that *pósadh nó lánúnas* is used to mean 'marriage or cohabitation', the latter acknowledging the status of those who live together without entering into marriage. Such usage is entirely in keeping with the sense of earlier *lánamnas*, for historically this term was applied to a number of different relationships that existed between people, the common factor in all of these being the presumption of sexual intercourse.

The formally recognised union of marriage was known in Early Irish as *lánamnas dligthech*, *dligthech* meaning 'lawful', and this and other unions are described in an eighth-century legal tract, *Cáin Lánamna*. The range of 'relationships' covered by *lánamnas* in this text extends so far as to include non-consensual encounters. *Lánamnas éicne*, for example, incorporates the word *éicen* 'force', while *lánamnas sleithe*, literally 'intercourse that is stolen', refers to sex with an unconscious woman. Clandestine affairs fell into the category of *lánamnas táide* 'secret intercourse', and this spawned a cluster of related terms such as *fer táide* and *ben táide*, which refer respectively to the male and female parties involved, and *clann táide*, the offspring of such a relationship.

Concern with specifying the nature of the relationship from which children arose is bound up, of course, with issues of inheritance. It is a query over the legitimacy of Christ, though, that provides us with perhaps the earliest extant example of imported *pósadh* being brought into association with the native vocabulary of *lánamnas*. A Late Middle Irish religious text attributes to Pontius Pilate the words *mac lánomna pósta* 'the son of a married couple', as he negotiates debate as to whether Christ was born in wedlock. In Modern Irish, *lánúin phósta* is still used to refer to 'husband and wife', but Scottish Gaelic opts instead for the term *càraid phòsta*. The latter has an interesting history, for the first element derives from Old Irish *córait* and originally appeared in references to the fastening or yoking together of two working animals. In a natural extension, the word came to be applied to the animals themselves and then to people who were bound together in some metaphorical way—medieval examples show *córait* used of companions, rivals and even saints who had the same feast-day.

Córait is remarkable in its survival, but through the centuries various aspects of marriage and betrothal have been conveyed in Irish using the language of binding and contract. *Commám* is best attested in the senses 'marriage' and 'wife' yet the basic meaning was 'joint yoke'. Similarly, early *ben chengail* meant 'a wife' and *ceangailte* is still used to mean 'joined in matrimony', yet in other contexts *ce(a)ngal* refers to a fetter. And the Old Irish verb *ar-naisc* is often defined as 'gives in marriage', but related *naiscid* could be both 'takes captive' and 'extracts a pledge'. In Modern Irish, 'becoming engaged' is expressed using an idiom which translates as 'giving hand and word' (*lámh is focal*). This is probably based on the idea of sealing a bargain by joining hands, as encapsulated in Old Norse *handfesta* and Middle English *hondfesten*, which had also the specialised sense of 'betroth'.

Medieval Irish preserves a rather different phrase incorporating the word *lám* 'hand' which is somehow connected with wedlock, although the exact connotations and usage are ill understood. The phrase in question is basically *feis láime ocus leptha*, though there are some variations. *Feis*, the key word here, refers to spending the night in ways that do not generally involve sleeping, and so this verbal noun covers a range of activities, including feasting, keeping watch and having sex. In its senses of 'feasting' and 'entertainment', it forms part of *banais* 'a wedding'. The start of the word *banais* derives from *ben* 'a woman; a wife', and so *banais* can be analysed as literally 'wife-feast'. *Feis láime ocus leptha*, on the other hand, seems to be a reformulation of expressions such as *foaid ar láim ocus ar lepaid lé* 'he spends the night, beside and on a bed, with her'. Notably, the thirteenth-century narrative *Acallam na senórach* employs a version of the phrase of interest to us to describe the interactions of the first couple to be married by St Patrick. The phrase appears here as *feis leaptha ocus lámdéirigthi* and seems intended to mean that the couple consummated their marriage; Whitley Stokes memorably translated it as 'the feast of bedding and handspreading'.

Although the early word *banais* 'a wedding' continues today as *bainis* in Modern Irish and *banais* in Scottish Gaelic, it is not particularly well attested in medieval sources. This is perhaps because marriage was not necessarily accompanied by a public ceremony or celebration in pre-modern times. That the word *caillech* seems to be used only rarely in its original sense of 'married woman' may be attributable to the same fact. *Caillech* stems directly from *caille* 'a veil' and means literally 'veiled one'. Thus early examples refer either to married women (as the veiling of the bride was an essential part of the Christian marriage ceremony) or to nuns (who were also associated with veiling or head-covering). Fortunately, such historical ambiguities have been resolved today: in its modernised spelling, *cailleach* is generally a term for an 'old woman', *bean rialta* has been adopted as the Irish for 'nun', and for 'married woman' the language avails again of borrowed *pósadh* and gives us *bean phósta*.

Sources

Information on the pre-modern language has been drawn mainly from the Royal Irish Academy's *Dictionary of the Irish language*, which was first published between 1913 and 1976 and is now available in a revised electronic version (released in 2013) at www.dil.ie. Modern forms are cited from Niall Ó Dónaill (ed.), *Foclóir Gaeilge–Béarla* (Dublin, 1977). The phrase attributed to Pontius Pilate can be found in Robert Atkinson (ed. and trans.), *The passions and the homilies from Leabhar Breac*, Todd Lecture Series ii (Dublin, 1887), l. 2669. For the extract from *Acallam na senórach*, see Whitley Stokes (ed. and trans.), '*Acallamh na senórach*', Irische Texte iv:1 (Leipzig, 1900), l. 7841 and p. 270.

2

Cáin Lánamna: 'the Law of Couples'

Charlene M. Eska

áin Lánamna 'the Law of Couples' is one of the most comprehensive legal sources we have for marriage and divorce in medieval Ireland. The law tract itself dates from *c.* AD 700 on linguistic grounds, and the accompanying legal glosses and commentary span the period from the eighth to the sixteenth century, showing a continuous interest in the topic on the part of medieval Irish lawyers. *Cáin Lánamna* is part of the *Senchas Már* 'Great Tradition' collection of law tracts. Only one complete copy of the text survives, and it is found in the fourteenth-century manuscript Trinity College Dublin MS 1316 [H.2.15A]. Fragments of the text are also found in later manuscripts, which is why we find a much wider linguistic range for the commentaries than that found in the main manuscript of the text.

It is important to state from the outset that the tract does not provide any information on any form of marriage ceremony, nor does it detail reasons for divorce. Rather the text provides a description of the number of recognised unions according to Irish law. A 'union' in the text is treated as any situation that can result in children, whether the situation is 'legal' or 'illegal'. Despite being written in a Christian context, the text largely ignores canon law and instead focuses on issues surrounding property. Marriage was considered to be a contractual arrangement between the spouses and their respective families. The legal language used to describe marriage is largely the same as that used to describe other types of contracts. Many readers approaching the laws for the first time are often struck by how similar they are to modern laws in several ways; for example, the text discusses and provides provisions for what would be considered the equivalent now of a 'no fault' divorce. Another fact that needs to be borne in mind is that whatever property each spouse brings to the marriage is the same property each spouse leaves with should the couple divorce. In the case where one spouse has grounds for divorce based on the behaviour of the other spouse, e.g. infidelity, then the profits from their household are awarded to the injured party. The tone of the text is never preachy; it is strictly practical.

The text discusses the following types of unions: *lánamnas comthinchuir* 'union of joint contribution', *lánamnas mná for ferthinchur* 'union of a woman on a man's contribution', *lánamnas fir for bantinchur* 'union of a man on a woman's contribution', *lánamnas fir thathigtheo* 'union of a man visiting', *lánamnas airite for eráil* 'union accepted at the instigation (of the man)', *lánamnas foxail* 'union by abduction', *lánamnas éicne* 'union by rape' and *lánamnas genaide* 'union of mockery'. In the first of these, *lánamnas comthinchuir*, the text presents a situation where each of the spouses is of the same social status and each brings the equivalent value of property, be it movable or non-movable property, into the marriage. In *lánamnas mná for ferthinchur*, the husband contributes substantially more property than the wife and thus has more control over aspects that affect the running of the household, such as making contracts and purchases. In *lánamnas fir for bantinchur* we find the opposite situation. Here the wife contributes most of the property and has the upper hand in terms of making contracts and purchases without her husband's permission.

The remaining unions discussed in the text are of declining respectability, and the text concludes with a series of unions that were considered illegal and reprehensible. In *lánamnas fir thathigtheo*, the text presents a scenario in which a woman is visited in her home by a man with the consent of her family. In *lánamnas airite for eráil*, the woman has entered into a relationship and gone away with the man but without the consent of her kindred. The next union, *lánamnas foxail*, presents a situation where the woman has been abducted with her consent and clearly without the consent of her kindred. These three types of union are not as formal as the first three discussed. The final two unions were considered highly illegal and heavy fines were imposed on those who committed or instigated the actions described. Regarding *lánamnas éicne* 'union by rape', the law recognised that rape could be perpetrated by an outright act of violence or by 'stealth', which included having non-consensual sex with a woman who had passed out from intoxication. Both scenarios were illegal and carried heavy fines for the perpetrator. Early Irish law also made special provisions for those of unsound mind. Those not considered legally competent could not enter into contracts, and anyone who brought together two such people for sport, i.e. in *lánamnas genaide*, would be responsible for any children that should result, along with paying heavy fines.

Further reading

Charlene M. Eska (ed.), *Cáin Lánamna: an Old Irish tract on marriage and divorce law* (Leiden, 2010).

Fergus Kelly, *A guide to early Irish law* (Dublin, 1988).

Fergus Kelly (ed.), *Marriage disputes: a fragmentary Old Irish law-text* (Dublin, 2014).

3

Cétmuinter: the Old Irish term for 'spouse' and its interpretation

Liam Breatnach

One of the earliest Old Irish law texts, the late seventh-century *Senchas Már*, consists of around 50 tracts concerning various legal issues, of which two are devoted to different aspects of marriage and one to the related issues of inheritance and paternity. The subject of marriage was thus fairly comprehensively covered, and in this text we find that the word *cétmuinter* is well established, with at least 25 instances. It is also well attested in other Old Irish law texts, and the examples are numerous enough to establish that it can be used either of the husband or the wife and that accordingly it means 'spouse'. An example which neatly illustrates the point is *Mád cétmuinter, is díles uile dond í bís inna mámaib téchtaib* 'In the case of a spouse, the profit from everything is forfeit to the party that carries out his/her marital duties', where the word *cétmuinter* will apply to either the husband or the wife as the case may be.

It continued in use in other texts, legal and non-legal, mostly from the Old Irish (AD 600–900) and Middle Irish (AD 900–1200) periods. The latest example I know of is in the seventeenth-century life of Aodh Ruadh Ó Domhnaill, where it is used of a wife, and the only example I know of in Classical Modern Irish verse is in an elegy on Domhnall Mac Carthaigh, earl of Clancarty (d. 1596), where it is used of a husband. In addition to *cétmuinter*, an abstract *cétmuinteras* is attested in the early law texts, and this can be translated as 'marriage'. Most occurrences, then, of both words are to be found in texts belonging to the pre-Norman period.

These are the basic facts regarding this word. As in the case of any other ancient language, however, the meanings of words in Old Irish can only be determined by a careful study of the way they are used in the texts in which they occur, and so the development of a dictionary of Old Irish must go hand in hand with the work of editing and translating Old Irish texts. The case of *cétmuinter* is an interesting example of how lexicographical standards can be overridden by unsubstantiated preconceptions. What is at issue here is that one often finds this word translated as 'chief wife', which implicitly underpins a notion of polygamy in Early Christian Ireland; the question then arises as to where it originated and whether there is any justification for it.

The best way to approach this question is to look at how the term *cét-muinter* was treated in the first modern editions of the law texts in which many of the examples of this word are found, namely in the *Ancient laws of Ireland*, published between 1865 and 1901. In the texts edited in volumes 1 (1865), 2 (1869) and 3 (1873), it is translated as 'first wife'. In those in volume 4 (1879) it is clearly used of both a woman and a man and is translated as 'first wife' and 'first husband'. By the time of publication of volume 5 (1901) the meaning of the word was much better understood, and a fairly accurate definition was given on p. 145 as 'Lit. "first-household" *prima familia*; but it is applied equally to the male or female spouse'.

We can see, then, as more examples came to light, a progress in understanding that it could apply to a husband as well as to a wife. Although it is not clear from the definition cited whether or not it was realised that the word means simply 'spouse', not 'first wife/husband' as opposed to 'second wife/husband', there is nevertheless no trace of the rendering 'chief wife' in any of these five volumes. The extraordinary thing, however, is that all of this was completely ignored by Robert Atkinson, the editor of the glossary which took up the final volume (6), published in 1901. The definition supplied there for *cétmuinter* is 'first, chief wife', plain and simple. In asserting that the word applied to the wife alone, he ignores the evidence of the preceding volumes, but much worse is the introduction for the first time of the notion of 'chief wife', with no explanation whatsoever. Now, while 'first wife' is erroneous it is not synonymous with 'chief wife'; the former presupposes a series of marriages, whereas the latter presupposes polygamy, specifically polygyny. One can only conclude that Atkinson took it for granted that polygamy had to have been normal in Early Christian Ireland, and was determined to embed this notion in the vocabulary of terms relating to marriage in Old Irish.

Worse still is the fact that the invented 'chief wife' did not remain as simply an aberration on the part of Atkinson in 1901. While a number of scholars, such as Kuno Meyer and Rudolf Thurneysen, subsequently pointed out that *cétmuinter* means simply 'spouse' and applied to both husband and wife, Atkinson's preconceptions were given a major boost with the publication in 1968 of the first fasciculus for the letter C of the Contributions to a *Dictionary of the Irish language* (Dublin 1913–75). The definition of *cétmuinter* supplied there is nothing other than a step backwards, in that precedence is given to the mistranslation 'chief wife' and the examples referring to the husband are downplayed. The formulation of its definitions ignores the work of previous scholars and is inconsistent. After all, if it is supposed to mean 'chief wife' when referring to a woman, then surely it should mean 'chief husband' when referring to a man. It would have been better if, in this extraordinarily regressive account, the *Dictionary* had drawn the line at all forms of polygamy rather than solely polyandry. This account is surely the main reason for the persistence of the rendering 'chief wife' or the variant 'primary wife' in works that appeared after its publication.

The compound word *cétmuinter* always refers to an individual and consists of two elements; the first element is *cét-* 'first' and the second element is *muinter*. The latter word is an Old Irish borrowing of Latin *monasterium* and can mean not only an ecclesiastical community but also a lay community or household, as well as an individual member of a household. The compound then means 'primary member of a household'. The ideal household will have at its head a married couple who will be the two 'primary members of the household'. In other words, marriage will ideally be between a husband and wife who are propertied and with a stable household. Only a *cétmuinter* is a wife or husband, and only their children are fully legitimate, as brought out in the legal term *macc cétmuintire* 'son of a spouse'. The creation of this compound, with its second element deriving from Latin *monasterium*, must surely be dated to the Early Christian period in Ireland, and it, as well as the compound *cétmuinteras*, form two crucial elements in the vocabulary of terms relating to marriage in pre-Norman Ireland.

The notion of polygamy in medieval Ireland is one that continues to be asserted, but no matter how often the mistranslation of *cétmuinter* as 'chief wife' is repeated it is no substitute for evidence. Over the last 150 years or so, we have had the fond notion of polygamy in competition with the actual evidence of the early Irish sources. One can only hope that the greater weight will be given in future to the sources.

Further reading

Liam Breatnach, *The Early Irish law text Senchas Már and the question of its date*, E.C. Quiggin Memorial Lectures 13 (Cambridge, 2011).
Liam Breatnach, 'On Old Irish collective and abstract nouns, the meaning of *cétmuinter*, and marriage in early mediaeval Ireland', *Ériu* **66** (2016), 1–29.

4

How early Irish canon lawyers dealt with St Augustine's indecent proposal

Thomas O'Loughlin

I doubt if many of those who saw the 1993 Hollywood blockbuster *Indecent proposal*—or, indeed, who read Jack Engenhard's 1988 novel on which the film is based—realised that the central element of the plot can be found in a book by Augustine of Hippo (354–430) written in 393. The novel's/film's basic idea is a simple one: a wife can save her husband from financial disaster if she accepts 'an indecent proposal' from another man to have sex, for which he will pay the enormous sum needed to cover her husband's gambling debts. The story's ups and downs made a great film but, on reflection, it raises some very interesting ethical problems about prostitution, sex outside marriage and, on a larger scale, what constitutes love, commitment and the place of the duty to help within a friendship. So what was Augustine's take on this?

Augustine in his book *On the Sermon on the Mount* (one of his earliest writings dedicated to the exegesis of the New Testament) has to comment on this statement: 'whoever marries a divorced woman commits adultery' (Mt. 5:32). This prompts Augustine to ask whether a woman marrying a divorced man would also have committed adultery. This leads to another question: could a man have sex with another woman, with his wife's permission, such that it would not constitute fornication? Augustine is aware that this happened in the past—there are instances in the Book of Genesis (e.g. 16:1–6)—and he wishes to point out that, while it was permitted then, it is no longer permitted in the new age of the Christ. Augustine then recalls that the same happened with wives when they had sex with others, with their husband's or father's permission (indeed, at their bidding) and without blame (e.g. Gen. 12:10–20 or 19:8). Could such instances amount to permission for a man to have guiltless sex provided that (a) he had his wife's permission, (b) the woman was not another man's wife and (c) the woman was not divorced? Augustine was troubled by the question, for his reply grasps at a straw: this could not be permissible because, if it were, a wife would have an equal right to have sex with another man (unmarried and not divorced) with her husband's permission. For Augustine, however, this idea of open sex for women is wholly morally repugnant to all! That Augustine was troubled by his grasping at straws can be seen in his statement that 'sometimes cases occur' when a woman has to have sex with another man *for her husband's sake* (this was the case with Abram in Gen. 12—and Augustine is not happy with an explanation that it was a different era) provided that it is with his permission.

He then tells of a case that he believed happened in Antioch about 50 years earlier—in the reign of the Emperor Constantius (reigned 337–61) and therefore in the current 'age of the Christ'—when a man was obliged to pay a pound of gold as tax to an enraged governor named Acyndinus. This wicked governor threatened the man with death unless the money was paid in full by a deadline. As the day came closer, the man was no nearer to assembling the gold and death loomed. As it happened, the man's wife was exceedingly beautiful but had not a penny she could give her husband in his hour of need. Luckily, there was a very wealthy man in the city who was madly in love with her and he sent her a message to say that he would pay the whole pound of gold for one night's sex with her. The woman submitted the offer to her husband 'because he had authority over her body and told him she was willing to do this for his benefit because her chastity belonged to him as her husband and he had dominion over her body'. The husband gave her permission, and she went and spent the night with the rich man, yielding to his carnal desires, but, Augustine notes, she only 'gave her body to her husband'. The story now takes on the whole character of a melodrama—or perhaps a farce. The rich man gave her the gold but then secretly substituted a pound of clay! The woman was not going to be outwitted: she proclaimed publicly what had happened, what the rich man promised and how he sought to defraud her. Then came the great denouement: the governor relented and the woman got possession of the land from which the clay was taken.

Despite this account having all the hallmarks of a yarn, Augustine believed that it was an actual event; and rather than finish the account with some statement like 'and they all lived happily ever after', he says: 'From this event I will make no case for either side of the argument. Each person must judge it for himself … for what that wife did becomes less repulsive when we know the whole situation … but … fornication is still a great evil' (*De sermone Domini in monte* 1, 16, 48–50). But what has all this to do with Ireland?

Sometime in the later seventh century a group of Irish clerics—we do not know where and we can only guess at some of their names—produced one of the most revolutionary books in the history of church law, which we now call the *Collectio canonum hibernensis* ('the Irish canon collection'). What was new about this collection was that it assembled legal materials (from the Bible—its principal source—and councils, popes and the writings of 'the fathers' such as Augustine) and arranged them not only under specific headings but also in such a way that they could be used in legal argument. This was the first collection that was systematically arranged under major topics and then specific problems, and it also comprised a built-in jurisprudence intended to give guidance when legal authorities were in conflict. As such, it was the first of a string of works produced in the Middle Ages, with sequels in church law down to our own day. One of the questions asked in the *Collectio* was, as one would expect, whether every occasion of extramarital sex—or, at least, in the case where a woman has sex with a man who is not her husband—is culpable?

The reply not only makes explicit the various biblical passages to which Augustine only referred obliquely—which shows how careful their biblical scholarship was—but also makes use of the 'indecent proposal' story from him. Here is the full text (*Collectio canonum hibernensis* 38, 7):

> *On breaking the marriage bond without blame.*
> It is asked if there is any occasion when a woman can have intercourse with a man who is not her husband, while her husband is alive, without it being a crime. There are three such reasons.
>
> First, if she is coerced into intercourse with another, this does not break a marriage bond.
>
> Second, if it is brought about by someone to avoid an evil such as what Sarah did lest Abraham be killed by the wicked king [Gen. 12: 11–20].
>
> Augustine says: 'Or as happened recently when a rich man demanded a gold coin from a man who had not got the money to give. Now a certain rich young man said to the wife of the man who owed the money that if she would have intercourse with him, he would give her the money. Now she, knowing that she had not power over her own body [1 Cor. 7: 4], spoke to her husband about this. The husband gave thanks, permitted her to do this, considering that there was no desire, it was not adultery.'
>
> Third, if she be sterile, just as it is read in Genesis that Abraham and Jacob took their maids as wives [Gen. 16: 1–7; 29: 21–35].

Both the story and its later use in Ireland by canonists raises even more questions about the history of Christian moral theology than watching the film raises today about interpersonal ethics. While we might frown upon both Augustine and the Irish canonists for their assumptions about male authority in a marriage, and perhaps be even harder on the canonists in that they ask the question only in terms of a married woman having extramarital sex while Augustine can at least think of it in terms of both the wife and the husband, we should also note that the canonists have moved some way towards linking culpability with intention by linking desire and adultery. A more profound question, however, is this: both Augustine and the canonists believed that they were dealing with manifest eternal laws in this whole area, yet their use of the story shows that they somehow knew that life was never as simple as the mere restatement of such 'laws'. Nevertheless, neither Augustine nor the canonists could grasp that nettle directly. It was just more than they could get their heads around to face up openly to the messiness of life, human limitations and frailties, and how behaviour is situated within a web of cultural assumptions.

Further reading

Thomas O'Loughlin, 'Marriage and sexuality in the *Hibernensis*', *Peritia* **11** (1997), 188–206.

Thomas O'Loughlin, *Celtic theology: humanity, world and God in early Irish writings* (London, 2000), 109–27.

5

Secrets of the medieval Irish marriage bed

Catherine Swift

edieval Irish literature, like fantasy literature today, is not good on the details of 'happy ever after'. Most encounters between men and women depicted in this corpus of texts are brief, generally between human heroes and beautiful women of the Otherworld who appear out of a transcendental mist, agree to have sex and disappear again almost immediately, leaving behind nothing but a smile. '*Inum-bia-sa úair coibligi latt?*' is a question posed to these women by more than one optimistic Irish hero— 'Will I get an hour (or a less specific period of time) lying down with you?'

Our longest and most famous saga, *Táin Bó Cúailgne*, does, however, provide us with a description of a marriage bed. The opening words of the twelfth-century Book of Leinster version read: '*Fecht n-óen do Ailill ocus do Meidb íar ndérgud a rígleptha dóib i Crúachanráith Chonnacht, arrecaim comrad chind cherchailli eturru*', which in Ciaran Carson's 2007 translation is rendered, 'One night when the royal bed had been prepared for Ailill and Medb in Crúachán Fort in Connacht, they engaged in pillow talk'. At great assembly sites such as Crúachán there were particular structures known as *cotaltigi* or *both leptha* 'sleeping houses', while in smaller settlements the sleeping area appears to have been a partitioned-off section within a house, often described as *irscartad* or *imdae*, a cubicle or compartment. Royal beds were made comfortable for their inhabitants with furs (*imscinge*—based on a Norse loanword for skins) and down (*clúm*), but at a more basic level they were made up of layers of heather, ferns and straw, apparently held in place with planks or wattles that slotted into corner bed posts, which could be carved and decorated. A number of accounts imply that both the posts and the intervening slats could be of precious metal rather than wood, but it seems most likely that such descriptions were always intended to be fantastical. The saga *Aislinge Óenguso* refers to a welcome visitor appearing on such bedposts. Óengus, the son of the Dagda and the goddess Bóann, was sleeping one night:

Co n-accae ní, in n-ingin cucci for crunn síuil dó. Is sí as áilldem ro boí i n-Ére. Luid Oengus do gabáil a l-lámae dia tabairt cucci inna imdai.

He saw something, a girl coming towards him over the post of the bed. She was the most beautiful who was in Ireland. Oengus went to take her hand to bring her towards him into his compartment.

Other visitors were less welcome. An eleventh-century satire describes a bed in a guesthouse: 'The covering … was rolled, bundled, in the bed, and was full of lice and fleas. No wonder, truly, for it never got its sunning by day, nor its lifting at night.' Archaeological excavation has illustrated the contemporary truth of this, with the bedding from the ringfort at Deer Park Farms and from the houses in Viking Dublin often containing large quantities of both pests.

Ailill and Medb's pillow talk focused on the dangerous topic of who had gained most from their marriage. Ailill opens with the statement, 'It's a true word, girl, it's a lucky woman who's the wife of a good man', and follows this up with '*ar it ferr-su indiu indá in lá thucus-sa thú*'—'for you are better off today than the day I took you'. Medb points out that she was well off before that and immediately they are drawn into a heated discussion of the status of their respective families, their qualities as individuals and their personal wealth. The upshot was that they proved to be equal in every respect except for a white-horned bull, which, while born to Medb's herd, could not countenance being a woman's possession and had migrated to Ailill's. It was to remedy this lack that Medb began her ill-fated expedition north to capture the *Donn Cúailgne*, the Brown Bull of Cooley.

Such independent ownership of goods, including farm animals, was a hallmark of the highest grade of marriage contract, in which the spouse was termed *cétmuinter* or 'first amongst the household'. The *banais* or 'woman-feast' was the celebration of an alliance made by the parents and was marked by the transfer of considerable gifts between families as well as to both spouses, and these included the provision of the *díllat ligi* or bed coverings, apparently made by the bride. It appears that the female *cétmuinter* continued to own her share of such goods throughout the period of a marriage and was largely free to exploit them as she saw fit, within the legal constraints imposed by the couple's responsibilities to entertain their lord, their church, their extended family and their friends. Infringements of the marriage contract were calculated by reference to the original gifts and could include a failure to provide bedclothes, or even the provision of ones which were inadequate to cover both parties. Perhaps because of this continued legal importance of the

original arrangements, a wry synonym for futility was '*tinnsccra iar n-indsma*'—
'[debating] a marriage-gift after riveting'.

Following the marriage, the couple had different areas of responsibility:
the woman was in charge of almost all domestic activity in the immediate
vicinity of the dwelling place, while the man had a primary role in those
duties which took him to the outer parts of the settlement. The ideal partner,
according to the author of *Tochmarc Becfhola* ('The Wooing of Becfola'), would
have provided his or her services in considerate silence:

> She went before him into the house. This was a fine house with both
> cubicles and beds (*Amra an teg hi-sin itir irscartad ocus dérgudha*). He sat down.
> Then she sat down beside him. He reached out his hand as he sat and
> brought forth a dish of food for them. They both ate and drank and neither
> of them was drunk. There was no one in the house. They did not speak to
> each other. He went to bed. She slipped in beneath his cloak, between him
> and the wall. However, he did not turn towards her throughout the night …
>
> 'Why don't I remain with you?', she asked. 'It is indeed a bad union
> (*drochbanais*) for you', he answered, 'to stay with me and to forsake the
> king of Ireland and to follow me in soldiering and in exile.' 'Why don't
> we have intercourse?', she asked. 'Not this time', he replied. 'However, if
> the island becomes mine and if we are alive, I shall go to fetch you and
> you are the woman who will be with me always.'

A key purpose of the social organisation of marriage in early Ireland was the
generation of offspring and, according to the lawyers, *bean doguidtar caemda*—a
wife whose marital bed is spurned—had the right to seek a divorce. Liam
Breatnach has recently elucidated a similar situation as described from the
man's point of view. Canon law from early Ireland makes it clear that the
Church favoured monogamous relationships that remained intact throughout
the lifetime of both participants, but early eighth-century Irish churchmen
recognised that this was a societal ideal which could not always be enforced.
More secularly minded lawyers explicitly recognised the difficulties involved
in sustaining relationships when the female spouse was too ill to contemplate
pregnancy. Such women were termed *cétmuinter cróligi* or a bedridden spouse;
while her husband remained responsible for making sure she continued to be
looked after, he was also entitled to seek another partner:

> There exist three [kinds of] spouses, i.e. a spouse of betrothal (*cétmuinter
> urnadma*), a bedridden spouse (*cétmuinter cróligi*) and a spouse on top of

another (*cétmuinter for muin araile*). The bedridden spouse, a woman who is dead with regard to the rightful state of marriage. The spouse on top of another, a woman who has been affected by an impediment with regard to the rightful state of marriage, and what is required for the period of medical treatment for her is the major [period of] medical treatment of the three years and the three months. And if she recovers, they are to be together. And if she does not recover, if he has anyone whom he can send her back to, let him do so, and if not, let him take care of her until death, and he takes another wife; and that is the spouse on top of another.

Sagas such as *Tóruigheacht Dhiarmada agus Ghráinne* ('The Pursuit of Diarmaid and Gráinne') illustrate the more positive context that such legal rulings were designed to promote:

> '*Ní gan ádhbhar do-rineas an mhoch-éirghe so, a Oisín*', ar Fionn '*óir atáim lé bliadhuin gan mhnaoi gan bhaincheile ... ní gnáth suan ná sádhail dá dheanamh don tí theangmhas gan mhnaoi a dhiongmhála aige.*'

> 'Not without cause have I made this early rising, Oisín', said Fionn, 'for I am a year without a wife and without a female companion ... he is not wont to have slumber or comfort who is without a fitting wife.'

According to *Agallamh na Senórach* ('The Colloquy of the Ancients'), '*is ó mnaib do gabar rath nó amhrath*'—'it is from [married] women that fortune or misfortune is derived'. Our medieval texts do not, however, provide us with many descriptions of the companionship which married couples enjoyed outside the marriage bed, except, paradoxically, in the case of St Brigit and her bishop. Despite being celibate, these partners clearly ran their collective settlement of Kildare within the traditional arrangements of male and female areas of responsibility, with St Brigit being in charge of the domestic arrangements and the provisioning. Together they governed their church, so her biographer Cogitosus tells us, 'by means of a mutually happy alliance and by the rudder of all the virtues. By the merits of both, their episcopal and conventual see spread on all sides like a fruitful vine with its growing branches ...'. Presumably many married couples in early Ireland enjoyed similar felicity, but they kept their own counsel and did not confide in poets and storytellers. After all, as the lawyers made sure to warn us, '*ni coir fo brataib fer forinnet coemdai*'—'it is not right for a man who talks of the marriage bed to be under coverlets'.

Further reading

Máire Breathnach, 'A new edition of *Tochmarc Becfhola*', *Ériu* **35** (1984), 59–91.

Liam Breatnach, 'On Old Irish collective and abstract nouns, the meaning of *cétmuinter*, and marriage in early mediaeval Ireland', *Ériu* **66** (2016), 1–29.

Ciaran Carson, *The Táin* (London, 2007).

6

'The Wasting Sickness of Cú Chulainn'

Gregory Toner

'The Wasting Sickness of Cú Chulainn' tells the story of how Cú Chulainn fell in love with an Otherworld woman called Fand. Unfortunately, Cú Chulainn was already married, and when his lover arrived in Ireland she was confronted by his wife, Emer, who was lying in wait along with 50 armed women ready to kill her rival. The resulting dialogue is one of the most poignant and remarkable commentaries on marriage in Irish literature.

The tale is found in the late eleventh-century manuscript *Lebor na hUidre* ('The Book of the Dun Cow'). This early manuscript contains a conflation of two different versions of the tale produced by successive scribes. The original scribe copied an eleventh-century version of the tale, but a later reviser erased parts of the story and partially replaced them with an earlier version. These two versions show a large degree of continuity but present notably different views of women, the older providing a stereotypically misogynistic portrayal while the later one offers a remarkably fresh portrayal of virtuous, strong women. The women of Ulster in the older version are shown to be unfaithful, vain and frivolous, and Cú Chulainn dismisses them as whores. One day he fell asleep beside a lake and was attacked by two women, one of whom turned out to be Fand. The women beat him with whips until he was nearly dead, causing him to take to his sickbed, where he remained for a year. The wasting sickness bears many of the typical features associated with medieval depictions of lovesickness and it is clear that the supernatural female assault is an imaginative representation of love as a violent and debilitating attack by the object of the man's desire.

The later version deals with the subsequent events of the story, notably a confrontation between the three members of the love triangle, Cú Chulainn, Emer and Fand. Early Irish law legislated for the taking of concubines who would have had reduced legal rights as compared to the wife (*cétmuinter*). Cú

Chulainn's relationship with Fand would seem to have been formally recognised, and the deal between Cú Chulainn and the Otherworld king, Labraid, by which Cú Chulainn agrees to assist Labraid in battle in return for Fand's hand, is tantamount to a betrothal. Such arrangements are described in the law tracts, which recognise a 'betrothed concubine' (*adaltrach airnadma*). Betrothal was marked by the payment of a bride-price (*coibche* or *tinnscrae*) and, while this is not paid here, Cú Chulainn's military service was clearly performed in exchange for the woman. Strangely, Emer seems not only to acquiesce in the initial arrangements but also to positively encourage her husband's extramarital adventure in the Otherworld. When she found him ill in bed, it was she who diagnosed the cause of his illness as 'love of a woman' and urged him to seek the object of his affections.

Emer's sudden change in attitude to Cú Chulainn's affair, reflected in the subtitle 'The Only Jealousy of Emer', may partly be attributed to her public humiliation. She asks, 'What caused you, Cú Chulainn, to dishonour me before the women of the province and before the many women of Ireland, and before all honourable men?' Cú Chulainn is unable to understand Emer's objections to his relationship with Fand and, in an audacious and seemingly boneheaded act, he lists Fand's many virtues in an effort to persuade Emer of her worthiness as a concubine. Confronted with her violent rage, he declares: 'I avoid thee, woman, as every man avoids his yoke'. He uses a pun here on the words for 'yoke' and 'friend', so that Emer is characterised both as his friend and as someone to whom he is yoked by marriage. He asks her why he should not have a while (*denus*) in the company of another woman, which seemingly refers to the practice of sleeping with a concubine for specific periods of time.

The bringing of another woman into the house was a recognised ground for divorce in early Irish law and Emer, knowing this, warns Cú Chulainn that divorcing her might not be to his advantage. 'Perhaps it would not profit you to abandon me, lad, if you tried', she says. Cú Chulainn's attitude changes after she utters the striking line: 'Everything red is beautiful, everything new is bright, everything unattainable is lovely, everything familiar is bitter, everything absent is perfect'. This truism sums up a universal problem of the human condition and Emer concludes, 'everything known is neglected until all knowledge is known'. Desire can never be satisfied and will always leave us wanting more. The final turning point comes when she reminds him that she once lived with him 'in dignity', at which point Cú Chulainn declares that he still desires her and always will as long as he lives. The resolution does not provide a happy ending, however. Fand, who has already been divorced by her husband, Manannán mac Lir, is left distraught, and although Manannán returns to her, she is still truly in love with Cú Chulainn. Cú Chulainn goes mad and takes to the hills, returning to his people only after the intervention of druids. Emer, too, is left broken-hearted and has to take a magic potion to forget her jealousy.

The tale, in short, is an exploration of the dangerous consequences of married men entertaining fantasies of other women. Although Emer initially encouraged Cú Chulainn to act on his fantasy in order to rouse him from his illness, seemingly tolerating his infidelity in the Otherworld, it became unbearable for her in this world. The story emphasises the supremacy of faithful, monogamous marriage, which is the only form of sexual union that can allow a woman such as Emer to live in dignity, if not in happiness, with her husband.

Further reading

Myles Dillon, *Serglige Con Culainn*, Mediaeval and Modern Irish Series 14 (Dublin, 1953).

Gregory Toner, 'Desire and divorce in *Serglige Con Culainn*', *Ériu* **66** (2016), 135–66.

7

Penis captivus: a strange tale of sexual taboo in medieval Ireland

Anthony Shanahan

The Church has always had a difficult relationship with sex. As early as the writings of Church Fathers such as Augustine of Hippo, sex was identified with sin, and living a chaste life as a virgin became the spiritual ideal. These attitudes continued into the Middle Ages, as Church authorities increasingly sought to regulate and even ban certain sexual practices. The medieval Church taught that sexual contact was only permissible between a man and woman within the confines of marriage, and even then the Church sought to regulate both the nature and the timing of these relations. Sex was prohibited during certain times of the year, such as Lent, holy days and during a woman's menstrual flow. The only sexual position that was allowed was the missionary, and the only cavity into which a man was permitted to orgasm was the vagina, as alternatives were considered to be a form of contraception. Indeed, such was the perceived importance and sanctity of the male seed that for it to be spilled and wasted anywhere outside of the vagina was strictly taboo.

Church authorities were also, it seems, concerned with where married couples chose to engage in sexual relations, as evidenced by a particularly bizarre tale recounted by a Franciscan preacher working in Ireland in or around the year 1275 and included in a book of preaching exempla known to us as the *Liber Exemplorum*. He tells the tale of a man named Richer, who was having intercourse with his wife in a cell adjoining a church. Upon completion of the act, however, the tale relates how the husband found that he was stuck inside his wife 'like a dog' and the couple couldn't be torn apart. This unfortunate incident, as far as the medieval reader would have been concerned, was not merely an example of bad luck: it served to illustrate the very real dangers of having sex on holy ground. The couple's embarrassing predicament was deemed to be a direct result of having sex in a holy place, and their punishment, apart from the probable physical discomfort, was also the inevitable shame of being discovered in this state.

The issue of people having sex on sacred ground was not just the concern of one particularly zealous and imaginative friar; indeed, the story appears frequently, in a variety of literary genres, right across western Europe during the period. In some versions, intercourse occurs in a graveyard or near a holy relic; sometimes the man and woman are unmarried or even religious, and in others the couple can only be released after specific prayers have been said over them. The common theme throughout all these accounts, however, is that sex is deemed to have occurred in some type of sanctified area and, as a result, the couple become entangled and can only be separated after some period of time has passed.

Just how common it was for people to engage in sexual relations in holy places during the period cannot be known. It is certainly possible, though, that it happened on occasion. Churches during this period were not just spaces within which to pray; the church was an important social and community hub, hosting fairs and games, housing the sick and providing shelter for travellers and pilgrims. This made it a far more likely space for sexual contact to occur than in modern times. Furthermore, in an era in which the majority of the population lived in open-plan homes, without interior walls, and when most people's lives would have been lived in a more communal and public way than in the modern western world, privacy would have been difficult to come by, and a church may have provided a relatively dry, quiet and rare private space to tempt the amorous.

While it is impossible to ascertain just how often couples engaged in sex in sacred spaces, what is very clear is that Church authorities certainly believed that they were doing so. Countless religious writers from the period warn of the dangers of sex in sacred places, and the Church even had in place a particular ritual which was carried out to cleanse a holy site after either blood or seed had been spilled in it. The contamination was considered so egregious that no religious ceremonies could take place in the building until it had been purified, and the rite of purification could only be undertaken by a bishop.

While it is certainly possible that people in medieval Ireland were having sex in churches, it is highly unlikely that any of them, in fact, ever became stuck together like breeding dogs. While it is possible for the muscles of the vagina to spasm during intercourse, the condition (known as *penis captivus*) usually lasts only moments; in fact, not a single case of prolonged entrapment has been recorded by a physician in the twentieth century. It is far more likely that the tale is a fictitious but carefully constructed warning to would-be lovers. Some scholars argue that the tale reflects a deep-rooted male fear of the female sexual organs and female sexuality, or a fear of castration and emasculation. Certainly, it does bear some resemblance to the common and persistent folk-tale of the *vagina dentata*, in which hidden teeth within the vagina can bite down on the penis during coitus. While the origins of the story may be mysterious, its function is clearly a warning to would-be lovers that the church is not an appropriate place for intercourse and that the consequences of such an act can be immediate, severe and extremely embarrassing.

Further reading

Ruth Evans (ed.), *A cultural history of sexuality in the Middle Ages* (London, 2012).

David Jones (ed.), *Friars' tales: medieval sermon exempla from the British Isles* (Manchester, 2011).

Ruth Mazo Karras, *Sexuality in medieval Europe: doing unto others* (New York, 2012).

8

The thirteenth-century marriage that never took place

Freya Verstraten Veach

Perhaps the most famous marriage in Irish history is that of Aoife and Strongbow (Pl. 1). It has come to symbolise the close but often troubled relationship between the Gaelic Irish and the English of Ireland that it anticipated. Intermarriages such as theirs have proved open to interpretation, and historians, antiquarians and commentators have wondered whether they took place for love, expediency, diplomacy or territorial gain. Some have taken a romantic view, assuming that the English conquerors could not resist the charm of Irish women. Most modern historians, however, are unwilling to project such emotions on characters about whom we know very little. The more statistically minded among them have suggested that a lack of female companions brought over by the English necessitated marriages with Irish women. This is not a widely held opinion either, however, partially because it ignores the ties that conquerors could maintain with England. All in all, mixed unions remain a little enigmatic, though the general consensus is that, as in most other societies at the time, marriages took place for practical rather than romantic reasons.

Nevertheless, romantic inferences have proved hard to resist for some: the early modern antiquarian Roger O'Ferrall, for instance. In his genealogical tract 'Linea Antiqua' (completed in 1709) he related how Richard de Burgh (d. 1243) took 'Una or Agnes', the daughter of Aodh Ó Conchobhair, king of Connacht, hostage, fell for 'his faire Captiue' and married her. Clearly, this peculiar case of Richard and 'Úna' (we have no contemporary mention of her name) was romanticised in O'Ferrall's account. In the absence of personal records, how can we know how Richard felt about her? There is nonetheless a kernel of verifiable fact in the assertions. O'Ferrall claimed that after Aodh's death both his daughter and his wife were taken hostage, and held by Richard de Burgh and Hugh de Lacy. This, at least, can be partially proven. The Irish annals report that Aodh's son and daughter had been held hostage by the

English. They also state that, shortly after their release, Aodh's wife, Raghnailt, was captured and handed to (again unspecified) foreigners. This, however, occurred while Aodh was still very much alive, and neither the annals nor any other contemporary source mention a marriage between Richard and Aodh's daughter. On the contrary, the contemporary sources that mention Richard's wife, the Close Rolls, unequivocally state that her name was Egidia de Lacy, daughter of Walter de Lacy, lord of Meath. Knowledge of their marriage has survived because it involved a gift of land. Richard is recorded as holding the territory around Cashel, Co. Tipperary, given to him and Egidia by Walter on the occasion of their wedding.

So why make the mistake of marrying Richard to Úna? O'Ferrall likely merely repeated a 'fact' found in one of his sources, but it may have been especially persuasive to him for what we might consider a personal reason. Had this marriage occurred, Richard's son Walter de Burgh, earl of Ulster, would have descended from the Uí Fhearghail (O'Ferrall), as Aodh's wife Raghnailt was of Ó Fearghail parentage. This, in turn, would have meant that, through later de Burgh connections with the English royal family, Ó Fearghail blood coursed through the veins of the kings and queens of England, a fact that O'Ferrall highlights in his tract. There was, however, a more weighty reason to link Richard to Úna, and this, presumably, was why the mistake was made in the first place. A marriage between these two people could explain the transfer of the land of Connacht from the traditional kings of Connacht, the Uí Chonchobhair, to the later lords of Connacht, the de Burghs. It made sense because Richard was in effect granted Connacht in 1227, when Aodh Ó Conchobhair was deemed to have failed to keep to the terms of his own grant of the province and was deposed by the English. And this was also the point at which Aodh's wife and children were held hostage. These coinciding events were enough to lead to the conclusion that Úna must have married Richard de Burgh and Richard then became lord of Connacht in right of his wife.

It is a neat explanation but, as mentioned, demonstrably false. Richard's claim to Connacht went back to 1215, when he had been given a speculative charter for the province, although it had been kept secret and on hold. This may have been done to avoid further unrest in Ireland but, whatever the reason, by 1226 the time was deemed right to officially enfranchise Richard. As a result, Aodh's position as tenant-in-chief of the same territory became untenable. He was summoned to Dublin and quickly set aside. In May 1227 Richard's twelve-year-old grant was put into effect. He became lord of Connacht, holding all but five cantreds, which remained reserved for the Uí Chonchobhair. Although the latter kept their title of kings of Connacht, they officially held a much-reduced area from the English Crown. The fact that Úna's captivity more or less coincided with Richard's enfranchisement had been misinterpreted.

The problem is that later antiquarians and historians such as John Lodge, Charles O'Conor Don, James Hardiman and John O'Donovan accepted the mistake. 'Úna's marriage' was consequently aired to a wider audience by being mentioned in their respective works and repeated as fact many times over. The error was further compounded by the inclusion of a thirteenth-century marriage between the de Burghs and the Uí Chonchobhair in several Irish genealogies, though it does not always concern Richard and Úna—and, in all fairness, such an alliance does seem plausible. We know beyond doubt, however, that Richard's wife was Egidia, and we know that Úna cannot have wedded Richard in or around 1227. Richard had married Egidia sometime between 1217 and 1225, while he waited for his grant of Connacht to be activated, and she was Richard's widow when he died in 1243 on an expedition in France.

In short, it seems that cause and effect have been inverted. O'Ferrall (or his source before him) assumed that a marriage had taken place (out of love, no less), and that this had led to de Burgh's possession of Connacht. In an effort to explain the transfer of landholding in Connacht from the Ó Conchobhair kings to the de Burgh lords, a point was sought at which a marriage might solve the puzzle. All the while, the truth was simpler. Conquest, with English royal backing, caused the transfer. Inferences such as 'Úna's marriage' can mislead many generations of historians. This, however, should not stop us from trying to interpret the evidence, work out who married whom and why. It should merely make us proceed with caution.

Further reading

G.H. Orpen, 'Richard de Burgh and the conquest of Connaught', *Journal of the Galway Archaeological and Historical Society* (1911–12), 129–47.

Helen Perros (née Walton), 'Crossing the Shannon frontier: Connacht and the Anglo-Normans, 1170–1224', in T.B. Barry, R. Frame and K. Simms (eds), *Colony and frontier in medieval Ireland: essays presented to J.F. Lydon* (Hambledon, 1995), 117–38.

9

'Kindly and honourable companionship': some medieval Irish marriages[1]

Colmán Ó Clabaigh, OSB

Contracting a marriage in medieval Ireland brought the partners into a jurisdictional minefield. Within the Anglo-Norman colony the participants were subject to the strictures of English common law. In Gaelic areas the arrangement was governed by the prescripts of brehon law, first codified in the eighth century but which enjoyed remarkable influence and resilience into the early modern period. Overarching both of these systems was the canon law of the Christian Church, which from the eleventh century increasingly sought to regulate marriages by ensuring that they were contracted by parties acting of their own free will, untrammelled by coercion or external pressure, and conducted in public in the presence of a priest and witnesses. In this ideal ecclesiastical world, the wedding party gathered at the door of the church in the presence of family and friends after a threefold proclamation of the banns of marriage in the weeks leading up to the ceremony. This allowed witnesses to come forward and indicate any impediments to the union. These most frequently arose in the context of ties of consanguinity whereby the partners were linked within the fourth degree of kinship. Less frequently, impediments arose from ties of affinity whereby the couple were impeded by a spiritual connection such as godparenthood, or because of previous sexual or marital connections between their relatives. These impediments could be surmounted by dispensations granted by episcopal or papal authority, but this was a costly remedy and was availed of only by the upper echelons of society.

Many—perhaps the majority—of medieval Irish marriages were private affairs conducted by the parties themselves. The speaking of the words of marriage in either the present or the future tense followed by consummation was sufficient, and these unions were regarded as valid if clandestine marriages

---

1 For Maeve and Maurice, 13 July 2019

by both religious and secular authorities. The problems generally arose when one or other party wished to withdraw from the contract, and the surviving records from ecclesiastical and royal courts are replete with references to the many ways in which relationships could collapse. Then, as now, court records are not the place to look for evidence of happy, successful marriages, which by their nature were less likely to be reflected in the sources.

Paradoxically, such evidence as survives for happy marriages often occurs in the context of the grief felt by the remaining spouse after the death of his or her partner. The register of the Dominican friary of St Peter and Paul at Athenry gives a lengthy account of the amounts spent by Joanna Uffler to commemorate her husband, David Weder, who died in Bristol while on a business trip in 1408. The couple were devoted to the Athenry friars and had already presented them with vestments and altar furnishings, but this was as nothing compared to the Widow Uffler's largesse. In addition to repatriating her husband's remains at great expense, she also entertained all the mendicant friars of Connacht for a fortnight as they celebrated her husband's exequies, for which she provided 100 pounds of wax. She then rebuilt the east end of the priory church, installing a new window over the high altar, and paid for the reglazing of all the windows in the choir of the church. In addition, she built a bridge to connect the priory precinct to the town, provided a wooden chest for the silk and cloth-of-gold vestments that she and her husband had presented to the community, and imported a stone tomb with sculpted figures from England to mark her husband's burial place in the church. She was buried in the same tomb herself with her second husband, Sir Robert Gardiner.

In a Gaelic context, the 1524 obituary in the Annals of Connacht of Gormlaith, daughter of Aed Rua Ó Domnaill, provides another oblique insight into a happy and fulfilling relationship:

> O Domnaill's wife, Gormlaith daughter of Aed Rua, wife of Aed, son of
> Niall son of Conn, a charitable and humane generous woman to whom
> God gave a fair, good name in this world, and surely the true Kingdom at
> the last, died in the month of March. And as this couple afforded a kind
> and honourable companionship to one another in the world to the time
> of their death, so may their souls give to one another a cherishing and a
> companionship of glory in the presence of the Lord.

Perhaps, however, the most moving evidence of marital harmony is the grief-stricken lament composed by the thirteenth-century bardic poet Muireadach

Fig. 1—Athassel Priory, Co. Tipperary: fourteenth-century grave-marker for a married couple. Edwin Rae © Triarc, Irish Art Research Centre. With thanks to Prof. Rachel Moss.

Albanach Ó Dalaigh on the death of his wife Maelva, beautifully translated by Frank O'Connor:

> I parted from my life last night,
>   A woman's body sunk in clay:
> The tender bosom that I loved
>   Wrapped in a sheet they took away.
>
> The ancient blossom that had lit
>   The ancient bough is tossed and blown;
> Hers was the burden of delight
>   That long had weighed the old tree down.
>
> And I am left alone tonight
>   And desolate is the world I see

For lovely was that woman's weight
    That even last night had lain on me.

Weeping I look upon the place
    Where she used to rest her head—
For yesterday her body's length
    Reposed upon you too, my bed.

Yesterday that smiling face
    Upon one side of you was laid
That could match the hazel bloom
    In its dark delicate sweet shade.

Maelva of the shadowy brows,
    Was the mead-cask at my side;
Fairest of all flowers that grow
    Was the beauty that has died.

My body's self deserts me now,
    The half of me that was her own,
Since all I knew of brightness died
    Half of me lingers, half is gone.

The face that was like hawthorn bloom
    Was my right foot and my right side,
And my right hand and my right eye
    Were no more mine than hers who died.

Poor is the shade of me that's left
    Since half of me died with my wife;
I shudder at the words I speak;
    Dear God, that girl was half my life.

And our first look was her first love;
    No man had fondled ere I came
The little breasts so small and firm
    And the long body like a flame.

For twenty years we shared a home,
    Our converse milder with each year;
Eleven children in its time
    Did that tall, stately body bear.

It was the King of hosts and roads
    Who snatched her from me in her prime:
Little she wished to leave alone
    The man she loved before her time.

No King of churches and of bells,
    Though never raised to pledge a lie
That woman's hand—can it be true—
    No more beneath my head will lie.

In the priory church at Athassel, Co. Tipperary, an incised double effigy is mounted on the east wall of the presbytery (Fig. 1). Dating from the early fourteenth century, it depicts a married couple. The husband, on the right, faces the viewer full on; his wife, on the left, coyly views his profile while holding the staff of a floriated processional cross that both unites and overshadows them. Both are smiling. It is a gentle visual reminder that then, as now, couples just got on with it, that some lived happily ever after and that many believed that love conquered everything, even death itself.

Further reading

Art Cosgrove, 'Marriage in medieval Ireland', in A. Cosgrove (ed.), *Marriage in Ireland* (Dublin, 1985), 25–50.

Patrick Crotty (ed.), *The Penguin book of Irish poetry* (London, 2010), 126–8.

Gillian Kenny, *Anglo-Irish and Gaelic women in Ireland c. 1170–1540* (Dublin, 2007).

10

Poems, poets and marriage

Pádraig Ó Macháin

The variety of interpretations of marriage and associated themes is one of the many pleasures of Irish literary tradition. Irish medieval poets, musing less than seriously on the nature of love, spoke of the futile jealousy of the married man, whose wife was Love's servant and who, should she stray, was not responsible for her actions. In a similar vein, Brian Merriman, the renowned Clare poet of the late eighteenth century, created memorable verse-pictures of the misery of mismatched marriage and the case for the abandonment of clerical celibacy in the cause of desire and procreation. Merriman's poem was inspired in part by the vernacular love tradition, as was, a generation later, that of the blind poet Raftery, who expressed his persona's unrestrained love for a local servant girl in the following terms:

is in ainneoin dlí na cléire
go dtoghfainn thú mar chéile,
is a Dhé nár dheas an scéal sin,
duine ag éaló lena ghrá?

(and in spite of the law of the clergy, I would choose you for my wife, and, O God, wouldn't that be a pretty tale, a man eloping with his love?)

Marriage in Ireland, as elsewhere, was subject to more than just canon law, however, and the dowry, for example, was a long-established custom, enshrined in early Irish law along with the bride-price and other forms of marriage arrangement. The value of these payments could be substantial, and they remind us of the serious, economic aspect of marriage. It is recorded that in 1560 one Ulick Ó Bruadair gave a bull, 21 cows and three horses as a dowry for his daughter. The document that recorded this was written and witnessed by a priest. Three centuries earlier, bands of fighting-men appear in the dowries of Scottish women marrying Irish chieftains, while the marriage of the daughter of Ó Catháin of Coleraine to Aonghus Óg of Islay, towards the end of the thirteenth century, was the occasion for the transfer of 24 sons of noble birth to Scotland as her dowry.

In some of their work the court poets of the bardic era took their cue, albeit expressed figuratively, from this element of exchange in marriage arrangements. At the same time, they were careful to emphasise the parity of esteem between the married couple, for wives could be important patrons of poetry in their own right, as well as conduits to the largesse of their husbands. A fifteenth-century poet, celebrating the marriage of Aodh Ó Néill and Fionnghuala, daughter of Ó Conchubhair Failghe, stresses that they are the perfect match for each other:

> Is meadh chomhthrom dá chéile
> mac Briain is a bhainchéile:
> tríd nach claon meadh don dá mheidh
> fear mar Aodh i n-a haigheidh.

> (Equally balanced are Brian's son and his wife so that neither side of the
> scale is lowered even when such a man as Aodh is weighed against her.)

Aodh, who was killed in 1444, was head of the Clandeboy branch of the family, based in south Antrim and north Down. Fionnghuala (d. 1493), the widow of an Ó Domhnaill, was daughter of An Calbhach Ó Conchubhair from present-day County Offaly. The poet argues that this Leinster–Ulster alliance reflects the settlement of a legendary debt. This is just a poetic device, of course, and, the Ó Néills being famous for their sponsorship of poetry, and Fionnghuala's mother being particularly noted for her generosity to poets, it is not surprising that such generosity receives the greatest attention in the epithalamium:

> Ní léir dóibh an díoghbháil chruidh,
> Aodh is inghean an Chalbhaigh;
> eire a n-oinigh, leath ar leath,
> le croidhibh eile is aidhbhseach.

> (Aodh and the daughter of An Calbhach are heedless of the depletion of
> their wealth, whereas others would think the weight of their respective
> generosity to be too much.)

One hundred years later, the marriage of another member of the Ó Néill clan—Máire, the daughter of Conn Bacach (of the main branch of the family)—to the famous Somhairle Buidhe Mac Domhnaill was again seen by a poet as a settlement of an old debt, this time one between Ireland and Scotland. The emphasis in this poem is on the bride, and the poet argues that Máire's superlative pedigree, which boasts 60 kings, means that, should she go to live in Scotland, Ireland will have got the worst of the bargain. Máire's beauty, however, will blind her husband and his followers to the attraction of their native country and will cause them to settle in Ireland, so that she will not be lost after all:

'Na bhfál eatorra is Alba
atáid na ruisg réallanda,
's an ghruaidh fhinngheal dá n-éir goil,
a inghean Í Néill nároigh.

(O daughter of noble Ó Néill, a barrier between them and Scotland are
your starry eyes and beautiful warm face.)

Just as poets viewed themselves as interpreters of the mythic, symbolic marriage of the rightful ruler with the land he ruled, so they also partook in equally ancient customs reflected in actual marriages. The bardic poet, for example, claimed the right to the bride's wedding clothes. To cite another example, in a type of wedding poetry greatly different from the formal epithalamia mentioned above, the weightiness of strategic family alliances is set aside for the more humorous, ribald concerns of the consummation of the marriage itself. This has to do with the communal celebration of marriage—an ancient concept—and the role of the jester (or *crosán*) in the bedding ritual: one of the outstanding Irish poets of the seventeenth century, Dáibhí Ó Bruadair, has left us memorable wedding poems of this type.

The wedding might also be a time of sadness and nostalgia for those for whom such events were but a distant memory. In one of a sequence of poems that achieved a wide circulation in Ireland and Scotland, the thrice-widowed and now destitute queen Gormfhlaith, a historic figure of the early tenth century, is depicted as expressing her grief at the sound of a wedding party:

Gáir bhainnsi san tighsi amuigh:
gibé dá dtabhair meanmuin

atá neach dá dtabhair brón
ag éisdeacht ris gach roghlór.

(The din of a wedding in the house outside: to whomever it brings happiness there is one to whom it brings grief listening to every loud voice.)

Gormfhlaith seems to be a real-life reflex of the ancient and much-married sovereignty goddess Sentane Bérre, the 'Old Woman of Beare'. In the famous tenth-century lament attributed to her, the Old Woman nostalgically contrasts her decrepit state with the excitement of young girls at May time. The association of marriage with the fertility and growth of summer was reflected in the later custom of demanding May Balls (decorated hurling balls)—together with money and refreshments—from recently married couples for the celebration of May Day, a custom attested to in Irish and English by commentators of the eighteenth and nineteenth centuries. The balls were competed for—sometimes not without bloodshed—and hung on maypoles. As with other marriage customs, we again find the poet on hand to document such an occasion. A renowned eighteenth-century poet of County Cork, Seán Ó Murchú na Ráithíneach, records how he himself used his poetry to request a May Ball of a neighbour, Pádraig Ó hÓgáin, who had been married in April 1725. He leaves the request until the final verse of the poem, which otherwise praises Pádraig's virtues and talents, and which demonstrates yet again the enduring and central role of the poet in so much of Irish tradition:

Táid taoisigh tofa an phobail d'aonfhóbairt,
dá mhaoimh gurb ort téid cothrom léarthóide
d'íoc led thoil gan doic dá n-aosógaibh,
chun grinn do nochtadh ar cnuic 's ar réidhmhóintibh.

(The elected community leaders are unanimous that you are the one to sponsor the Ball for the young people, freely and cheerfully, so that fun may be had over hills and moors.)

Further reading

Osborn Bergin, *Irish bardic poetry: texts and translations with an introductory lecture* (ed. D. Greene and F. Kelly) (Dublin, 1970).
Kevin Danaher, *The year in Ireland* (Cork and Dublin, 1972).
Dubhghlas de hÍde, *Abhráin agus dánta an Reachtabhraigh* (Dublin, 1933).

Margo Griffin-Wilson (ed.), *The wedding poems of Dáibhí Ó Bruadair* (Dublin, 2010).

Lambert McKenna, *Aithdioghluim dána* (Dublin, 1939–40).

Torna [Tadhg Ó Donnchadha], *Seán na Ráithíneach* (Dublin, 1954).

11

Marriage and the ecclesiastical courts in mid-fifteenth-century Ireland

Sparky Booker

Popular imaginings of medieval women, arising in large part from depictions of the medieval world on the stage, on screen and in works of fiction, tend to give these women little control over their fate, especially in terms of choosing their marriage partners. This vision of medieval women and marriage is not entirely groundless, and in many instances, perhaps particularly among élite families, marriages were contracted without much input from the women involved: marriage was a crucial strategic tool, used to cement alliances, acquire lands and pursue other practical aims rather than to suit a woman's wishes. Of course, the two are not mutually exclusive, and there is no reason to think either that women's wishes were always ignored or that women and girls were not just as invested as their male relatives in making a good strategic match. Moreover, in those cases in which a woman was dead set against the husband her family chose, there were some avenues of resistance open to her. One was the ecclesiastical courts. Canon law held that marriages were not valid unless both parties freely consented to them. If one party could prove that he or she had been forced into a marriage, either through threats or the use of violence, or both, an annulment could be obtained. This meant, in essence, that the church court would rule that the marriage had never been valid, since it was based on 'force and fear' rather than true consent, and both parties were therefore free to separate and marry elsewhere.

These canonical ideas about marriage and consent governed the actions of ecclesiastical courts in Ireland just as they did elsewhere in medieval Christendom, and women who sued for annulments in the English colony in Ireland in the later Middle Ages were well aware of what they had to prove in order to be successful. They (and their legal counsel) knew that they had to emphasise their fear, the threats made against them, and the coercive and violent actions of those who pushed them into marriage. Annulments based on 'force and fear' were also available to men; there are cases from later medieval England in which men entered this plea, but only female plaintiffs appear in these suits in the records of the archbishop of Armagh's consistory court, from which most of our information about marital litigation in Ireland in the later Middle Ages comes.

Since a strict standard of proof was needed to demonstrate 'force and fear', witnesses (who were only called for the plaintiff) were carefully briefed to ensure that they told their stories in a certain way. Each witness was deposed privately and did not hear the testimony of the others, so they would have had to agree on the facts of the case and how to present them before they arrived in court, most likely prepared by the plaintiff's counsel. The records of the witness depositions for an annulment case instigated by Isabelle Heyron from near Kells, Co. Meath, c. 1449 show how well prepared her witnesses were, as they replicated closely much of the same information and emphasised the violence and compulsion that she endured from her father when he forced her to marry William Drake.

Isabelle's first witness, John Collynge, stated that 'he knew of the marriage between Isabelle and William and said that it was against her will, and that her father beat her and indeed dragged her and made her come to the church. He was asked if he was at the church door [during the marriage ceremony] and he said that he was not, that he was preparing food, but that he knew well what her [Isabelle's] wishes were, and that she wept all day and felt great sorrow'. He added that he did not know whether William knew her carnally after they were married. This was an important question, and one that court officials invariably asked in these cases, since subsequent consent to sex or cohabitation after a marriage, even one that was initially forced, could scupper the chances of a successful annulment. The next witness was Connacius McBrady (*Conchobair Mac Bradaigh*), who said that 'he was at the church door but he couldn't hear if Isabella consented because of the noisy crowd at the door, but he knows well that her father beat her and dragged her and compelled her and that she wept and felt great sorrow'. These first two witnesses used the same trio of words to describe Isabelle's treatment at her father's hands: that he beat, dragged and compelled her to come to the church. These words are well chosen—and were probably selected deliberately by Isabelle and her counsel—to highlight the doggedness of her resistance and the physical pain that she endured because of it.

The witnesses in the annulment case of Catherine McKesky of Termonfeckin, Co. Louth, in 1436 also emphasised the violence that Catherine suffered: all six witnesses agreed that her parents beat her in order to make her marry John Cusack and that she lamented greatly. One witness, Patrick McGyll, added the detail that Catherine's mother beat her grievously with 'a bedoke' (which may be a wooden slat from a bed), striking her with so much force that the 'bedoke' broke. Catherine had a legal representative named John Rybard, who would have advised her on how to frame her petition and would have directed her witnesses to focus on these elements of force and fear that were necessary to her case. This is not to suggest that she or her witnesses were lying, and there is no reason to suppose that they were, but just that they, like Isabelle Heyron and her witnesses, knew which facts had to be emphasised to fulfil the requirements of proof in these cases.

Both Isabelle and Catherine were also described as weeping or lamenting. Two witnesses in Isabelle's case agreed that she felt great sorrow at being made to marry, and that she demonstrated this visually by weeping during the ceremony and, according to one witness, for the entire day. Catherine was also described as lamenting. These descriptions of weeping and sorrow are not strictly necessary to the legal case, since they do not support the two evidentiary requirements for pleas of coercion (fear/threats or force/violence). They do, however, add substance to the overall picture that these women and their witnesses painted of a deep reluctance and unwillingness to consent to marriage. This weeping may have been a result not only of the genuine emotional distress of women in these difficult situations but also perhaps of their understanding that their neighbours must be left in no doubt of their feelings about the marriage, since they were future witnesses. They could use their tears to openly demonstrate their lack of consent to their community, and witnesses evidently saw these tears as important proof of coercion. Thus visible displays of sorrow and resistance were a way for women who were unable to stop an unwanted marriage from going forward to bolster their chances of being able to secure an annulment at a later stage. For these women, their tears, signalling their non-consent and sorrow, helped them to retain some control over their fate and resist the efforts of their families to make them marry.

Further reading

Art Cosgrove, 'Marriage and marriage litigation in medieval Ireland', in P. Reynolds and J. White (eds), *To have and to hold: marrying and its documentation in western Christendom, 400–1600* (Cambridge, 2007), 332–59.

P.J.P. Goldberg, 'Gender and matrimonial litigation in the church courts in the later Middle Ages: the evidence of the court of York', *Gender and History* **19** (1) (2007), 43–59.

R.H. Helmholtz, *Marriage litigation in medieval England* (Cambridge, 2007).

12

Impotence, violence, dowries and drinking: married couples in court in sixteenth-century Ireland

John McCafferty

In the Public Record Office of Northern Ireland there is a manuscript known as 'Cromer's Register', which contains the only surviving 'Act Book' of a pre-Reformation church court from Ireland. Covering the years 1518–22, this is the record of a body that mainly sat in Drogheda and concerned itself with legal business from an area slightly larger than modern County Louth. Perhaps the most striking aspect of this court for a modern reader is its wide cognisance, as it takes in many matters that have since become the business of civil jurisdiction. In the early sixteenth century, however, ecclesiastical courts were central to a number of legal facts of life. They had sole jurisdiction for marriage cases, defamation, bastardy and wills, and all matters pertaining to the clergy and extensive church properties, as well as sexual, moral and religious discipline. They were heavily used, busy bodies with real power.

Marriage cases made up much of this business. Of the 145 entries in the Act Book, 28 are concerned with marital affairs. Suits range from those to enforce marriage (the largest single category, with twelve entries) to those seeking annulment on the basis of impotence, and taking in issues such as bigamy, desertion, domestic violence and consanguinity. Marriage in later medieval Ireland, as elsewhere in Europe, did not usually take place in a church. A wide variety of locations—ranging from a drainage ditch to a cook-shop to the garden of a house—are recorded in the manuscript. A number of contracts were entered into in the house of the woman, such as the disputed marriage of Patricius Ohoy and Patricia Ny Yvy, or in the man's house, such as that between Nicholaus Conyll and Anisia Gowin. While none of the depositions make reference to the giving of a ring, several of them do mention the joining of hands. Phillipus McEward and Katerina Nywoldoyn joined hands while uttering the words of consent. In one case heard in 1520 there is an interesting variation. A witness to the contract, Petrus O'Regan, deposed that the groom had placed his hand in his, saying: 'Take my hand and the woman's hand so we can thus contract marriage'. This may point to a belief that a layman could 'officiate' rather than simply witnessing the consent of the parties. At another marriage wine and ale were purchased by the groom, and in several cases there are references to dowries. At another contract made on the Meath–Louth border, the man agreed to pay the woman threepence to have her belt mended. We do not know, unfortunately, why or how this came about.

Litigation is never a mark of a happy marriage. The Act Book is replete with people trying to get out of their contracts or attempting to change the conditions of their life. In two of the cases the desire of the wife to be a mother is mentioned, while in a third she openly begs the court for the freedom to marry another man. Claiming impotence on the part of the husband was one route open to women. In February 1520 Anisia Gowin attempted to sue Nicholaus Conyll for impotence. Anisia had form, though, as two months earlier she had been involved in a case with one Thomas Palmer, claiming pre-contract as a device to have her union with Conyll annulled. At first the judges kept adjourning the impotence case in the hope that Gowin and Conyll would resolve their difficulties, but eventually they appointed a commission of nine men to examine Conyll's genitals. These men were satisfied that Nicholaus was adequately endowed and functional. Anisia was then ordered to sleep with him in one bed without any further disturbance under threat of excommunication. The judge also made explicit what had been implicit in the suit all along by decreeing that Thomas Palmer was to stay away from Anisia in all 'suspect places'.

The 1518 case of Margeria Kelly of Ardee versus Patricius Murghe of Ardee gives a sense of the kind of violence that one partner might inflict on the other. Canon law allowed a judicial separation for *saevitia* (cruelty) and it was for this that Margeria took her husband to court. His physical violence towards her was severe and apparently uncontrolled. He had flogged her with a stick and beaten her on the head and back with an iron rake, breaking one of her ribs. In his sentence (pointedly delivered in English rather than Latin) the judge drew particular attention to the instruments used. Margeria secured her separation.

Church law upheld the notion of individual consent as integral to valid marriage. Sixteenth-century societies, however, were ones in which family considerations were of overwhelming importance. A dowry case in 1518, involving Walterus Galtrim against Iohannes White and his wife, Christina Pippard, shows the family at work trying to limit the choice of the individual. White and Pippard claimed that they had forbidden the marriage of their daughter Anisia to Walterus Galtrim. If she did marry him, she would be disinherited. Galtrim won the case, however, and his wife's parents were ordered to pay him the dowry. In the 1521 case of the union between Anisia FyJohn and Iohannes McCan, there was pressure on McCan from his father to deny his existing contract with Anisia. Iohannes chose defiance, telling his father that even if he cut his head off he would still not deny that Anisia was truly his wife.

It is only possible to offer a small sample of a large number of complex and often difficult cases here, but the surviving evidence from this Irish court suggests that its services were in demand. It also appears that its proceedings usually combined legal rigour with efforts at conciliation, and that its sentences in marriage cases were both clear and timely.

Further reading

John McCafferty (ed.), *Act Book of the diocese of Armagh, 1518–1522* (Dublin, 2019).

13

Serial marriage in Tudor and early Stuart Ireland

Clodagh Tait

The Gaelic Irish and Scots had long evidenced relaxed attitudes towards the making and dissolution of marriage, the acceptability of subsequent partnerships, and the legitimacy and inheritance rights of children of irregular unions. Medieval Irish brehon law recognised wide grounds for the ending of marriage and permitted remarriage after divorce. In the 1500s, 'serial' marriages persisted in the west and north of Ireland and in Highland Scotland. The writer Fynes Moryson claimed that 'till the end of the last Rebellion' (1603) divorces 'upon pretence of Conscience' were frequent in Ireland, 'nothing being more ordinary than to take a wife with a Certayne number of Cowes (their Common Portion [dowry]) and to send her backe to her friends at the yeres end with some small increase of them, which Divorces the Brehounes or barbarous Iudges among them esily admitted, upon a brybe of Cowes, and that upon trifling causes'. It is unclear, however, how common such divorces were, how they worked in practice and to what extent observers like Moryson exaggerated reports of marriage irregularities.

Members of the Gaelic nobility—men in particular—might get through several spouses during their lifetimes in the course of managing shifting political associations. For example, Shane O'Neill, claimant to the earldom of Tyrone, divorced his first wife, Catherine MacDonald, and offered to put away his third, Catherine O'Donnell, when better alliances came along. His numerous sons from these marriages and other relationships were subsequently to cause considerable trouble in the north of Ireland. His main opponent, Hugh O'Neill, later earl of Tyrone, married four times. He divorced his first wife, a daughter of Brian MacPhelim O'Neill, in about 1574 (the same year her father was accused of treason and murdered), and married Siobhán (Joan) O'Donnell, daughter of Hugh, lord of Tyrconnell. She died in early 1591, but when he married Mabel Bagenal that summer his first wife was still alive and had herself remarried. During an investigation by Lord Deputy Fitzwilliam, prompted by Mabel's furious brother, Nicholas, who accused him of bigamy, Tyrone supposedly presented his divorce decree 'under the seal of the judges that pronounced it' for inspection. Those 'judges' were possibly from the brehon tradition or may have been Catholic bishops. Tyrone seems to have claimed the latter, and Catholic scholars from Peter Lombard onwards assumed so, crediting Tyrone with only three marriages (his final marriage was to Catherine Magennis), since under canon law a bishop or ecclesiastical court would technically have issued an annulment, not a divorce. Tyrone doesn't seem to have had many religious scruples about the matter, however, since he described Joan as his second wife, and contemplated putting her away as well when a marriage with the daughter of Turlough Luineach O'Neill was mooted in 1579/80. It was later alleged that in 1605 Tyrone planned to put away his fourth wife, Catherine, 'for that purpose having gotten together all the priests of the country'. The countess retaliated, insisting that 'if he desisted not from such courses against her, she would discover him, so far as to enforce him again to rebellion, or to lose his head; whereupon the earl dismissed his priests'.

Tyrone's associates also used divorce politically. His daughter Rose, wife of Hugh O'Donnell, earl of Tyrconnell, was frequently threatened with divorce when the earls disagreed. When O'Donnell finally divorced her she married Donal Ballagh O'Cahan, who had already put away his first wife, Rose's former husband's sister, Mary O'Donnell; Mary also remarried. Eight years later, when O'Cahan 'was set on to withdraw himself from the earl', he turned Rose away 'without any kind of exception or interruption of any', and married Honora O'Cahan, with whom he may formerly have had a relationship. He refused to return Rose's dowry and Tyrone complained on her behalf to Lord Deputy Chichester and the assize court. O'Cahan and Chichester counter-claimed that the matter 'should be decided by the lord bishop of the Derry'. This was George Montgomery, whom O'Neill saw as 'the chief author of her putting away', having advised O'Cahan on his break with the earl. That an English-style court should collude with a Church of Ireland bishop regarding a divorce he had encouraged but which was impossible under Anglican canon law and illegal under common law exemplifies how local officials contrived to frustrate and provoke Tyrone after the Nine Years War.

Though some cast-off wives remarried, as we have seen, the implications for others may have been dire. Those who could not retrieve their dowries or extract maintenance might find life especially difficult. Gráinne O'Malley complained in 1595 that women could become impoverished after being 'divorced upon proof of precontracts [that one of the parties had previously contracted to marry another], and the husband now and then without any lawful or due proceeding do put his wife from him and so bringeth in another'. She argued that sureties should be put in place to guarantee the return of dowries 'for fear of the worse'.

The undermining of the Gaelic élites, especially after O'Neill and his associates left in 1607, is reflected in the subsequent decline of serial marriages. Greater scrutiny of titles to land meant that proof of heirs' 'legitimate' birth within legally contracted marriages was increasingly important. The expansion of English legal systems and Anglican administrative structures meanwhile meant that divorces in the guise of Catholic annulments or sanctioned by brehon judges became difficult to secure. Counter-Reformation Catholicism also discouraged the overfree granting of dissolutions of marriages. Nevertheless, Lord Deputy Wentworth claimed that even in the 1630s 'there is nothing so common for a Man to deny his Wife and Children, abandon the former and betake him to a new Task'. He saw opposition to bigamy legislation in the Irish parliaments of 1634 and 1640 (also rejected in 1613–15) as clerically led, 'the Friars and Jesuits fearing that these Laws would conform them to the Manners of England, and in Time be a means to lead them on to a Conformity in Religion'.

The decline of serial marriage was one emblem of the passing of the old Gaelic order and shifts in the authority and theology of the Catholic Church. Nevertheless, this development, along with the extension of elements of English marriage law such as rights to dower (the third of deceased husbands' movable goods customarily allowed to widows), may have been welcomed by Irish wives concerned about securing their livelihoods.

Further reading

Jerrold Casway, 'The decline and fate of Donal Ballagh O'Cahan and his family', in M. Ó Siochrú (ed.), *Kingdoms in crisis: Ireland in the 1640s* (Dublin, 2001), 44–62.

Art Cosgrove, *Marriage in Ireland* (Dublin, 1985).

John Kerrigan, *Archipelagic English: literature, history, and politics 1603–1707* (Oxford, 2008).

C.P. Meehan, *The fate and fortunes of Tyrone and Tyrconnel* (Dublin, 1868).

Mary O'Dowd, *A history of women in Ireland, 1500–1800* (Abingdon, 2005).

Paul Walsh, *The will and family of Hugh O'Neill, Earl of Tyrone* (Dublin, 1930).

14

The politics of domestic violence in Elizabethan Ireland

Valerie McGowan-Doyle

D omestic abuse, like sexual violence, is notoriously underreported. It is perpetrated overwhelmingly by men against women, and recent statistics suggest that one in seven women in Ireland will experience domestic violence, though only 21% of those women will report it. Reconstructing the scale of domestic violence in sixteenth-century Ireland is even more difficult, hindered by the significant loss of this period's records, notably court records. What few records remain offer no insight into the levels of or attitudes towards domestic violence within the Gaelic world or the non-élite classes. Rather, they emanate from the highest levels of English administration during this period of intensified English conquest and reference élite members of the Old English colonial community. Descendants of the Anglo-Norman conquerors, the Old English were in the midst of displacement from office and influence as newly arrived administrators, military personnel and landholders, known as the New English, gained power over Old English and Gaelic Irish alike. The few references to domestic abuse from this period each bear the mark of colonial politics in one form or another, whether in their chance recording or their prosecution, and especially in allegations of domestic abuse used to undermine the Old English.

A lone reference to domestic homicide from late in the Elizabethan period provides one example of this. In 1603 it was recorded by Sir George Carew, almost in passing, that John Delahide had killed his wife. Carew, president of Munster, was an avid collector of manuscripts and deeply interested in landownership—a central concern of many new arrivals, as Gaelic and Old English holdings came under the control of the New English. Carew's concern in this case was to document the transfer of the attainted Delahide's lands to the English-born Richard Cooke, chancellor of the exchequer in Ireland. This unnamed woman's death at the hands of her husband meant little to Carew. Her fate merited mention only as a factor in land transfer.

The use of ambiguous language, compounded by the loss of detail, veils what may have been other women's experience of domestic violence. In 1594, for instance, it was reported that Henry Fitzgerald, 12th earl of Kildare, 'ill-used' his wife, Lady Frances Howard. Though the precise nature of Kildare's 'ill use' is unknown, it was probably Lady Frances's status as the daughter of an English nobleman, the earl of Nottingham, and crucially as a relative of the queen, that led to news of Kildare's mistreatment reaching the queen. Elizabeth wrote a lengthy letter to the viceroy, ordering him to reprimand Kildare and to send Lady Frances home, as her parents had requested.

Vague though suggestive language was also used in a 1575 reference to the 'ill-dealing' used by Thomas Butler, 10th earl of Ormond, against his wife. Whereas Lady Frances Howard's welfare was the principal concern in the above case, the allegations against Ormond suggest colonial politics at play. Ormond was once again at odds with a viceroy, on this occasion Sir William Fitzwilliams, and, as in the past, Ormond was defended by both the queen and Lord Burghley. Such an accusation may thus have been a last-ditch effort by Fitzwilliams to discredit a political rival at court.

When political problems arose, such as accusations of disloyalty or treason, allegations or the exposure of domestic abuse were often used to blacken character. The political and the domestic were deeply intertwined in early modern English conceptions of the relationship between the patriarchal, ordered household and the stable, ordered state, a cultural system extended to Ireland along with English law and control. Husbands were expected to apply physical punishment when necessary, though always within limits. Clear distinction was made in law and prescriptive literature between a patriarch's obligation to administer reasonable punishment and a beating perpetrated in anger and without restraint. The Old English nobility would have been expected to model ordered households as a fundamental requisite of English civility and governance, for in order to govern one first had to govern one's self and one's household. As Cynthia Herrup noted for several high-profile and highly sensationalised cases in early modern England, though domestic abuse may well have been occurring and for some time (as well as culturally defined sexual improprieties such as adultery, incest or sodomy), it was often only when political charges arose that prosecution occurred.

Such was precisely the case against Christopher St Lawrence, 7th baron of Howth. Brought to trial in 1579 before the Court of Castle Chamber, the disturbing detail recorded by the court provides our most vivid portrait of one woman's experience of domestic violence in Elizabethan Ireland. Howth was charged with multiple brutal beatings of his wife Elizabeth Plunket, an unnamed servant and his thirteen-year-old daughter Jane, who died subsequent to her father's beating. Like Herrup's cases, Howth's involved a triad of domestic abuse, sexual impropriety and political discredit. Though his activities purportedly stretched back twelve years, it was only in the aftermath of his opposition to the viceroy, Sir Henry Sidney, for which he had been imprisoned in 1577 and again in 1578, that his domestic abuse case was prosecuted.

Howth was found guilty, imprisoned in Dublin Castle for a third time and fined £1,000, but the political needs of the Dublin administration soon changed. He was released after only nineteen weeks and his fines reduced. Howth's restoration then went further, as he took a seat on the Irish council and was reinvested with judicial and military powers, ultimately holding a seat on the very court that had so recently prosecuted him. His wife's renewed complaints following his release counted for little.

It is indeed unfortunate that we know so little of what must have been the tragic and violent marriages of countless unnamed women and whether they received assistance from family, friends, neighbours or the courts. Such information would dramatically enhance our ability to reconstruct the social history of family, violence and the law in this period. The few cases we do have indicate rather how these women's experiences were used to discredit political rivals, serving the colonial ends of English conquest in the later Tudor period.

Further reading

Susan Dwyer Amussen, '"Being stirred to much unquietness": violence and domestic violence in early modern England', *Journal of Women's History* **6** (1994), 70–89.

Cynthia Herrup, *A house in gross disorder: sex, law and the 2nd earl of Castlehaven* (Oxford, 1999).

Valerie McGowan-Doyle, *The Book of Howth: Elizabethan conquest and the Old English* (Cork, 2011).

15

John Leslie, 'the oldest bishop in Christendom', and his eighteen-year-old wife

Patrick Comerford

When Bishop John Leslie died on 8 September 1671, he was just a few weeks short of his 100th birthday and was reputed to be the oldest bishop in Christendom. He was also pugnacious and was known as 'the fighting bishop' because of his active role, despite his years, in the wars that raged throughout Ireland in the 1630s, 1640s and 1650s.

Bishop Leslie must have been a very happy man, though. When he died, his wife Catherine was half his age, and in their 33 years of marriage they had ten children. John Leslie may have thought that he was at the end of his career when he came to County Donegal in June 1633 as bishop of Raphoe. He was then almost 62 and single, and was moving from Scotland, where he had a difficult time as bishop of the Isles, a far-flung diocese, but Ireland brought its rewards in church, in politics and in marriage.

Leslie was born at Crichie in Aberdeenshire on 14 October 1571. He was educated at Aberdeen but left Scotland in 1588 and studied in Padua, Leipzig, Madrid, Salamanca and San Sebastian. He continued to live on the Continent for decades, and in Spain he was acclaimed for his learning in Latin.

He was in his late 40s when he moved to England, and he was admitted to read in the Bodleian Library in Oxford in 1618. He was ordained deacon that year by John King, bishop of London, and at the age of 50 was ordained priest in 1621. On the nomination of King James I, he received the degree of Doctor of Divinity (DD) at Trinity College Cambridge in 1624 and was also made a privy councillor of Scotland and one of the royal chaplains. That year Leslie also received his first church appointment, as rector of Hartlebury in Worcestershire. He remained there for only three months, however, and returned to London as rector of St Martin Vintry on St Patrick's Day, 17 March 1625, ten days before the king died.

Leslie was now dabbling in politics and war, and he was with George Villiers, duke of Buckingham, at the siege of Isle de Ré in 1627 in support of the Huguenots fighting against the French crown. The siege was a disaster, but Leslie continued to enjoy royal favour; he returned to Scotland at the age of 56 when King Charles I appointed him bishop of the Isles in August 1628. In Scotland, neither episcopacy nor a far-flung diocese along the western coast had their attractions, as there was strong Presbyterian resistance to Charles I's efforts to impose a brand of Anglicanism on the Church of Scotland. When Charles I was finally crowned in Edinburgh in June 1633, he rewarded Leslie's loyalty with a new appointment as bishop of Raphoe, Co. Donegal, and he had Raphoe Castle built.

By then Leslie was almost 62, but Ireland offered a fresh start, in life and in love. Leslie found that many of the diocesan estates had been acquired illegally by laypeople, and he used the force of law to recover some of these lands. He had no official residence and so he built a new, fortified episcopal palace. In his disputes he found a ready ally in John Bramhall, bishop of Derry and later the Restoration archbishop of Armagh. Then in 1638 the bishop married Catherine Cunningham, daughter of Alexander Cunningham, dean of Raphoe Cathedral. There was a gap of almost half a century in their ages— he was almost 67 and she was only eighteen.

When the rebellion of 1641 broke out, Leslie went to battle for Charles I. Although he was now 70, he raised a company of soldiers, brought ammunition from Dublin to Derry and relieved a besieged Sir Ralph Gore at Magherabeg in north-west Donegal.

When most of his fellow bishops of the Church of Ireland abandoned their dioceses and moved to England or Scotland, Leslie remained in Raphoe and did not go to Scotland until 1642. After the execution of Charles I in 1649, he returned again to County Donegal and defended Raphoe against the Cromwellians. He was one of the last royalists to submit in 1653, and was the only Anglican bishop to remain in his diocese in Ireland during the Cromwellian era. During those years he confirmed children in Dublin and ordained priests and deacons.

At the Restoration in 1660, Leslie—by now an elderly but sprightly man of 88—rode from Chester to London in just 24 hours to declare his loyalty to Charles II. He then returned to Ireland and resumed his role as bishop of Raphoe. A year later, with Bramhall's reorganisation of the Church of Ireland, Leslie's loyalty was recognised once more, and at the age of almost 90 he was appointed bishop of Clogher in June 1661. On the recommendation of Charles II, the Irish parliament voted him a reward of £2,000. Leslie said that he hoped 'that whatever the house hath given to a prophet may receive a prophet's reward.'

Fig. 2—View of Old Castle Leslie, *c.* 1850s. Permission granted by Castle Leslie Estate. With special thanks to Sammy Leslie and Yvonne Murphy, Cultural Heritage Manager, Castle Leslie.

Leslie used the money to buy the Glaslough estate in County Monaghan and renamed the house Castle Leslie (Fig. 2; Pls 2 and 3). Despite his age, he remained bishop of Clogher for another decade. When he died on 8 September 1671, he was buried at St Salvator's, the church he had built on his estate.

Catherine and John Leslie seem to have been happily married, and they had ten children. Their eldest surviving son, John Leslie, became dean of Dromore, while their sixth son, the theologian Charles Leslie (1650–1720), chancellor of Connor Cathedral, was a leading non-juror, refusing to take the oath of loyalty to William III and following the Jacobite court into exile.

The descendants of this happy marriage continue to live at Castle Leslie in Glaslough—which is, appropriately, a popular wedding venue today. The Castle Leslie Estate has recently launched a new gin in honour of Bishop John Leslie; named 'The Fighting Bishop', it is produced from beech leaves and botanicals hand-picked from the trees planted by the bishop on the estate over 300 years ago.

16

Inter-confessional marriage in early modern Ireland

Bronagh McShane

In his will, proved on 17 April 1650, William Parsons (c. 1570–1650), lord justice of Ireland, exerted considerable control over his children's choice of spouse and was blatantly prescriptive regarding the confession of any potential marriage partner. He stipulated that his children were 'not to marry Irish papists' and 'to marry only with the consent of their grandmother or any three of my overseers'; they were also to incur a penalty if they married without consent. Regarding the betrothal of his daughter, Dorothy, Parsons's guidelines were even more stringent. Reminiscent of the Protestant divine Luke Challoner's deathbed instructions to his daughter Phoebe in 1613 that she should marry no man other than James Ussher (1581–1656), later archbishop of Armagh, in his will Parsons decreed that Dorothy was to receive a marriage dowry of £1,500 on condition that 'she marry the man [that] I have chosen'. Sir William Parsons's admonitions to his children not to marry outside the confessional community were echoed later in the century by the overtly Catholic Robert Barnewall (d. 1689), ninth Baron Trimleston. In a letter written to his sixteen-year-old son Matthias in 1686, Trimleston cautioned against the perils of inter-confessional marriage (or exogamy), warning Mathias to 'Never bring a Protestant wife into your family'.

While heads of families such as Trimleston and Parsons may have deemed inter-confessional marriage unacceptable, marriage across the religious divide *did* occur and, from the sparse evidence that has survived, it appears to have been remarkably widespread throughout society. Indeed, the prevalence of inter-confessional marriage down to the mid-seventeenth century is demonstrated by the fact that in 1651 and 1653 the Cromwellian authorities in Ireland prohibited intermarriage between Catholics and Protestants, a move emulated in 1658 by the Catholic synod, which even conceded that when unions with Protestants occurred the Catholic spouse should have liberty to practise his or her faith and that any children resulting from the marriage should be raised as Catholics. Nevertheless, despite attempts on the part of the state and the Catholic Church to legislate against inter-confessional marriage, repeated clerical fulminations against it suggest that the injunctions may not always have been as effective as the church (on both sides of the confessional divide) would have wished.

While inter-confessional marriage may have posed a challenge to church authorities, it could also be problematic for those who chose to marry across the religious divide, and the success of these unions depended on a wide range of factors, including the personalities and the social status of the individuals involved. Clearly, couples dealt with the challenges of mixed marriages in a range of ways. For some, inter-confessional marriage could be successful, and it is evident that certain couples developed a particular *modus vivendi* that allowed them to enjoy harmonious relationships based on mutual respect despite religious variance. That contemporaries believed that inter-confessional unions could be successful is intimated by Randall MacDonnell (1609–83), the staunchly Catholic marquis of Antrim, who hoped to secure the marriage of one of his elder daughters to George Fitzgerald (1612–60), the Protestant heir of the house of Kildare. In the lengthy negotiations, MacDonnell expressed the hope that the marriage would prove congenial and that both spouses could live 'contentedly' despite their divergent religious perspectives:

> Your Lordship need not doubt that any will attempt to alter your opinion in religion, and I hope your Lordship will not seek to force whosoever shall be your wife from hers. You both may live contentedly and each one use their own conscience, for which (thanks be to God) you want not an excellent precedent.

The marriage of Susanna Brabazon and Luke Plunket (c. 1602–37), Lord Killeen and later first earl of Fingall (1628), in 1611 proved successful despite the confessional variance of the couple. Susanna was the younger daughter of Edward, Lord Brabazon (d. 1625), son and heir of Sir William Brabazon (d. 1552) and his wife, Elizabeth Clifford. By the early seventeenth century the Brabazons had distinguished themselves as one of the most prominent servitor families of Elizabethan and Stuart Ireland and were staunch advocates of religious reform. By contrast, Luke Plunket, son and heir of Christopher Plunket (d. 1612/13), lord of Killeen, was a well-known recusant; his younger brother, Patrick Plunket (d. 1679), became Catholic bishop of Ardagh (1647–69) and Meath (1669–79), while another brother,

Nicholas (d. 1680), a barrister, later rose to political prominence within the Roman Catholic Confederation.

Susanna's marriage into the strongly Catholic Plunket family contrasted sharply with the marriages of her sisters, all of whom contracted unions with members of the Church of Ireland community. For example, Susanna's older sister, Elizabeth (b. 1568), married as her first husband George Montgomery (d. 1621), Church of Ireland bishop of Meath and Clogher, while her younger sister, Ursula, married Sir James Hamilton (*c.* 1560–1644), first Viscount Claneboye. In spite of their different religious backgrounds, however, Susanna and Luke's marriage appears to have been a successful union. Susanna was permitted by her husband to 'enjoy the full exercise of her religion' and on her death in 1623 was afforded burial according to Protestant ceremonial rites, her husband 'suffering the minister at her death to dispose her soule religiously and Christianly to God'. It is noteworthy, however, that after Susanna's death the earl (who remarried twice) chose spouses from strongly Catholic backgrounds, including Margaret Preston (d. 1637), widow of Jenico Preston (d. 1630), fifth Viscount Gormanstown, whose daughters, Elizabeth and Jane Preston, were members of the Irish Poor Clare order.

While relations between spouses of diverging confessions may have been harmonious, determining the faith of a couple's offspring could lead to feuds. For example, the birth of a son, Thomas, *c.* 1600 to the devoutly Catholic Lady Margaret Esmonde (née O'Flaherty) (d. 1626) and her husband, Sir Laurence Esmonde (1570–1645), occasioned a dispute between the couple which ultimately resulted in the breakdown of their marriage. Fearing that her husband, a zealous proponent of the reformed religion, would raise their son in the Protestant faith, Margaret fled with the infant to her family home in County Galway, whereupon she was repudiated by her husband. The couple remained permanently estranged but never formally separated, despite the fact that Sir Laurence later married Elizabeth Butler (d. *c.* 1645), a granddaughter of James Butler (d. 1546), ninth earl of Ormond.

Further reading

David Cressy, *Birth, marriage and death: ritual, religion and the life cycle in Tudor and Stuart England* (Oxford, 1997).

Donald Jackson, *Intermarriage in Ireland, 1550–1650* (Montreal, 1970).

Margaret MacCurtain, 'Marriage in Tudor Ireland', in A. Cosgrove (ed.), *Marriage in Ireland* (Dublin, 1985), 51–66.

Jane Ohlmeyer, *Making Ireland English: the Irish aristocracy in the seventeenth century* (New Haven, 2012).

17

'Why don't you love me like you used to do?' Marital discord in early modern Ireland

Brendan Scott

Robert Boyle, the bachelor son of the earl of Cork, whose two sisters were trapped in unhappy marriages, once noted that 'I have so seldom seen a happy marriage, or men love their wives as they do their mistresses, that I am far from wondering our law givers should make marriage undesolvable'. The prevalence of arranged matches surely influenced Boyle's attitude, and this short article aims to uncover some examples of marital discord in Tudor and Stuart Ireland.

At a time when arranged marriages were the norm, particularly among the wealthier sections of society, it is not difficult to understand the tensions that sometimes developed between a husband and wife. Indeed, those who experienced marital difficulties of various types in the sixteenth century only had to look at the exploits of Henry VIII, who divorced two and executed a further two of his six wives, or Mary Queen of Scots, who was strongly suspected of having been involved in the assassination of her husband, Lord Darnley, for prime examples of the dangers of bad marriages—or, rather, marriage to an incompatible partner.

Of course, disagreements are an ordinary part of married life and can often be exacerbated when difficulties of various kinds are encountered. The reported argument between Hugh O'Neill and Catherine Magennis, his fourth wife, on the eve of the Flight of the Earls in 1607 gives us some insight into their relationship and the pressures they were under. According to Sir John Davies, while *en route* from Dungannon to Rathmullan Catherine, 'being exceedingly weary, slipped down from her horse, and, weeping, said she could go no farther; whereupon the earl drew his sword, and swore a great oath that he would kill her in the place, if she would not pass on with him, and put on a more cheerful countenance withal'. Catherine did indeed resume the journey, but her countenance and mood thereafter are not reported. Part of Catherine's unhappiness probably stemmed from the fact that they could not locate their youngest son, Conn, who had been fostered out to another family. (Conn later died in the Tower of London sometime after 1622.) Catherine's unhappiness continued in Rome; even after her husband's death in 1616, financial problems and personal tragedy (her second son, Brian, was found hanged in 1617) plagued her life until her own death in 1619. Marriage to the 'Great Earl' had not been a happy experience for Catherine.

Poor marriages—or, rather, what were seen from the outside as poor marriages—were sometimes commented upon by observers of the union, mystified by the reasons for the marriage in the first place. Bishop William Bedell of Kilmore, when referring to the wife of Murtagh King, who helped him to translate the Old Testament into Irish, wrote that she was King's 'greatest crosse; so unreasonable a woman, as I have often thought her possessed by a wicked spirit and set on by Sathan, to vexe him [King] and disgrace his person'. King's thoughts on his marriage were never recorded, however, and perhaps it is unfair to damn the union as being unhappy on the word of one outside observer, Bedell, whose own marriage was a happy one.

These marriages, although not without their problems, did not end in separation, but some marriages were so unhappy that one of the parties might even deny that it had ever occurred, as happened in the case of the union between Thomas Cusack, an important political figure in the mid-Tudor Pale who was made lord chancellor in 1550, and his first wife, Joan Hussey. Despite having three children with Hussey, the union deteriorated to such an extent that in 1537 Thomas applied for a divorce on the grounds of consanguinity (they were third cousins). Gossip abounded in relation to this separation, and a document from 1547 that listed complaints against Lord Deputy Anthony St Leger, who was a close associate of Cusack, accused Cusack of persuading a servant of his to 'enter into familiaritie with his wif [Joan Hussey] whereupon he had a divorse betwixt him and hir'. This extraordinary claim does not seem to have been repeated anywhere else and was probably part of a wider attempt to damage St Leger and his associates, but it does demonstrate the prevalent gossip of the period. Time did not mellow Cusack's attitude towards his first wife, and in his will he referred to Maud Darcy as his first wife; Joan was mentioned but was obliquely referred to in vague terms as 'sometime my wife'. Furthermore, his funerary monument, part of which survives in Tara Church, Co. Meath, displays the coats of arms of the Darcy and Sarsfield families (his third wife, Janet Sarsfield, herself married six times, survived Thomas), with no mention of the Hussey family.

Prior to her marriage to Cusack, Maud herself was also involved in marital scandal: it was alleged that she had her first husband, James Marwarde, baron of Scryne, murdered by Richard Fitzgerald, who replaced Marwade to become her second husband. Fitzgerald's execution in the wake of the Kildare Rebellion put Maud back on the market, and she was swiftly married to Cusack; this union seems to have been a happy one, and they had thirteen children together.

So although Robert Boyle was correct in pointing to the prevalence of arranged marriages as being a reason for unhappy unions, we can see at least in the case of the marriage between Thomas Cusack and Maud Darcy that occasionally these arranged unions could result in happy and fruitful lives together. The course of true love never did run smooth!

Further reading

Jerrold Casway, 'Heroines or victims? The women of the flight of the earls', in D. Finnegan, É. Ó Ciardha and M.-C. Peters (eds), *The Flight of the Earls: Imeacht na nIarlaí* (Derry, 2010), 227–36.

Christopher Maginn, 'A window on mid-Tudor Ireland: the "matters" against Lord Deputy St Leger, 1547–8', *Historical Research* **78** (202) (2005), 465–82.

Jane Ohlmeyer, *Making Ireland English: the Irish aristocracy in the seventeenth century* (New Haven, 2012).

Brendan Scott, 'Career wives or wicked stepmothers?', *History Ireland* **17** (1) (2009), 14–17.

18

The wages of bigamy (1663)[2]

Thomas O'Connor

She was an attractive woman, Leonora Nugent—young, unmarried, conveniently Catholic, living with her uncle in Lisbon. The old boy was a Garvan, strict on family honour, avuncular and well connected. It would have taken more than that, though, to deter Christopher Bremejan. Since coming to Lisbon to serve the king as lieutenant general, the Meath man had been feeling lonely and out of kilter. As he prepared to leave Lisbon for a commission up north, he'd seen Leonora in the street and was smitten. He couldn't help hanging around Garvan's, hoping to catch sight of her or, better still, to catch her eye. And he wasn't entirely persuaded that it wasn't reciprocal. What young woman wouldn't crave liberation from the cage of her guardian's reputation? In the end their passion, or at least Bremejan's, got the better of them. They eloped to Oporto, a staging post to his commission and maybe, he hoped, to something more.

But the old man was not so easily thwarted. Seized with enormous indignation, *tío* Garvan joined pursuit, armed with a royal arrest warrant order for the eloping parties. They could only be living in sin, a scandalous smear on the Garvan escutcheon. Bremejan, as the male and the senior, was, of course, the culprit. The wronged uncle could look forward to the criminal's humiliation, the loss of his commission, maybe even a spell behind bars—prospects that cooled Bremejan's ardour and spurred him to evasive action. Comrades were willing to put their shoulders to the wheel, with advice at least. Some, apparently experienced in such matters, counselled matrimony. Not that they were theologians, but it figured. If he put the sacrament between himself and

---

2 On 16 January 1663 Christopher Bremejan, of Corballis, Co. Meath, handed himself in to the Lisbon Inquisition and confessed to the crime of bigamy. See *Cristóvão Bremejan [réu], casado, duas vezes: Ilicia Clancy e com Leonor Nugen, tem 47 anos de idade. É Tenente General de Infantaria. É natural de Corbally, Irlanda e morador em Guimarães. Filho de Guilherme Bremejan e de Ana Hilon, ambos irlandeses* (Archivo Nacional Torre do Tombo [Lisbon] TSO–IL–28–12519).

her uncle's outrage, there was nothing the old man could do. The only trouble now was bi-location. His commission had taken him to a garrison on the Spanish border, leaving the lovely Leonora alone in Oporto. Time being of the essence, it was essential to perform the wedding before the uncle got up from Lisbon. Again his comrades came to the rescue. What about a proxy marriage? Perfectly legal. All he needed was someone in Oporto, well placed and willing to execute the proxy. Not one of the usual Irish suspects, but perhaps another foreigner. How about the English counsel, William Maynard? Inconveniently Protestant, yes, but legally apt and a very obliging fellow. Having everything to lose, Bremejan calculated and took the plunge. Paperwork came courtesy of contacts in Oporto. An amenable cleric was procured. A suitable church venue was arranged. Maynard, decent fellow, did the decent thing. By the time her uncle arrived in Oporto, his niece was Mrs Bremejan. Clad in their matrimonial armour, the couple settled down and, in time, the diasporic community in Oporto was augmented by two little Bremejans. Despite the shaky start, the little household was turning into a model of matrimonial propriety.

Or was it? Conjugal bliss was attenuated in December 1661 by news of a new arrival. Not another baby Bremejan but rather a new Mrs Bremejan. Recently arrived from Paris, Alicia Bremejan (née Clancy) wielded a certificate of marriage naming, as contracting party, a certain Christopher Bremejan. Her description of her putative husband fitted that of the man married to Leonora Nugent. And this woman was not for turning. The 'new' Mrs Bremejan intended to rejoin her lawful husband and to apprise him of his obligations to her and their three children. News travelling fast along the Irish diasporic grapevine, a concerned Bremejan got wind of the inconvenience. A relative, the Dominican Gerard de Hilon, was engaged to check out the details. He met the woman; he saw the certificate; he confirmed its authenticity. The cat was out of the bag. Suddenly Christopher Bremejan had a lot of explaining to do—and not just to his two wives. The first Mrs Bremejan experienced her husband's bigamy as the alienation of affection and a failure to honour obligations to herself and her children. The second Mrs Bremejan no doubt entertained similar sentiments. For the Inquisition, however, the offence to the women was dwarfed by the offence to Holy Mother Church. Bigamy distained a sacrament and suggested heresy.

Bremejan realised the gravity of his situation and turned to colleagues for succour. The advice proffered came in many versions but all boiled down to a simple counsel: better to call on the inquisitor before he calls on you. Quite. But how did one 'call' on an inquisitor? And in what would such a call consist? These were matters beyond the ken of his martial mates but not of Malachy

Carron, a friar of Saõ Pedro. He seemed to know all one needed to know about the Inquisition. Yes, he advised, a visit to the inquisitor was in order. What should be said? Only what needed to be said. What would that be? A believable version of the truth—in Portuguese, preferably. Bremejan left it to Carron, and on the morning of 16 January 1663 he found himself standing in the antechamber of Inquisitor Correa de Lacerda. A porter ushered them in and Bremejan delivered himself of his confession, punctuated by Carron's Portuguese translation. Between them they gave the best possible account of the Irishman's predicament, as apologetically and repentantly as Bremejan's ignorance of Portuguese permitted.

Bremejan had opted, as advised, for a believable version of the truth. He was a bigamist. That much was true. But his bigamy was attended by a host of mitigating factors—concerning the first wife, for instance. The inquisitor had to understand the special circumstances: how, six years previously, he had been under French colours, a sergeant-major at Arras, and she, future wife number one, a camp-follower. Nothing improper, of course; chaperoned by her brother and another relation, soldiers like himself—a common enough circumstance for the diasporic Irish, which Cromwell had recently scattered. An ill wind, you could say, as the couple had taken a liking to each other. Everyone being agreeable, and a peripatetic friar performing the sacramental honours, they committed matrimony. Four years of marriage and three little Bremejans later, the 1659 Peace of the Pyrenees brought a military lull to France, obliging Bremejan to hawk his martial skills elsewhere—this time in Portugal, where, lodged in Lisbon, his eye fell on the lovely Leonora. The rest was, well, history, though he took pains to give an account of the requited love, the flight to Oporto, the angry uncle, the threat to his commission, the danger of imprisonment and, of course, the misleading intelligence from his well-intentioned but ignorant friends. The inquisitor cocked his head. What sort of *misleading* intelligence, he enquired? Bremejan had to be careful. Unintelligent intelligence: that wife number one at that time was, reportedly, *in extremis* in Paris and not expected to live, and that a doubt existed, inchoate and unsubstantiated, that his battlefield marriage was invalid.

Like the good inquisitor that he was, Dr de Lacedra jumped on the doubt of sacramental validity. Why had the Irishman failed to pursue so grave a matter with competent authority? A sticky one, but Bremejan was ready, pleading the pressures of the time and a noble concern to preserve the children of his first marriage from bastardy. But why had he lived with his first wife if there were doubts concerning validity? There was no doubt, Bremejan explained, prior to the advent of future wife number two. But why, when threatened with the loss of his commission and imprisonment, had he failed to acquaint himself with the particulars of his first wife's state? But he had, the Irishman elaborated. He wrote unanswered letters to knowledgeable persons in Paris to inquire about wife number one. But if there was a doubt about the validity of the first marriage when contracting the second, de Lacerda continued, why did the defendant desist in attempts to inform himself of his first wife's situation? Because he couldn't bear to leave his second wife alone and because, if it turned out that wife number one was still alive, he'd be subject to civil proceedings and the loss of his commission.

Impaled on the horns of such diverse dilemmas, Bremejan made a poor canonical spectacle. It was a predicament that an inquisitor might understand but not, of course, condone. Notwithstanding the Irishman's protestations, for Dr de Lacerda the suspicion remained that the second marriage had been contracted in distain of the first. His sentence, confining Bremejan to Portugal and obliging him to report any change of address, might seem lenient—but then he also had the two wives, five children and the still-smarting *tío* Garvan to deal with.

Further reading

Thomas O'Connor, *Irish voices from the Spanish Inquisition: migrants, converts and brokers in early modern Iberia* (Basingstoke, 2016).

19

'Come kisse me': the troubled marriage of Mary Sackville and Roger Boyle

Eamon Darcy

In the mid-1660s two aristocrats, Roger Boyle, the first earl of Orrery, and Richard Sackville, the fifth earl of Dorset, became well acquainted with one another over the course of their negotiations in the summer of 1665 for the eventual marriage of Roger Boyle junior, second Baron Broghill, and Mary Sackville. Both men had been pivotal in the process of restoring Charles II after the tumultuous events of the mid-seventeenth century. Consequently, Boyle was elevated to the earldom of Orrery and Dorset became lord lieutenant of Middlesex to aid his impoverished title. The political advantages of this match to both men were clear. Orrery provided much-needed financial resources while Dorset could cement Orrery's political and financial networks in England.

In the initial stages of the marriage, Orrery and Dorset became close and frequently commented in a cordial way upon the state of their children's marriage, particularly concerning prospective grandchildren. Upon the birth in June 1668 of a daughter, Dorset congratulated Orrery but also expressed the hope that the next would be a male heir for Orrery and his son. Mary eventually bore two sons who would live to adulthood, Lionel and Charles. Although at first her marriage was a happy one, in time her relationship with Broghill became acrimonious. Both families were eventually dragged into a feud that would outlive the marriage.

At first glance, one could be tempted to understand the tribulations of this marriage through contemporaries' clear definitions of marital roles. At Church of Ireland marriage ceremonies, new brides were ordered to 'submit yourself unto your own husband' by the minister. There was a growing concern in the latter half of the seventeenth century, however, that women were undermining traditional social roles. Broghill's cousin, Francis Boyle, Viscount Shannon, would later lament that Irish husbands were oppressed by their wives: 'In truth one need go no further than the streets to meet many men that do not govern their wives, but one must travel the whole Kingdom over to meet a few that do'. In the light of what is discussed below, one wonders whether Shannon had Broghill in mind, although Shannon too had an unhappy marriage.

Mary Sackville, Broghill's wife, was a formidable woman who was unhappy living in Ireland. Her husband was no match and had a rather, shall we say, delicate and sensitive disposition. In the autumn of 1672 (according to Broghill's admittedly pathetic account), the two had a seemingly irreconcilable falling out. Broghill alleged that he asked his wife: 'I pray my dear come kisse me'—a request that he repeated 'three or four' times, only to be ignored by his wife. Unimpressed by her husband's advances, Mary eventually responded by taking 'up a bibell that lay on ye table & swore … that she would never come to kisse me'. Broghill retaliated by claiming that he would have been happier if he had married a 'kitchen wench', only to receive the stinging rebuke that 'she had bin fitter for you'.

This insult, although uttered in the heat of a private row between a husband and wife, cast aspersions on Broghill's, Orrery's and Dorset's honour. Orrery reminded his daughter-in-law of her duty as a wife: 'you should striue to give the loue to him from whom by all decisions & humours tyes you ought to receiue it'. Mary denied ever stating such words and maintained that she had not dishonoured her family nor failed 'of any duty' as a wife. She explained that the latest dispute emerged because her husband refused to listen to her advice. In the end, Orrery and his wife invited their son and daughter-in-law to his home in Ballymartyr so that an open conference could be held to clear the air.

While the exact outcome of this particular dispute is unknown, we do know that Orrery was unimpressed by their behaviour. His will, attested in 1679, showed a clear preference for Henry, Broghill's younger brother, by granting his widow's jointures to him. This failure, in Mary's eyes, of Orrery's family to provide for her children caused further tension within her marriage, which was beset with financial difficulties. By January 1680, Broghill (by now the third earl of Orrery) no longer wanted to live with his wife, especially as she castigated him for his lack of political nous. Despite the efforts of Dorset's and Orrery's widows to bridge the divide, the two families had fallen out by this point. Broghill refused to attend English doctors (despite his rapidly declining health) for fear that his brother-in-law would have him imprisoned. In the end, Broghill lamented that he and Mary could not recapture the happiness of their first four or five years of married life, before the row concerning the 'kitchen wench'.

The marriage of Roger Boyle and Mary Sackville provides us with an invaluable insight into the trials and tribulations of aristocratic marriages in seventeenth-century Ireland. While we are aware of the intense process of negotiations between families, less is known about how both sets of families subsequently provided a support network for the married couple. Furthermore, despite public protestations of female subservience, Orrery and Dorset engaged as equals with their wives during this dispute, and Mary, perhaps knowing this, lambasted her husband for repeatedly ignoring her perspective on his political affairs. Thus the evidence discussed here also provides a more nuanced view of gender relations. Mary, despite social rhetoric that demanded her subservience, was grudgingly respected by her father-in-law and she refused to bow to his or her husband's wishes. Orrery probably recognised Roger's character flaws, as evidenced by his preference for his younger son, Henry, which was designed to protect his estate in the light of the acrimony that subsequently developed between the Boyle and Sackville families. While Broghill presumably sought companionship with his wife such as that which his father and grandfather had enjoyed with their wives (and subsequently discussed by historians), his experience reminds us of what many of his contemporaries thought of marriage: that it was for better or for worse, but not necessarily for the happy ever after.

Further reading

David Cressy, *Birth, marriage and death: ritual, religion and the life cycle in Tudor and Stuart England* (Oxford, 1997).

Jane Ohlmeyer, *Making Ireland English: the Irish aristocracy in the seventeenth century* (New Haven, 2012).

20

Quaker marriage in Ireland

John Glynn Douglas

In Ireland, the recording of the births, marriages and deaths of Friends started in the 1660s after Men's and Women's Meetings had been set up to look after the affairs and discipline of the Society. The Quaker Monthly Meeting is the unit that manages church affairs, keeps the records and handles the discipline of the Society. It may or may not have subsidiary meetings. For instance, Dublin Monthly Meeting has six subsidiary meetings. George Fox encapsulated the marriage procedure in 1667 when he wrote: 'For the right joining in marriage is the work of the Lord only, for it is God's ordinance and not man's; and therefore Friends cannot consent that they should join them together; for we marry none; it is the Lord's work, and we are but witnesses'. Fox's marriage procedures stressed three principles: adequate preliminaries, an open ceremony that included an exchange of declarations to be recorded in a certificate, and an efficient method of registration. These principles have been carefully guarded and are as valid today as they were 350 years ago. Since 1844, Friends have complied with the state's requirements to register their marriage registering officers. They are now registered as 'Solemnisers' in the Republic of Ireland and 'Officiants' in Northern Ireland. These titles do not really suit George Fox's marriage definition.

The restoration of Charles II led to the setting up of church courts with their responsibility for legal matters, including the proving of wills. The established church did not recognise Quaker marriages and they could be disputed by non-Quaker relatives who wished to prove the illegitimacy of children and thus claim a family inheritance. From 1661 onwards, Friends had secured successive civil law judgements upholding their marriages as good in law. Nevertheless, the precarious position of Quaker marriage made Friends very careful to ensure that they could demonstrate their three procedures. Early preliminaries were cumbersome, requiring both parties to appear repeatedly before Women's and Men's Meetings, and if there was no objection the marriage could be solemnised at the mid-week Meeting for Worship in the Meeting House to which the woman belonged. Once the preliminaries had been completed, the Meeting for Worship in which the marriage was solemnised was relatively simple. Up to the nineteenth century the meeting routinely lasted two hours or more. After some time, during which various Friends minister, the couple would stand up and make their declarations, the man usually first: 'Friends, I take … to be my wife, promising through divine assistance to be unto her a loving and faithful husband until death shall separate us'; and the woman in a like manner: 'Friends, I take … to be my husband, promising through divine assistance to be unto him a loving and faithful wife until death shall separate us'. The marriage certificate included the declarations, date and time, the names of the couple and of their parents, and the Monthly Meeting (or Meetings) involved. It was signed in the meeting by the couple and by everyone attending the marriage, thus producing a valuable historical document.

Lord Hardwicke regularised the Quaker marriage situation in England and Wales. His Act of 1753 provided that all marriages, other than those of the royal family or covered by special licence of the archbishop of Canterbury, should be conducted in the parish church, and publicity was ensured by public banns or common licence. There were two exceptions: the act did not apply 'to any marriage amongst the People called Quakers or persons professing the Jewish Religion'. Quaker marriage, where both parties were in membership, was thus recognised implicitly in England and Wales and eventually explicitly in the Marriage Act of 1836.

Things were very different in Ireland. The Irish parliament did not emulate Lord Hardwicke, and the marriage problem was to persist for another hundred years. It was not until 1844 that an act establishing registration districts in Ireland, similar to those in England and Wales, made Quaker and Jewish marriages 'good in law'. Recognition of those Quakers who had married earlier was to take another two years. All of this only applied where both parties to the marriage were members of the Society. In 1860 an act recognised Quaker marriages where only one party was in membership provided that the other was 'professing with Friends', and in 1872 the 'professing with Friends' was replaced by a certificate of permission from the Quaker registering officer involved.

The disestablishment of the Church of Ireland in 1869 had interesting repercussions. The Church of Ireland archbishop, like the archbishop of Canterbury, could issue a special licence for a marriage at any time and place on behalf of the established church. The act of 1870 extended this privilege to the heads of most other churches, including the clerk to the Yearly Meeting of the Society of Friends in Ireland. The privilege applied only when both parties were in membership.

Surprisingly, the setting up of the separate Irish jurisdictions in 1922 did not affect marriage legislation and they both continued to use the nineteenth-century Westminster legislation. The special licence provision was modified in 1954 by the Northern Ireland parliament and in 1972 by Dáil Éireann so that it applied to marriages where only one party was in membership.

Irish Quaker marriage has not changed fundamentally in 300 years. The preliminaries have been simplified and no longer require repeated appearances at meetings. Legal requirements have to be complied with, and the three months' notice required by state registrars suits Quaker administration nicely. The wording of the marriage declaration is still prescribed, although a number of alternative wordings are now allowed; the couple, however, must each use similar wording. The Meeting for Worship solemnising the ceremony now lasts usually one hour or slightly less. Only the couple and the witnesses sign during the meeting and everyone else signs afterwards.

The organisation of the Society of Friends in Ireland, initially circulated to meetings in manuscript form, was first published in 1811 and has been revised several times since. The current version, entitled *Organisation and Christian Discipline*, was adopted in 2000. It sets out the necessary arrangements and regulations connected with the civil and religious requirements of the Society. The marriage regulations enshrined therein have become extraordinarily complex. Each revision of legislation since 1844 had to incorporate earlier clauses because the earlier acts had not been withdrawn. This unsatisfactory situation continued in Northern Ireland until the Marriage (Northern Ireland) Order of 2003 superseded most of the previous enactments. In the Republic of Ireland the situation continued until 2007, when the Civil Registration Act of 2004 became law. These acts greatly simplified the legal requirements for traditional marriage and recognised civil partnership. A number of Quaker civil partnerships have since taken place and have been frequently followed by special Meetings for Worship celebrating and blessing the partnership, but no Quaker registration was involved.

In the Republic of Ireland the 2015 Marriage Act removed the requirement that the couple getting married be of opposite sexes. In the autumn of 2016, Dublin Monthly Meeting received a request to marry a well-known Friend and his partner. It was realised that there was nothing preventing the Monthly Meeting from sanctioning this marriage other than the gender-biased wording of the Quaker marriage regulations and the attitude of Friends to same-sex marriages. All the preliminary forms and the actual wording of the declaration can easily have their gender bias removed.

All changes to the Society's Discipline have to be agreed by the Yearly Meeting of the Religious Society of Friends in Ireland. Proposed new marriage regulations for the Republic of Ireland, in which the gender-sensitive wording has been altered, were accepted by Dublin Monthly Meeting in January 2017.

Quaker marriage is peculiar to the Religious Society of Friends. It is defined in *Organisation and Christian Discipline* as follows: 'Quaker marriage is not an alternative form of marriage available to the general public, but is for members and those who, whilst not in formal membership, are in unity with the principles of the Society. Usually one or both of the parties being married will be in membership or closely associated with Friends.'

21

An eighteenth-century wedding manuscript

Bernadette Cunningham

In County Clare, in 1711, celebrations were held to mark the marriage of Séamus Mac Fhlannchadha and Mairghréag Nic Conmara. It was probably quite a high-profile social event in the locality, and a wedding poem (an epithalamium) was composed for the couple by the renowned west Clare scholar Aindrias Mac Cruitín (*c.* 1650–1738). The poem, which opens with the line '*Créad fa n-uaibhrid a chéile*' ('Why do you take pride in one another?'), was almost certainly recited as part of the wedding celebrations, perhaps by the poet himself. Mac Cruitín also compiled pedigrees of the couple, tracing their ancestry through eighteen generations in time-honoured tradition. Perhaps the genealogies, too, were read aloud to the assembled relatives and friends.

Such poems and pedigrees were rather ephemeral things, intended to enhance the celebrations that marked the marriage. Other examples of Irish wedding poems survive from the post-bardic Gaelic tradition. Among them are two for a Limerick patron composed by the seventeenth-century poet Dáibhí Ó Bruadair (1625–98), one by Aogán Ó Rathaille (*c.* 1670–1729) for the wedding of Sir Valentine Browne of Killarney and Honora Butler of Kilcash in 1720, and another by Aindrias Mac Cruitín to mark the marriage of Brian O'Loghlen and Isabel Casey in County Clare in 1728. Mac Cruitín's 1728 poem has the same opening line as the one he had provided for the McNamara/Clancy wedding in 1711, but they are otherwise quite different compositions.

The wedding poem and pedigrees prepared for Séamus Mac Fhlannchadha and Mairghréag Nic Conmara are now preserved as part of a very substantial Irish manuscript of over 320 pages in the Royal Irish Academy (MS 23 G 9). The entire manuscript is in the hand of Aindrias Mac Cruitín but, curiously, most of it had been written a few years before the wedding at which it was probably presented as a gift. The main part of the manuscript is a transcript of *Foras feasa ar Éirinn*, the history of Ireland compiled by Geoffrey Keating in the early seventeenth century. A scribal colophon gives the date of completion of this copy of *Foras feasa* as 5 March 1708/9. Keating's history was much in demand through the seventeenth and eighteenth centuries, and was in circulation in English and Latin translations as well as in the original Irish. In the absence of any printed edition in Irish before the twentieth century, *Foras feasa* circulated through a process of 'scribal publication'.

Aindrias Mac Cruitín was among the most prolific copyists of Keating's prose works, and the manuscript associated with the McNamara/Clancy wedding is one of three extant copies of *Foras feasa* in his hand that date from the first decade of the eighteenth century (RIA, MS 23 O 10, completed 1703/4; RIA, MS 23 G 9, completed 1708/9; National Library of Ireland, MS G 599, completed 1709). Many years later he made another transcript of the same text in 1736 (RIA, MS 23 E 10), while a fifth copy is undated (British Library, Additional MS 27,910) but may well date from Mac Cruitín's earlier phase of transcription before 1710.

The 'wedding manuscript' (23 G 9) offers an insight into the business of scribal publication. Mac Cruitín had completed this particular transcript of *Foras feasa* in March 1708/9, and made a second copy of the same text in the same year. It seems, however, that it was only on the occasion of the wedding more than two years later that he found a taker for one of those copies. In 1711 he undertook to customise his transcript of *Foras feasa*, which also contained a selection of poems from the early seventeenth-century 'contention of the bards', to make it into a distinctive wedding gift. In the customisation, an additional four leaves were added at the beginning of the manuscript, comprising a small selection of poems, followed by the pedigrees of the bride and groom and the specially composed wedding poem.

The manuscript is bound in leather, with gilt lettering on the spine, in what appears to be its original binding. This was a prestige, personalised item, intended to commemorate a significant marriage by reference to a long historical tradition. Centuries after the last surviving memories of the wedding had evaporated, the manuscript survives, a tangible witness to a little piece of the social and cultural history of County Clare. *Verba volant, scripta manent.*

Further reading

Bernadette Cunningham, *The world of Geoffrey Keating: history, myth and religion in seventeenth-century Ireland* (Dublin, 2000).

Bernadette Cunningham, 'The Book of O'Loghlen: an unwanted wedding gift?', in R. Gillespie and R.F. Foster (eds), *Irish provincial cultures in the long eighteenth century: making the middle sort* (Dublin, 2012), 181–97.

Margo Griffin-Wilson (ed.), *The wedding poems of Dáibhí Ó Bruadair* (Dublin, 2010).

22

The Delanys: a marriage of 'perfect friendship'

Kristina Decker

When Dr Patrick Delany (1685/6–1768) wrote to Mary Pendarves (née Granville) (1700–88) on 23 April 1743 proposing marriage, he said: 'I have been long persuaded that perfect friendship is nowhere to be found but in marriage, I wish to perfect mine in that state'. This would be the second marriage for both of them, and it couldn't have been more different from Mary's first marriage to Alexander Pendarves in 1718. Mary came from an élite background, her family having many connections at court and beyond. One uncle was Lord Lansdowne, another was Lord Carteret, lord lieutenant of Ireland (1724–30), and yet another was Sir John Stanley, one of the commissioners for customs. After their family fell from favour following the death of Queen Anne, her first marriage was arranged through her uncle Lord Lansdowne for financial and political reasons. Mary's autobiography is very clear that she had married Pendarves out of a sense of familial duty. She was only seventeen; Alexander Pendarves was 60. It is perhaps unsurprising that when he died in 1724 Mary didn't rush into marriage again but enjoyed a happy widowhood of almost twenty years.

She met Patrick Delany through Jonathan Swift on a visit to Ireland from 1731 to 1733. Patrick Delany was about to be married, but they remained friends and corresponded for years before his wife's death and his subsequent proposal of marriage. Patrick Delany came from a relatively humble background. He went to school in Athy before securing a place at Trinity College and, in addition to holding university offices, he was chancellor of St Patrick's, Dublin, vicar of Davidstown, Kildare, rector of Derryvullen, Fermanagh, and finally dean of Down. Some members of Mary's family opposed the match, believing that he was not of sufficiently high standing. For the first and perhaps only time in her life, Mary resisted that sense of familial obligation and married Patrick Delany, for, as Delany mentioned in his letter, his proposal offered the prospect of something that appealed to Mary Pendarves: a marriage built on friendship and companionship.

From the point of view of a modern reader, the values of friendship and companionship seem like they should form the obvious foundations of marriage, but, as is evidenced by Mary Delany's first marriage, this was still far from the norm in the eighteenth century, particularly among the élite. In this light, Mary and Patrick Delany's marriage comes across as quite modern. They enjoyed spending time together; Mary's letters are full of references to the activities they liked to share. Walking and passing time in the garden were among their prime enjoyments. On one trip, exploring a place that they had never visited before, she describes him as a Don Quixote setting forth with a cane instead of a sword, she herself following behind with her shepherdess's crook. In another letter she mentions one of her favourite spots in the garden, a seat that they called the 'Beggar's Hut', and specifically points out that it only had space for just the two of them to sit. Little instances like this scattered throughout her letters paint a picture of companionship and a couple who treasured their time together.

Mary and Patrick Delany also provided each other with emotional support, which was not a feature of her first marriage at least. Mary records in her letters how her husband would cheer her up when she was feeling melancholy by talking of things that she enjoyed, such as the planning of a future trip to England. She also wrote about his support of her creative pursuits. While perhaps best known for her 'paper mosaics', a series of cut-paper flower collages now in the collection of the British Museum, she didn't start making these until her second widowhood, and in one letter from that time even talks about using her work to attempt to fill the gap left by Patrick's death. During his lifetime she was just as involved in creative projects, such as needlework, shellwork, sewing, interior decoration, drawing and painting, and wrote of how his encouragement helped her to complete this work, even when her spirits were low. Mary was equally devoted to her husband. She refused to embark on a trip to England to visit much-missed family and friends when it was apparent that Patrick Delany couldn't accompany her for health reasons. Although he urged her to go on her own for a few months, she declared that she would be miserable without him.

Through Mary Delany's letters we see a contented couple who enjoyed each other's company. Perhaps the best indicator of their happy marriage is in one of the few letters that remain from Patrick Delany to his wife, written during a prolonged period of separation owing to his responsibilities as dean of Down. He implores her not to count the days until they see each other again, as this will make the time seem to pass agonisingly slowly, and suggests instead a less painful way of measuring its passage: 'My dearest life ... you should only count by months, whilst there is any part of another month to come and then you may begin to count by weeks. The last week of the next month will, I hope bring me to you, care of my greatest happiness; but I desire I may not be expected to a day.' It is clear from the terms he uses to address her that Dean Delany was as devoted to his wife as she was to him. This was truly a marriage of mutual happiness.

Further reading

Katherine Cahill, *Mrs Delany's menus, medicines, and manners* (Dublin, 2005).

Mary Delany, *Letters from Georgian Ireland: Mary Delany 1731–68* (ed. Angélique Day) (Belfast, 1991).

Ruth Hayden, *Mrs Delany: her life and her flowers* (London, 1988).

23

Mid-eighteenth-century Irish marriage as portrayed in *The Bordeaux–Dublin letters*

Thomas M. Truxes

Iirst a disclaimer: the author of this essay is not an authority on marriage in early modern Ireland. The observations presented here are based entirely on letters from wives to husbands and husbands to wives that survived unopened in the mailbag of an Irish wine ship—the *Two Sisters* of Dublin—captured in March 1757 returning home from Bordeaux during the first year of the Seven Years' War.[1] Published in 2013, *The Bordeaux–Dublin letters: correspondence of an Irish community abroad* contains 125 letters, 100 of them in English between Irish correspondents, seven of which are between married couples separated by the circumstances of war. All of these individuals fell into the middle tier of Irish society and each of the men was a mariner, serving in roles ranging from common sailors to captains of vessels engaged in Franco-Irish trade.[2] Three of the seven letters provide rare insights into the married lives of their authors.

The first of these was written in October 1756 by Mary Dennis of Dublin to her husband, Capt. John Dennis, master of the *Two Sisters*. Evidence elsewhere in the collection—a December 1750 letter from John's mother concerning his relationship with a Protestant woman—suggests that John and Mary (both Roman Catholics) were in the early years of their marriage and that his livelihood kept them apart for weeks at a time. Mary Dennis's letter

---

1 The contents of the mailbag of the *Two Sisters* of Dublin survive in the 'Prize Papers' of the High Court of Admiralty (HCA) in the British National Archives (Kew). This massive collection is concentrated on times of war — from the mid-seventeenth to the early nineteenth century — when British warships and privateers scoured the seas in search of trading vessels serving the enemies of the Crown. A ship's mailbag, along with whatever papers were found in the captain's cabin, were sources of evidence in prize proceedings against captured vessels in the High Court of Admiralty (TNA, HCA 32/259 and HCA 32/249 [1]).

2 L.M. Cullen, J. Shovlin and T.M. Truxes (eds), *The Bordeaux–Dublin letters, 1757: correspondence of an Irish community abroad*, Vol. 53 of the British Academy's *Records of Social and Economic History* (Oxford, 2013), 112–15, 137–9, 141, 143–6, 170, 195–6 (hereafter cited as BDL). See also T.M. Truxes, *Ireland, France, and the Atlantic in a time of war: reflections on the Bordeaux–Dublin Letters, 1757* (Abingdon, 2017).

is a powerful expression of love and concern for the welfare of her husband. 'I have bean very uneasey Abbout this Bad Whether', she wrote, 'but I trust in ye great God to preserve you from all Dangers & send us a hapy meetting wich is all I ambishon on this Earth.'[3]

The real significance of Mary's letter lies in its portrayal of their marriage as a partnership and in the evidence it presents of a woman playing an independent role as a contributor to the support of the family. Combined with news of goings-on in Dublin are her requests for goods to stock the shelves of her shop on Aston's Key, an enterprise that served the needs of mariners frequenting the port of Dublin. Mary turns to the requirements of her business with the confidence of a wife on an equal footing with her husband: 'I thought it Proper to advise you', she wrote, 'to Bring Reasons & prunes ye sell ye latter 6^d pr^{lb} & anny thing you think Fit for ye ships are stopd hear [because of a wartime embargo] & if you Bring nutts & ollifs you will not luse & you May Remit ye munny'. Mary was a shrewd businesswoman, but she was a wife first: 'I beg you will not omit Riting as it is ye onely Pleasure I Can have in y^r abstance'.[4]

Ten of the letters in the Bordeaux–Dublin collection were from Irish prisoners of war in France. One of them, Capt. Walter Codd, was free on his own recognisance in Marseilles. Like Mary Dennis's letter to her husband John, that of Walter Codd's to his wife Catherine—whom he addresses as Catty—is rich in detail suggestive of a marriage grounded on love and respect. Mary Dennis's letter pulsated with romantic love, whereas that of Walter Codd—after at least fifteen years of marriage—centres on domestic concerns, principally the challenges of raising three adolescent children. Codd's letter is one side of a conversation between a husband and wife seeking the best for their children but experiencing frustrations along the way.

The couple's son, Tom, is in Marseilles with his father, while the two daughters are at home in Dublin with their mother. According to Walter Codd, Tom is lazy but capable, more interested in dancing and drinking than in learning the French language (as his father wishes). 'He is really Idle in regard to The French', Walter told his wife, 'But I intend to send him to the Country, Wher he must Speak it or keep his mouth shut.' As for the daughters at home with their mother, 'above all I expect they will avoid

---

3 Mary Dennis, Dublin, to Mr Jo^n Dennis, Com^{dr} of ye Two Sisters, to be left at Mr Gernon's, Merch^t, Bordeaux, 14 October 1756, *BDL*, 138–9 (quote on p. 138); Margaret Dennis, Waterford, to Mr John Dennis, at Mr John Shaws, Livin in Hawkings Street, Dublin, 10 December 1750, *BDL*, 139–40.

4 Mary Dennis to John Dennis, 8 and 14 October 1756, *BDL*, 137–9 (quotes on p. 138).

the too Common Custom of Dublin Girls', he admonishes his wife, 'Such as Gadding Abroad &c, which is the fore runner of many Evills that attend Girls'. The father has taken a clear stand on the education of women. 'Theyr Needle & Improving Books shoud be Theyr great study, And lett me tell you its as great a Scandall For Girls to be ignorant of theyr needle as it is for men not to understand The use of the pen.' Other matters of importance to the family arise in this letter, but it is clear that launching their three children into mid-eighteenth-century Irish society is the central focus of this marriage.[5]

The third letter, that of Richard Exham, a prisoner of war in the notorious Bayonne Castle, to his wife Betty in Cork, stands in stark contrast to those of Mary Dennis and Walter Codd. Exham's letter exposes a marriage blighted by anger, resentment and distrust. His attacks begin with the very first sentence: 'Your Remissness in not writeing to me Since the 22^d Novr past is a very great Crime and a barefaced Couldness'. Exham's accusations ignore the difficulties of maintaining correspondence in a time of war (a point underscored by the fact that this letter never reached its destination). In addition to not writing with greater frequency, he blames her for failing to achieve his release through a prisoner exchange, for his having missed an opportunity to escape (which he had turned down on the expectation that his wife would arrange for his parole) and for the jail fever that brought him low. 'You see what a Just Reason I have to Condem you', Exham tells his wife in Ireland, 'in this my great Affliction being shut up from all Communication Except our fellow Sufferers whose Number are upwards of 500.' He concludes with an outpouring of venom: 'You have your easey bead by night and your warm house and Searvants at Command, Whils I am Confined within this dark Castle where is nothing but beare Walls and a Could flowr to Ly on Except^t boards under us for which we pay Extravigently. You night and day have Ease and pleasure Whilst I have nothing but Bitterness and Affliction.' We know only one side of this collapsing marriage but it is likely that the well was poisoned before Richard Exham left Ireland.[6]

To a lesser degree, each of the four remaining letters also sheds light on married life in Ireland. The correspondence of two common sailors, written to inform their wives of the capture of the *Two Sisters*, is carefully composed so as not to cause alarm: 'My Dear Kepe a Good hart aad Don't frate your Self',

5 Walter Codd, Marseille, to Catherine Codd, [Dublin], 21 October 1756, *BDL*, 112–15 (quotes on pp 113 and 114).

6 Richard Exham, Bayonne Castle, to Mrs Richard Exham, Georges Street, Cork, 15 February 1757, *BDL*, 143–5 (quotes on pp 144 and 145).

John Johnson told his wife Molly in Dublin.[7] Both he and Archibald Farris signed their letters, 'Loving husband'.[8] Another prisoner of war, the mariner Robert Moore, has become desperate, as his wife faces homelessness in Cork because of his lack of financial support. 'I am but in a poore Condision', he wrote, 'nor is itt in my power to Releave you att This Time my D[r] you most Strive to Gett y[r] Bread till please God I Get my Liberty to Com home.'[9] On a lighter note, there is an unmistakable conspiratorial tone in the letter of Capt. David Donovan to his wife in Limerick. Whereas Donovan's customs documents show that he departed Ireland for Spain, his true destination was France, in direct violation of the law. 'Arrived here the 23th', he tells her, 'the Name of the please I cant Let you know but you may well guse it.'[10]

What are we to make of these few letters touching on marriage in mid-eighteenth-century Ireland? The correspondence presented here may—or may not—be representative, but it speaks eloquently about the married lives of the individuals involved. It is also worth noting that social historians have had little access to what went on behind closed doors in the middle ranks of Irish society. One promising path to uncovering that hidden middle world—in Ireland and elsewhere in western Europe—will be through documents in the massive High Court of Admiralty 'Prize Papers' at the British National Archives (Kew), a collection containing as many as 85,000 personal and business letters (many unopened) in nearly every European language (c. 1650–c. 1815).[11] For historians of early modern marriage, the HCA Prize Papers provide unparalleled opportunities to access the lives of ordinary men and women. Many of those men and women are Irish.

---

7 John Johnson, from on board the *Caesar*, privateer of Bristol, Captain Nash, to M[rs] John [Mollay] Johnson, at the Sine of the hapy Bug, in Gorge's Quay, Dublin, 27 March 1757, *BDL*, 170 (quoted).

8 *Ibid.*; Archibald Farris, at Sea, aboard the Caesar of Bristol, to Mrs Archibald Farris, Living at the Sine of the Bare, in pool Beg Stret, Dublin, n.d., *BDL*, 146.

9 Robert Moore, La Réole, to Marey Moore, att Mr James marins, in Pals Street, near ye Cousthomhouse, Corke, 27 February 1757, *BDL*, 195–6 (quote on p. 195).

10 David Donovan, place not stated, to Mrs[s] Donovan, [c/o] Mr Thomas MacInerheny, Merchant, Limerick, 28 February 1757, *BDL*, 141 (quoted).

11 The bulk of the High Court of Admiralty's 'Prize Papers' reside in TNA, HCA 30; TNA, HCA 32; and TNA, HCA 65.

Further reading

L.M. Cullen, John Shovlin and Thomas M. Truxes (eds), *The Bordeaux–Dublin letters, 1757: correspondence of an Irish community abroad*, Vol. 53 of the British Academy's *Records of Social and Economic History* (Oxford, 2013).

Thomas M. Truxes (ed.), *Ireland, France, and the Atlantic in a time of war: reflections on the Bordeaux–Dublin letters, 1757* (Abingdon, 2017).

24

Bigamy and betrayal: the making of marriage in eighteenth-century Ireland

Leanne Calvert

> *David Clements of the Congregation of Sixmilecross about two Years and a half ago went off with one Scot a Member of the established Church & was married to her by a degraded Popish Priest which Marriage he acknowledged was consummated by cohabiting repeatedly. And some Time after he abandoned said Scot & fell in Courtship with one Love a Dissenter & applying for Marriage with her in the Congregation of Sixmilecross being refused he obtained Licence & was married to the last mentioned agreeable to the Form prescribed by law established. The Synod having spoken to the Affair at full length it was resolved that the said Clements at present by his Conduct hath shut the Door upon himself & excluded himself from Communion with us.*
>
> (Minutes of the Secession Burgher Synod, June 1782)

The case of David Clements offers a fascinating insight into the making of marriage in eighteenth-century Ireland. It is a complex tale, involving desertion, betrayal, bigamy and defiance of church authority. Key to unravelling this tangled web of broken relationships and multiple attempts at marriage is an appreciation of the role that religion played in the making of marriage in eighteenth-century Ireland.

During the period in which David Clements lived, the majority of Ireland's inhabitants belonged to one of three religious traditions: Anglican, Roman Catholic or Presbyterian. While each of these traditions had its own set of rules governing the making of marriage, in the eyes of civil law only that of the Anglican Church was legally valid. This was because Ireland in this period was a confessional state, in which access to political power and the enjoyment of full civil rights was dependent on membership of the Established Church—in this case the Anglican Church. Those who dissented, such as Roman Catholics and Presbyterians, suffered discrimination as a result. One area in which this was evident was marriage.

Marriages performed by Presbyterian ministers were subject to various forms of legal disabilities throughout the eighteenth and nineteenth centuries. For example, until 1782 marriages performed by Presbyterian ministers, between two Presbyterians, were deemed invalid. Moreover, it was not until 1845 that marriages performed by Presbyterian ministers were confirmed as legally unassailable under the Marriage (Ireland) Act. This included those between Presbyterians as well as those between a Presbyterian and a member of the Anglican Church. Marriages performed by Roman Catholic priests were also subject to discrimination, though to a much lesser extent than their Presbyterian counterparts. While marriages between a Catholic and a Protestant performed by Roman Catholic priests were regarded as null and void until 1870, the marriages of two Roman Catholics performed by a Roman Catholic priest were never subject to regulation by statute law. Such marriages were valid in civil law as long as they were celebrated by a validly ordained clergyman, which a Catholic priest was in the eyes of both civil and canon law.

As a member of the Presbyterian community, David Clements's decision to marry was also shaped by the rules of his faith. The Presbyterian church differentiated between what it termed regular and irregular marriage—conforming to Presbyterian rules or not. For a marriage to be regular, it had to conform to three main stipulations: the parties were to be free from any previous contract; the banns of marriage were to be read on three consecutive Sabbaths; and the marriage was to be celebrated by the minister of the local congregation. Persons who contravened these rules were charged with having done so 'irregularly' and many were subject to church discipline. This usually involved the couple reaffirming their marriage before the congregation according to the Presbyterian form. Importantly, however, while the presence of a Presbyterian minister made a marriage 'regular', his absence did not make the union invalid. The role of a minister was only to bless the union. In its simplest form, Presbyterian marriage was made by the exchange of free and mutual consent between the persons to be married. Moreover, the Presbyterian Church could not invalidate marriages celebrated by Anglican clergy, as such marriages were valid in civil law.

It was against this background that David Clements embarked on his route to marriage. Around 1780 Clements procured the services of a Roman Catholic priest and married a woman named Scot, who was a member of the Anglican Church. The newly married couple then moved in together and consummated their marriage. Within three years, however, the relationship had ended. Clements abandoned Scot and entered into a courtship with another woman named Love, a fellow Presbyterian. Clements then decided that he wanted to marry his new love interest and applied to the minister of his congregation. His application, however, was refused. Undeterred by the decision, Clements obtained a licence from the Anglican bishop of his local diocese and married Love regardless.

Why was David Clements's application to marry Love refused by his Presbyterian minister but subsequently granted by the Anglican Church? The answer to this question lies in each church's interpretation of marriage law. In the eyes of the Presbyterian Church, Clements's second application for marriage was potentially bigamous. While his first marriage had been celebrated 'irregularly', it was still valid: both parties had exchanged their free and mutual consent to the union and they had consummated the marriage thereafter by living as husband and wife. It is for this reason that Clements's application was turned down by his minister.

The case was viewed quite differently from the perspective of the Established Church. Under civil law, Clements's marriage to Scot (his first wife) was invalid because it had been celebrated by a 'degraded Popish Priest'—that is, a priest who was not in regular orders. The priest who celebrated this first marriage did not have the proper authority to do so, making it invalid. This point was recognised by the Established Church, which then granted Clements and Love a licence of marriage.

David Clements's case reveals how some individuals were able to take advantage of the ambiguities that were inherent in marriage law in eighteenth-century Ireland. The existence of three competing religious traditions, each of which had their own rules regarding marriage, gave women and men a greater degree of autonomy in their pursuit of marriage. For those (like David Clements) who wished to end one marriage and enter another, a previous contract was not an obstacle. Indeed, while the Presbyterian Church could not rule that Clements's second marriage was invalid on the grounds of bigamy, it was able to subject him to discipline. As a result of his defiance, Clements was excluded from Presbyterian communion.

Sources

Minutes of the Secession Burgher Synod, 1779–1814 (PRONI, CR3/46/1/1).

Further reading

J.C. Beckett, *Protestant dissent in Ireland, 1687–1780* (London, 1948).
Patrick J. Corish, 'Catholic marriage under the Penal code', in A. Cosgrove (ed.), *Marriage in Ireland* (Dublin, 1985), 67–77.

A.R. Holmes, *The shaping of Ulster Presbyterian belief and practice, 1770–1840* (Oxford, 2006).

Mary O'Dowd, *A history of women in Ireland, 1500–1800* (Abingdon, 2005).

25

Love, marriage and
The Midnight Court (1780)

Ciarán Mac Murchaidh

One of the best and most humorous Irish-language texts that deals with the topic of love and marriage is *Cúirt an Mheán Oíche* (*The Midnight Court*), which was composed by the County Clare poet Brian Merriman in 1780. The 1,026-line text takes the form of a quasi-legal debate about the issue of love, sexuality and marriage chaired by Aoibheall (or Eevul), queen of the fairies. The definitive edition of the original Irish-language text is *Cúirt an Mheon-Oíche*, edited by Liam P. Ó Murchú, who spent his career teaching in the Department of Modern Irish at University College, Cork. Ó Murchú considered Frank O'Connor's translation of the text, *The Midnight Court* (which first appeared in 1945), to be the best of all that have appeared either before or since, primarily because of the manner in which he succeeded in capturing and relaying to the English-reading public the spirit, rhythmic virtues and rollicking impact of the original poem.

The story of *The Midnight Court* is quite straightforward: the poet, while out strolling in a rural setting, is overcome by fatigue, falls asleep and has a dream in which he is visited by a fearsome woman, Aoibheall, who summons him to a court sitting:

> And she cried in a voice with a brassy ring
> 'Get up out of this, you lazy thing!
> That a man of your age can think 'tis fitting
> To sleep in a ditch while the court is sitting!'

The reason for the court is Aoibheall's contention that the country is failing because of the lack of a vigorous manhood that is attentive to the needs of its womenfolk:

'A plea that concerns yourself as well,
That the youth of the country's gone to hell,
And the population in decline
As only happened within your time …
Shame on you there without chick nor child
With women in thousands running wild …
What matter to you if their beauty founder,
If belly and breast will never be rounder,
If ready and glad to be mother and wife
They drop, unplucked, from the boughs of life.'

Thus Aoibheall convenes the court to address the injustices of the time against the women of Ireland.

In the second part of the poem, the case of Irish womanhood is put forward by a young woman who gives an account of her woes and those of her contemporaries to the assembled court—that while she has youth and beauty on her side she has no mate because of the refusal of the young men to marry:

'A man that's looking for a wife,
Here's a face that will keep for life!
Hand and arm and neck and breast,
Each is better than the rest.
Look at my waist! My legs are long,
Limber as willows and light and strong,
There's bottom and belly that claim attention
And the best concealed that I needn't mention.'

The fact that young men put off marrying till they are older or marry older women for love of land and property as opposed to love of a good woman their own age is no way for love and marriage to blossom, as far as the young woman is concerned:

'A boy in the blush of his youthful vigour
With a gracious flush and a passable figure
Finds a fortune the best attraction
And sires himself off on some bitter extraction,
Some fretful old maid with her heels in the dung
And pious airs and venomous tongue.'

In Part Three of the poem an old man steps up to present a defence of Ireland's manhood, and he blames the young women of the time for the predicament in which they find themselves. He recounts the circumstances of his own marriage, at the time of which (unbeknownst to him) his wife-to-be was already pregnant by someone else:

> 'Your worship, 'tis women's sinful pride
> And that alone has the world destroyed!
> Every young fellow that's ripe for marriage
> Is hooked like this by some tricky baggage.'

From that moment on, the old man's carefree existence disappeared:

> 'But you see the troubles a man takes on;
> From the minute he marries his peace is gone …
> I lived alone as happy as Larry,
> Till I took it into my head to marry;
> Tilling my fields with an easy mind
> And going wherever I felt inclined.'

His claims do not go uncontested, however, as the young woman returns to the fray in the final part of the poem with a withering condemnation of the old man and his ilk. She mocks his inability to satisfy his young, passionate wife:

> 'What possible use could she have at night
> For dourness, dropsy, bother and blight,
> A basket of bones with thighs of lead,
> Knees absconded from the dead,
> Reddening shanks and temples whitening,
> Looking like one that was struck by lightning?'

The young woman pleads for a ruling that will require all young men to marry and force the clergy to abandon celibacy:

> 'Has the Catholic Church a glimmer of sense
> That the priests won't marry like anyone else?
> Backs erect and heavy hind quarters,
> Hot-blooded men, the best of partners,

Freshness and charm, youth and good looks
And nothing to ease their mind but books!'

As the poem draws to a close, Aoibheall issues her judgement on the matters before the court. She allows the women to seize and tie up the men while their fate is decided, and she predicts the end of the waste that is clerical celibacy. The poet, to his horror, finds that he will be the first to meet this judgement, but as he awaits his new destiny he awakens—with immense relief—from his dream.

As well as its value as an influential text from the canon of eighteenth-century writing in Irish, *The Midnight Court* is a poem by turn bawdy, humorous and ribald. It nevertheless treats of the age-old tension between the sexes in a clever and imaginative manner and provides a mine of information about herbs and potions and aspects of eighteenth-century rural life, as well as addressing—in a surprisingly prescient manner—the many issues that still bedevil contemporary discourse on this key aspect of human interaction.

Further reading

Brian Merriman, *The Midnight Court* (trans. Frank O'Connor; illus. Brian Bourke) (Dublin, 1989).

Brian Merriman, *The Midnight Court* (trans. Ciaran Carson) (Dublin, 2005).

Liam P. Ó Murchú (ed.), *Cúirt an Mheon-oíche le Brian Merriman* (Dublin, 1982).

26

Eloped to Maynooth

Penelope Woods

Grafton Street in the Dublin of 1785 sold all the trappings of respectability. From College Green, which fronted the Houses of Parliament and Trinity College, the street rose gradually to St Stephen's Green, where Dublin society paraded itself, there to see and be seen. Maxwell Boyland, cutler, was at No. 1; next door was Peter Lafont, perfumer, then Thomas O'Leary, peruke-maker; beyond them were chandlers, apothecaries, a printer, a glass-seller, a goldsmith, tailors, confectioners, watch-makers, a miniature-painter, a stay-maker … up one side of the street and back down the other to No. 112, Quin and Cummins, haberdashers and milliners.

Towards the top of the street at No. 69, between Francis Battersby, grocer, and George Draper, haberdasher, was wine merchant William Witherington, who had sold his woollen business the previous year. The house itself belonged to the Reverend Edward Fanning, a wealthy widower, who lived there with his two daughters and their families. His elder daughter, Catherine Witherington, wife of William, was in charge of the household, and it must have been a noisy one. The couple had six, possibly seven, surviving children at this stage: Edward, the eldest, was twenty; next came Joanna, followed by fifteen-year-old Martha, our heroine; then Harriet (thirteen), Catherine (ten) and Henry (six), with Elizabeth, born in 1780, who may or may not have survived. Mrs Witherington's sister Matilda (who married as Martha), wife of Blennerhasset Grove, a linen-draper, had been widowed early when expecting her second child in 1773. She and her daughters Elizabeth and Anna were also of the household, their not-insubstantial wealth having accrued to Edward Fanning as guardian. So, eight or nine children, four adults and servants to boot. According to her nephew, Thomas Reynolds, Mrs Witherington was passionately fond of her children and devoted to her ailing, elderly father, who unsurprisingly kept to his room.

And the children, what of their upbringing? Edward Witherington was sent to the school six doors down at No. 75, Samuel Whyte's English Grammar School. Whyte offered a good classical education but also set great store by a proper understanding of English, of the meaning of words, their pronunciation, use and delivery, and for this he encouraged his pupils in the dramatic arts, with such productions as Addison's tragedy *Cato* and Gay's *Beggar's opera*. His views echoed those of the two Thomas Sheridans, father and son, and also John Walker, he of the pronouncing dictionary; their ideas were much in vogue at this time. In 1772 Whyte published *The shamrock, or Hibernian cresses*, a collection of poems by himself and his pupils. The book also contained a list of his pupils, both young ladies and young gentlemen, which included Edward Witherington, then aged seven. In his *Modern education* (1775) Whyte strongly promoted his school for the education of young ladies. In order to give them a 'liberal cast' they would study the *belles lettres* and have a good classical education through English, with a strong emphasis on the knowledge and use of the language. Parents were urged to send their daughters to school and not bury their 'golden talent in the earth'. At the very end, his eloquence gave way to deep indignation. Who would wish to be accused of being 'some muck-worm of a parent who had not the heart to pay for a meritorious daughter's education'? It is not known whether any of the Witherington daughters or nieces attended Whyte's school, but the parents would have been very aware of Whyte's precepts. Certainly Martha was to become an intimate letter-writer, and was described later, in 1802, as affectionate, with 'an understanding of every accomplishment', and as having books on her sitting-room shelves by French, Italian and English authors, with a harp, guitar and pianoforte there besides.

It was Martha who was sitting by the window in Grafton Street one evening early in 1785 looking out at the passers-by. The students at Trinity College had finished dining at Commons, and one of them, accompanied by a friend, was strolling up the street when he caught sight of Martha and cast a lingering glance. She was, by his own later account, 'as beautiful as an angel'. Thereafter he passed the house each evening, exchanging glances with the girl in the window until they had become much enamoured of each other without having spoken a word together. The student was Theobald Wolfe Tone, bright, intelligent and articulate, son of a Dublin coach-maker turned Kildare farmer. At this stage, aged 22, he was studying with no great enthusiasm for a Bachelor of Arts degree and longing instead for a military career.

How was Theobald to contrive the means to meet the girl in the window, not just once but regularly? He needed an introduction to the family. A little investigation and he discovered that Martha's brother Edward had recently graduated from Trinity College with a BA. He found him an 'egregious coxcomb', but needs must. Thankfully, the two had music as a common interest. Edward played the violin and Theobald played the instrument that was then most popular amongst his peers, the flute. The songs sung in the comic operas, which were regularly performed at the theatres in Smock Alley and Crow Street, were very fashionable at this time; so too were sprightly Scottish dances and the music of Carolan, frequently adapted for song settings. These were all typically arranged for combinations of German flute, violin, harpsichord or guitar. Excellent! It proved to be a happy means of introduction to the family, and according to himself Theobald became a firm favourite. Not far away, in Dame Street, leading music publisher John Lee sold numerous arrangements, with romantic song titles which might well fan youthful ardour, such as 'I loved him for himself alone' or 'Sweet transports' from Frances Brooke's recent popular opera *Rosina*. Theobald was a great devotee of the theatre.

Mrs Witherington failed to keep her eye on what was happening. Under her very nose, Theobald managed to propose secretly to Martha and to be accepted. He wrote later that he had not sought consent from anyone, 'knowing well it would be in vain to expect it'. The Witherington family's parish church was St Ann's in nearby Dawson Street. The church was built in 1720 and still thrives today. The vicar, Dr Thomas Leland, was in failing health—he spent much of his time in his second parish of Ardstraw in the northern diocese of Derry and had not performed a marriage in Dublin since April 1783—and so the church of St Ann, a fashionable one, was managed by two curates. Edward Ryan had been curate there since 1776. He was living close by at No. 4 Clarendon Street and would have known the Witheringtons well, yet he apparently carried out the marriage without the family's knowledge. The calling of the banns, which was supposed to take place on three consecutive Sundays in the parish church of each, could be avoided by payment of a fee, and this was a common practice. The required marriage licence was issued by the consistorial court of the diocese. It was a printed document, filled in by the priest, with his name, the name of the parish and of the couple. It was then sent to the consistorial court, where it was registered and the great seal of the court applied, signed by the seneschal. According to the parish register of St Ann's, which no longer survives in the original, Theobald Wolfe Tone Esq. and Martha Witherington were married by consistory licence by the Reverend Edward Ryan on 21 July 1785. Names of the witnesses were not recorded. Theobald, with tender memory, wrote 'one beautiful morning in the month of July we ran off together and were married. I carried her out of town to Maynooth for a few days.' Martha became known as Matilda ever after, a name much favoured for heroines in novels and plays of the day—*Reginald Du Bray*, Godwin's *Italian letters*, Cumberland's *The Carmelite* and Walpole's *Castle of Otranto*. She had just turned sixteen on 17 June.

Maynooth was the estate town of the duke of Leinster—this was ten years before Maynooth College was founded. The town was not such a great distance away. It lay on the main road west, fifteen miles from Dublin, in County Kildare, and was easily reached. Theobald's own family were ten and a half miles cross-country from Maynooth, at Bodenstown. So the couple did not flee but merely hid away to give the families time to recover from the initial discovery—'when the first éclat of passion had subsided, we were forgiven on all sides'. The marriage proved to be a loving and very successful one in the turbulent times that lay ahead.

Sources
Dublin Consistorial Court records were destroyed in 1922; an example of a consistorial licence, recording a Dublin marriage of 1798, is held in the National Library of Ireland (MS 49,433). The National Library of Ireland also holds a large collection of eighteenth-century music printed in Dublin.

Further reading
D.A. Chart (ed.), *Marriage entries from the registers of the parishes of St Andrew, St Anne, ... Dublin, 1632–1800* (Dublin, 1913).

T.W. Moody, R.B. McDowell and C.J. Woods (eds), *The writings of Theobald Wolfe Tone, 1763–98* (3 vols, Oxford, 1998–2007). [Detailed indexes in vol. 3.]

H.F. Reynolds, 'Irish family history: Fanning of Dublin', *Notes and Queries* (12th ser.) **7** (16 October 1920), 307–8.

H.F. Reynolds, 'Irish family history: Witherington of Dublin', *Notes and Queries* (12th ser.) **9** (16 July 1921), 43–5.

C.J. Woods, 'Tone, Matilda (Martha)', in *Dictionary of Irish Biography*, vol. 9 (Cambridge, 2009), 406–8.

27

The criminal conversation suit in Ireland

Diane Urquhart

lthough claims of exalted Irish morality were long-lived, evidence of extramarital affairs spans the centuries. This often came to light in marital disputes. Such disputes took various forms and not all resulted in a legal dissolution of marriage. Indeed, only *divorce à vinculo matrimonii*, secured by a parliamentary act from the mid-seventeenth century, dissolved the matrimonial bond to allow the parties to remarry. By comparison, a church-based or civil nullity suit denied that a legitimate union had taken place; separation, known as *divorce à mensâ et thoro*, allowed divorce from bed and board so that the parties could not be compelled to live together but could not remarry; a restitution of conjugal rights suit compelled a spouse to return to the marital home, and a civil criminal conversation suit allowed a husband to sue a wife's paramour for trespass. The latter, popularly abbreviated to crim. con., implied adultery. This was one of the most notorious marital suits, as it not only financially compensated a husband whose wife had been adulterous but was also a legal recourse that was only available to men. The gender-specific access to criminal conversation suits was a consequence of married women's legal status as the 'property' of their spouses. Romanticised and sensationalised in equal measure, this suit's foundation lay in thirteenth-century writs for ravishment and trespass which developed into trials for loss of services. Trespass and compensation for the loss of consortium were the most significant inheritances from these early origins. Developing at common law in the late seventeenth century, the first widely publicised criminal conversation case was that of the duke of Norfolk, who sought £100,000 in damages for his wife's adultery in 1692.

A criminal conversation suit was a stand-alone legal action, but its history is closely entwined with that of parliamentary divorce: by 1780 a criminal conversation suit was a preliminary step to a parliamentary divorce, and from 1798 it or a sufficient explanation for not having brought such a case (owing to the death or unknown whereabouts of a paramour, or if he was outside of the court's jurisdiction or too poor to pay damages) was a prerequisite. Initially, as the duke of Norfolk's case indicates, this was an upper-class preserve, but the class composition of the criminal conversation plaintiff broadened from the mid-nineteenth century onwards to include the middling and eventually the lower social orders. Unlike some solutions to marital discord, criminal conversation suits were used by both Catholics and Protestants.

A criminal conversation suit often brought unsolicited notoriety. These cases attracted considerable attention, and proceedings, often illustrated, were frequently published. Such publications sought to entertain and excite with intimate details of private lives, but they also served to alert would-be adulterers of the consequences which could accompany their actions. The newspaper coverage of these trials was also extensive. Courtrooms hearing these cases were regularly packed to capacity and, on occasion, admission was on a ticketed basis.

Damages awarded in criminal conversation suits highlighted that not all wives were considered of equal value. Amounts awarded in Irish cases ranged from nominal damages of a farthing to £20,000. The legal pendulum deciding the amount of damages to be awarded thus swung over what a woman's infidelity denied her spouse. Nominal amounts could also be awarded when a husband was considered negligent or abusive, and damages could be reduced if a jury suspected connivance. Class was another central consideration; a woman from so-called respectable stock would merit a higher award of damages in the eighteenth and nineteenth centuries, and the wealth of the parties still featured in Irish twentieth-century criminal conversation suits. Although the level of damages decreased from the late nineteenth century onwards, awards of damages in Ireland during the 1970s could still amount to thousands of pounds. The lowering of damages was possibly a covert way of deterring criminal conversation suits; criticism of the action increased, especially in relation to women's perilous legal state and concerns that 'evidence', often given by servants, was being purchased. Neither the husband nor the wife's alleged lover could testify in person in these cases until the passage of the Evidence Further Amendment Act of 1869. This act also allowed women to be cross-examined and to be represented by a lawyer who could call witnesses, but it was the 1880s before this occurred with any regularity in Ireland. Giving such evidence was understandably traumatic: women are often described as distressed and weeping in the coverage of these trials.

Ireland's history of criminal conversation has a long chronology. The Divorce and Matrimonial Causes Act of 1857 ended the criminal conversation action in England and Wales, although its spirit lingered in the damages which could be claimed from a co-respondent in court until 1970. Scotland never adopted the practice although damages could be levelled in court. Ireland's exclusion from the 1857 act allowed criminal conversation to survive. Criminal conversation was only abolished in Northern Ireland in 1939 and in the Republic of Ireland in 1981. Although not an overly popular action, it never became defunct: in the 1970s, for example, the decade preceding the action's repeal in the Republic of Ireland, six cases were brought. As a legal suit it therefore stands as testament to the longevity of the sexual double standard and the variance of law between England and Ireland whilst under the Act of Union and within Ireland in the post-independence era.

Further reading
Art Cosgrove (ed.), *Marriage in Ireland* (Dublin, 1985).
David Fitzpatrick, 'Divorce and separation in modern Irish history', *Past and Present* **114** (1987), 172–96.
Niamh Howlin and Kevin Costello (eds), *Law and the family in Ireland, 1800–1950* (London, 2017).

28

Clandestine marriage in eighteenth- and early nineteenth-century Dublin

James Kelly

On 1 May 1788 the Catholic archbishop of Dublin, John Thomas Troy (1739–1823), circulated among the priests of the diocese a short document containing three questions on the subject of 'clandestine marriage'. Acutely conscious of the fact that such marriages were a cause of 'serious scandal' (*ingenti scandalo*) and 'extremely detrimental' (*summo detrimento*) to the authority of the Church (*disciplinae ecclesiasticae*), Troy sought not just information but also guidance. Since *Tametsi*—the decree regulating marriage approved by the Council of Trent in 1563—had never been promulgated in Dublin, Troy was not merely going through the motions. Clandestine marriages conducted by ordained clergymen who operated outside of the regular parish structure were not just commonplace but also a symptom of the limitations of the rule and authority of the Church, and one which Propaganda Fide, which was responsible for the propagation of the faith, was anxious to address by encouraging its promulgation in those dioceses, Dublin included, that had failed to do so. To this end, since the 1770s it had sought to encourage Irish bishops to take the appropriate steps to bring the Irish Church into line, and was unconvinced by the reservations expressed by various Irish bishops, who were well disposed in principle, that the moment was not opportune.

Troy had come to Dublin in 1786, having previously ministered for a decade in the diocese of Ossory, with a deserved reputation as a reforming pastor and (as a Dominican friar) a loyal prince of the church. To this end, beginning in 1788, Troy embarked on regular parish visitations and required his clergy to report annually on the state of the Church in their parishes. While the issues upon which priests were requested to comment reflect the enduring preoccupation of the Church authorities with schism and heresy (the issues of proselytism and conversion and the relative numbers of Catholics and Protestants feature prominently), Troy also contrived to apply the decrees and doctrines of the Church through improving the doctrinal knowledge of his priests by requiring them to attend instructional meetings, and through enhancing clerical discipline by identifying what was inappropriate behaviour and occasions they should avoid. He made sufficient progress in this respect during his long episcopate to prompt a modern authority to describe him as 'the father of the modern Irish church and the author of many of the initiatives … attributed to [Cardinal] Paul Cullen'. This may overstate the extent and impact of his reformist endeavour, since the caution with which he proceeded when the matter at issue involved the state meant that there were not only problems that he failed to resolve but also solutions, provided for by the decrees of the Church, that he declined to pursue. One of the most emblematic matters was the ongoing problem of what contemporaries, churchmen included, denominated 'clandestine marriage'.

According to *Tametsi*, a Christian marriage was invalid unless it was conducted by a bishop, a parish priest or a priest duly authorised to act in their place before two witnesses. Approved along with a great number of other reforms in a conscious attempt to provide for doctrinal and disciplinary conformity, the fitful and local promulgation of the decree in Ireland in the late sixteenth and early seventeenth centuries mirrored the diminishing authority of the Church in that jurisdiction, with the result that a variety of irregular practices were commonplace during the eighteenth century, when the Church functioned in the shadow of the Penal Laws. Some of these—the forced marriage of abducted heiresses, for example—were sufficiently egregious to elicit legislative intervention. Capital sanctions were also provided for to discourage Catholic clergy from officiating in the marriage of Protestants and of Protestants and Catholics. Since a marriage performed by an ordained clergyman (of any denomination) was recognised as legal, however, the Church authorities were unable to enforce the provisions of *Tametsi*, and since the Catholic populace was unwilling to be bound by its restrictions, 'clandestine marriages' were commonplace. Though an island-wide phenomenon, it was most prevalent in Dublin. This can be attributed in large part to the fact that Dublin was the most populous and important diocese in which *Tametsi* had not been promulgated, but it could not have flourished as it did in the absence of 'couple-beggars'—ordained clerics no longer in good standing with the Church who were commonplace in the capital—who would perform the rite of marriage with no questions asked (see Katie Barclay's contribution elsewhere in this volume). It is also important to point out that they did so for a fee smaller than that requested by the parish clergy, since it also highlights a social dimension of this phenomenon—that clandestine marriage was the preference of the poor and marginalised.

This is not to suggest that members of the élite—Protestant as well as Catholic—did not avail themselves, on occasion, of the opportunity to marry secretly when it was convenient to do so. Nevertheless, the observation of Fr Richard Callaghan, the parish priest of St Nicholas Without, in 1788 that clandestine marriage would greatly decrease 'if it were published that the poor would be married *gratis*' indicates not only that the phenomenon possessed an economic rationale but also that it was favoured by the less well-off for whom the standard 'marriage dues' were 'more than they could afford'. It also possessed a social rationale, given the power of veto that parents asserted over whom their children married, since it provided young couples with the means of circumventing the opposition of parents or guardians, and, when they arose, the 'canonical impediments' that the Church identified. Amongst the latter, 'the intermarriage of Catholicks with Protestants' was identified as a particular issue in Dublin, for though it galled some clergy that 'the marriage of a Catholic with a heritick [*sic*]' conducted by a 'couple-beggar' was recognised in law, it was a critical consideration in causing four-fifths of the nearly 40 respondents who engaged with Troy's queries to advise that it was 'unseasonable and dangerous' to promulgate *Tametsi*. Most apprehended that it 'would justly irritate the government against us', since it would inevitably mean that marriages recognised in law would be deemed invalid by the Church. It was not self-evident what the consequences of this might be, but even the suggestion that it must 'open the way to recantations, lawsuits, discords, enmities and deceits' encouraged caution. There were few among the clergy, and still fewer on the episcopal bench, who did not see the risks if the Church set itself at odds with the law of the land. Indeed, it was pointed out by one respondent that since the Church traditionally sought the 'support of the civil power to enforce obedience to her mandates, [and] never to slight it, much less to induce an opposition', to do otherwise would be contrary to established practice.

Given the number of Troy's respondents who counselled caution, it is a matter of little surprise that Archbishop Troy did not promulgate *Tametsi* in 1789 or at any moment during the remaining 34 years that he oversaw the archdiocese of Dublin. He did not ignore the matter, however. He was heartened by the advice he received from many quarters within the diocese that 'the evils of clandestine marriage may be remedied' by the 'unremitting and impartial exercise of the spiritual authority [of the Church] in publick admonitions, threats, excommunications, etc.' to persist with this strategy, which he had already elaborated in his Lenten pastoral in 1789. It did not save him (and his fellow archbishops) from a stern admonition from Propaganda Fide in 1791, but it dovetailed with the greater willingness publicly to censure those who appealed to couple-beggars and the incremental increase in discipline in the laity and clergy that was a feature of Troy's episcopate. It also ensured that considerable progress was made in applying Tridentine forms in respect of marriage in advance of the formal adoption of *Tametsi* nationally in 1827, after which the once-prevalent problem of clandestine marriage effectively disappeared.

Further reading

Cormac S. Begadon, 'Laity and clergy in the Catholic renewal of Dublin, *c.* 1750–1830' (unpublished Ph.D thesis, Maynooth University, 2009).

Patrick J. Corish, 'Catholic marriage under the penal code', in A. Cosgrove (ed.), *Marriage in Ireland* (Dublin, 1985), 67–77.

Dublin Diocesan Archive, Troy papers, AB2/29/1 (1–40).

Dáire Keogh, 'John Thomas Troy', in J. McGuire and J. Quinn (eds), *Dictionary of Irish Biography* (9 vols, Cambridge, 2009).

Vincent J. McNally, *Reform, revolution and reaction: Archbishop John Thomas Troy and the Catholic Church in Ireland, 1787–1817* (Lanham, MD, 1995).

29

Buckle-beggars, bribes and brides

Laurence Kirkpatrick

I rish Presbyterians are 'blow-ins' in terms of the ecclesiastical history of Ireland, only arriving in significant numbers, and then mostly in Ulster, in the early seventeenth century. For much of their existence they have occupied a second-class middle ground between their majority third-class Catholic and minority first-class Protestant neighbours, agreeing and at times disagreeing on a plethora of issues with one or both. As Dissenters, they frequently experienced the opprobrium of the minority Protestant élite, who were often paranoid in their determination to retain power and control at all costs in this alien land. It is the purpose of this short paper to examine aspects of how this conflict and other factors impinged upon the Presbyterian concept and celebration of marriage.

A product of the Reformation, and particularly following the teaching of John Calvin of Geneva via John Knox and Scotland, Irish Presbyterians did not regard marriage as a sacrament but rather as a creation ordinance, and it was invariably celebrated in simple form. Generations of Irish people of all religious persuasions and none have fallen in love and committed to living together. All the churches have their peculiar rubrics for such ceremonies, though often their enforcement was conducive to complicating nuptials for prospective couples. For over 200 years Presbyterians struggled to gain legal recognition for marriages conducted by their own ministers. The root issue from an episcopal church perspective was that Presbyterian ordinations were invalid, as no bishop was involved. To accept Presbyterian marriages as valid meant also to accept the Presbyterian Church as valid, a step too far in seventeenth-century Ireland. In consequence of episcopal disapproval, Presbyterian ministers did everything in their power to ensure that Presbyterian marriages were decent and sober occasions.

The earliest extant Presbyterian Church record relates to the congregation of Templepatrick, Co. Antrim, from 1646, and a warning was issued on 28 December 1647 against any misdemeanours such as drunkenness or squabbling at marriages. There was also a decided preference for marriage to be celebrated *facie ecclesiae*. In 1702 Revd John McBride published *A vindication of marriages as solemnised by Presbyterians in the north of Ireland*, in which he complained bitterly of episcopal attacks on Presbyterian marriages. He mocked the episcopal clergy who took fees in respect of Presbyterian marriages while at the same time declaring the marriages invalid.

The implication of the invalidity of Presbyterian marriage was that Presbyterian couples married by their own minister were regarded in law as fornicators and their children as bastards. In addition to the *obloquium* of the terminology, expensive legal difficulties could be raised regarding land inheritance in such circumstances. For more than a century, the crux of the Presbyterian case for legal recognition was that in the early 1600s the government had invited Scottish Presbyterian ministers to Ireland to minister in the Established Church and their sacraments and marriages were then recognised as valid. Additionally, since 1672 Irish Presbyterians were in receipt of *regium donum*, an important annual Westminster contribution to ministerial comforts yet anomalous if their ministry was invalid. Extant Irish Presbyterian records abound with troublesome references to marriage. For example, in 1716 four members of Tullylish congregation in County Down were 'handed over to Satan' by episcopal authority for the crime of having been married by their own minister, Revd Gilbert Kennedy.

In an attempt to deflect criticism, the Presbyterian Synod ruled in 1701 that the banns of marriage should be pronounced for three preceding Sabbaths, but this was not popular among the Presbyterian people. Frequent ignoring of this unpopular decree is indicated by the fact that it was reinforced in 1755 and again in 1761. Rather than submit to this rule, many couples reverted to local buckle-beggars for marriage. The term 'buckle-beggar' refers to a deprived or unlicensed minister or priest who made his living by offering cheap marriages, the couple marrying being 'buckled'. Such marriages were irregular and Presbyterian authorities usually required a couple so married to show subsequent contrition before a congregation for two Sundays as penance, but they were thereafter regarded as a married couple. It was only in 1825 that the Presbyterian Synod declared all such marriages to be null and void. Presbyterian ministers performing irregular marriages faced the ultimate sanction. Between 1710 and 1775 ten ministers were suspended for this crime, and eight of these were permanently deprived. The infamous buckle-beggar Samuel D'Assigny, who died in 1737, is reported to have married many thousands of couples. Presbyterian minister Revd William Blakely was suspended from his congregation in Carrickfergus in 1779 and thereafter pursued a career as a buckle-beggar until his death in 1810. Such generally inexpensive marriages were relatively popular and it is known that 28 registers containing records of some 30,000 buckle-beggar marriages perished on 30 June 1922 when the Public Records Office was destroyed during the Irish Civil War.

Every extant Presbyterian congregational record which records marriages contains references to 'irregular marriages', indicating how widespread the practice was. Revd James Cochrane was ordained in Larne in December 1815, having previously served as tutor to a family called Craig in nearby Carrickfergus. He 'married' a daughter of that family, but when malevolent rumours circulated it was discovered that Mr Cochrane had performed the marriage himself in May 1815, with no witnesses present and without any prior public announcement—all highly irregular. He was suspended from office for one year, but his congregation, in a show of solidarity, refused to pay any of the supply preachers. More common irregularities included breach of promise, no banns read, elopement, and no parental permission for younger brides. Kirk Session punishment for such misdemeanours varied but usually consisted of a measure of 'rebuke and admonishment', though 'irregular' did not equate with 'invalid'.

'Mixed marriages' were a particular source of *angst*. As late as 1840, Armagh Consistorial Court ruled that a marriage between a Presbyterian and an Anglican, performed by a Presbyterian minister, was illegal. In the following year, a man convicted of bigamy successfully appealed to a higher court on the grounds that his first marriage to a Presbyterian by her minister was not a valid marriage. In Queen's Bench the accused won his case on a split decision but the matter came to the House of Lords, which upheld the decision of the lower court. Outraged, the Presbyterians held a special General Assembly to register their disapproval, and in 1844 the government conceded that marriages conducted by Presbyterian ministers where only one party was Presbyterian were legal.

One of the most notorious cases of difficulty concerned Alexander McCann (a Catholic) and Agnes Barclay (a Presbyterian), who were married in Antrim by Presbyterian minister Revd McCheyne Gilmour on 16 May 1908. They set up home in Belfast and joined Townsend Street Presbyterian congregation. Local priest Father Hubert called regularly at their home and informed them that they were not properly married because of the recent *Ne Temere* decree (see Oliver Rafferty's contribution in this volume). Agnes refused to submit to 're-marriage' by a priest, and in 1910 Alexander absconded with their two young children and she never saw them again. It is now known that Alexander and his children sailed from Derry and settled in Philadelphia, changing their surname to Madden. Thankfully, the main churches generally co-operate on a much better level today and 'mixed marriages' can usually be accommodated with common sense and a spirit of ecumenical co-operation. True love always trumps ecclesiastical rules, but in parts of Ireland such marriages still provoke deep anguish within family circles.

The latest perceived challenge to the marriage standards of the Presbyterian Church in Ireland was sparked by the Irish referendum on 22 May 2015 which approved the 34th amendment to the Constitution in the following terms: 'marriage may be contracted in accordance with law by two persons without distinction as to their sex'. As a direct response, the 2016 Presbyterian General Assembly ruled that all Presbyterian marriage celebrations must now include the following statement: 'Since the beginning of creation God, in His gracious purpose, provided marriage as the accepted way in which a man and woman may come together as husband and wife'.

30

Marriage, ministers and Irish Presbyterians

Janice Holmes

The history of Irish Presbyterian marriage traditions has still to be written. We have some understanding of popular Presbyterian marriage habits, especially in the eighteenth century, but we know more about the marriage practices of Irish Presbyterian ministers, even though their biographies and memoirs tend to present their marriages in an idealised way. A closer reading of these and other sources shows that the marriages of Presbyterian clergy reflected the full spectrum of possible relationships, from companionable and affectionate to authoritarian and distant. The nature of the ministerial role—with its requirements to be teacher, leader, mentor and counsellor—could put ministers and their marriages under considerable pressure.

It is estimated that between the eighteenth and twentieth centuries several thousand men were ordained as Irish Presbyterian clergymen. Of those who were appointed to Ulster-based congregations (which would be the large majority of this figure), about 61% were married. Most of these men married between the ages of 31 and 33. This was because the average age at ordination was 27, and ministers would not have married until they had a position and income with which to support a wife. Most ministers married only once; only 12% married more than once. In a separate survey of Presbyterian clergy in Belfast between 1800 and 1900, approximately 78% (96) were married and a similar proportion as above were married more than once. Anecdotal evidence suggests that ministers tended to marry within the Presbyterian tradition and that there was a small but noticeable tendency to marry women from clerical families.

Presbyterian guidance on marriage and the form a marriage service should take drew on the precepts outlined in the Westminster Confession of Faith. Marriage should be allowed if it was based on mutual consent, did not break the laws of consanguinity or create partnerships with 'infidels, Papists or other idolaters'. In the eighteenth century new guidelines required marriages to be conducted by a minister, in the meeting-house, and with three weeks' notice (or 'banns') being announced in the relevant parties' home congregations. Many couples sought to avoid these regulations and contracted 'irregular' marriages based on a verbal declaration. Changes to the Irish marriage laws in the early nineteenth century meant that by the 1850s most Presbyterians, and certainly all Presbyterian clergymen, were being married in church by a minister and according to the official Presbyterian form of service.

The official Presbyterian marriage service was quite simple. The minister would begin with a prayer that asked God's blessing on the marriage at hand. He would then address the bride and groom and their assembled friends and family. He outlined the scriptural basis for marriage: that it was the husband's duty to 'love, protect, and provide for his wife', that it was her duty to 'love her husband and obey him in the Lord', and that it was their mutual duty to 'bear with each other's infirmities, sustain and comfort each other under the various trials of life, help each other in the service of God, and live as heirs together of the grace of life that their prayers be not hindered'. The bride and groom would then hold hands and, in front of their witnesses, say their vows. The minister then declared them married and closed the service with prayer.

As for what actually happened in practice, we still have only fragmentary evidence. We know, for instance, that ministers tended to meet their future wives through family and Presbyterian circles. The Revd Henry Cooke met Ellen Mann, his future wife, when he was appointed to his first charge at Duneane in 1808. The Revd John Edgar met his wife in 1828 when preaching in one of the villages around Belfast where his pastorate was based. The Revd Robert Barron renewed his friendship with his wife Mary in 1893, several years after the death of her first husband. We know, too, that ministers had some notion of a 'wedding party'. The Revd David Hamilton, for instance, had a 'best man' at his wedding to Eliza Weir in the 1830s. Ministers also seem to have taken honeymoons. Most of these were quite modest, but for the Revd William Fleming Stevenson, minister at Rathgar in Dublin between 1860 and 1886, his was a month-long cultural tour through Switzerland, Italy and London.

When reflecting on their married lives, Presbyterian ministers and their wives used highly idealised language. Jane Toye, the Revd Thomas Toye's third wife, declared that it was her 'privilege to spend seventeen years of happiest days in the closest and most endearing of all human relationships, with one of the tenderest, best and most affectionate of husbands'. Such paeans disguise the complexities and nuances of ministerial relationships. The Revd

William Johnston's biographer describes Johnston's marriage to his wife Sarah as 'thirty-nine years of unclouded domestic sunshine', and Johnston himself admitted that his professional success was due to Sarah's 'loving co-operation' and her 'unwearied sympathy and effort'. Yet, as Sarah herself recalled after his death, 'he took occasion at an early date [after they were married] to teach me once for all, in a very amusing incident, that "wives should submit themselves until their own husbands as is fit in the Lord"'. Ministerial marriages may have been loving and affectionate, but they were firmly based on a traditional model of male head and obedient wife.

Although the evidence is scarce and harder to interpret, some accounts can be seen to suggest that not all ministerial marriages were entirely happy. The Revd Hugh Hanna's wife, Fanny, is rarely mentioned in connection with any of his extensive public activities. The Revd John Kinghan sounds harsh and autocratic in the provisions he made for his wife in his will. Several biographical accounts suggest that ministers had significant friendships with other women and that they spent a great deal of time away from home, attending meetings or on preaching tours. Although Ellen Cooke wrote to Henry while on a lengthy trip to Dublin, asking him to come home, Cooke put her off and returned when he had decided his work was finished. Pressures of congregational work and fund-raising to eliminate congregational debt triggered nervous breakdowns in a number of ministers. Their long bouts of ill health must have created a whole new set of stresses and strains on their marital relationships.

Taken together, these accounts show that marriage was an important part of the Presbyterian ministerial profession. Ministers were expected to model the ideal Christian family, and while many of them demonstrated great affection and respect towards their wives, they operated with considerable autonomy and determined the terms upon which their marriage was based. It was only in the twentieth century that there was a growing recognition that marriages could, in the words of the Revd John Barkley, go through significant 'grey patches' and that the Presbyterian Church, as an institution, should do something to help.

Further reading

Linda May Ballard, *Forgetting frolic: marriage traditions in Ireland* (Belfast, 1998).
Andrew Holmes, *The shaping of Ulster Presbyterian belief and practice, 1770–1840* (Oxford, 2006), chapter 8.

31

Four weddings, two funerals and a divorce: or, the lives and loves of the Tennent family

Jonathan Jeffrey Wright

The story of the Tennent family of County Antrim and Belfast contains much of interest to the historian. Prominent in the political, religious and intellectual life of Ulster in the late eighteenth and early nineteenth centuries, their number included, in three successive generations, the Revd John Tennent, a Presbyterian minister; William Tennent, a founding member of the United Irish movement, who was also one of the wealthiest Belfast businessmen of his day; and two members of parliament, Robert James Tennent and James Emerson Tennent. Public life aside, however, the family's marital history is of equal interest, revealing, as it does, the varied trajectories—not all of them happy—that marriage could follow.

The Tennent family was established in Ulster by the Revd John Tennent, a Scot who was ordained as a Presbyterian minister in May 1751 and who settled in Roseyards, Co. Antrim. Five years later, in January 1756, the Revd John took a wife—one Ann Patton, of Limavady, Co. Londonderry. If not without its difficulties—family letters suggest that Ann was a woman of sharp tongue and quick temper—their marriage was, by the standards of the day, a successful one. It lasted just under 50 years (Ann died in 1805, the Revd John in 1807) and produced at least nine children, eight of whom survived infancy. Moreover, if there were moments of conflict, there was also affection, and the Revd John wrote movingly of his loss when Ann died in 1805. In short, the pairing of the Revd John and Ann marked an auspicious start to the Tennent family's marital history. Regrettably, not all of the family's marriages proved to be so successful.

The story of John and Ann's son Robert (b. 1765) provides a case in point. Having spent time working as an estate manager in Jamaica in the 1780s and '90s, Robert Tennent was a man with a past—a past which included his fathering of an illegitimate child. By the early 1800s, however, he had returned to Ireland a changed man. Having experienced a religious conversion, he was determined to start his life anew, and in August 1802 he married a young woman named Eliza MacCrone. Both serious about religion, the two were well matched and very much in love; indeed, on one occasion the Revd John was moved to chide them for their excessive affection. All bade well for the future, but tragedy soon struck. Shortly after their wedding Eliza had become pregnant, and late in May 1803, just weeks after having given birth to a son, Robert James, she died. Robert was never to remarry, and was marked by his loss for the rest of his life. Thus, on the occasion of his death in 1837, one friend remarked that he had witnessed 'his whole frame shaken by an unintentional allusion to his bereavement'.

Four years later, in 1807, tragedy would strike the Tennents again, cutting short the marriage of Robert's elder brother, William (b. 1759). William, too, was a man with a past. Present in October 1791 when the Society of United Irishmen was established in Belfast, he appears to have played an important, if shadowy, role in the organisation, and was imprisoned without trial between 1798 and 1801. More pertinent here, however, is his private life, for prior to his marriage he had fathered at least thirteen illegitimate children. Why William decided to marry in 1805 is unclear, but decide he did—much to the dismay of Ann Henry, the mother of four of his children, who is known to have been living in his Belfast home early in 1805 and who wrote to him, revealing her disappointment, as he made arrangements for his marriage. If moved by these letters, William pressed on regardless and in March 1805 was married to Eleanor Jackson of Ballybay, Co. Monaghan. Quite what Eleanor made of William's past is unknown, but shortly after the marriage she became pregnant and a daughter, Letitia, was born in March 1806. Letitia would prove to be William's only legitimate child, for the following January her mother, Eleanor, died. William lived on until 1832 and like his brother, never remarried. For the remainder of his life he appears to have lived respectably and to have fathered no further children, though his continued acknowledgement of, and provision for, his illegitimate children speaks of a man who, whatever the opinions of society, lived life on his own terms.

Compared to the near 50-year marriage of the Revd John and Ann, those of William and Robert were short-lived. That said, insofar as it is possible to tell, they appear, during their short spans, to have been happy unions. Two generations later, the Revd John and Ann's great-granddaughter, Annie Tennent, would not be so fortunate.

The daughter of Robert Tennent's son Robert James and his wife Eliza, whose father was the Belfast merchant John McCracken, Annie Tennent was married to Nicholas Delacherois on 16 June 1864. On paper the match was a good one: Nicholas came from a prominent and long-established County Down family. It soon became clear, though that the marriage was a far from happy one. On 25 June 1864, not two weeks after their first wedding anniversary, Annie's brother, Captain Robert Tennent, visited her husband at their home in Donaghadee and, 'excited by reports which had reached him that his sister … had been ill-treated', attacked him 'with a walking-stick, striking him on the head, face, and nose … until the stick was broken into pieces'. In due course Tennent was tried for assault and found guilty, whereupon he was fined £100 and imprisoned for a year. As might be imagined, things did not end there. Annie and Nicholas's already troubled union deteriorated still further and by November 1869 it had reached the provincial court of Armagh, where Annie sought 'divorce *a mensa et thoro* from her husband … on the ground of cruelty'. Annie's testimony suggested a deeply dysfunctional marriage, characterised by verbal and emotional abuse, and the case proved lengthy. 'The Delacherois diverse case', the *Belfast News-Letter* complained on 7 December 1869, 'which has for several days been dragging, without exhausting, its weary recital of miserable squabbles, was again at hearing yesterday.' By the following April, however, it had drawn to a close and 'resulted in judgement for Mrs Delacherois, decreeing a separation between the parties with permanent alimony of £250 a year, and costs'. Not six years old, Annie's unhappy marriage was at an end.

There were, of course, other, less eventful marriages involving members of the Tennent family, but what of those presented here? Are they, in any sense, typical? In some respects not. After all, divorce, if possible, was rare indeed in the nineteenth century, and marriages lasting nearly 50 years, such as that of the Revd John and Ann, were not common. Set against this, in an age of high natal mortality, many marriages were cut short by early death, and widowhood was a common experience. Moreover, at a time when the possibility of marital separation was limited, the experience of an unhappy marriage was surely not rare. Thus if there is any lesson to be drawn from the Tennent family's marital fortunes it is, perhaps, that not all weddings end in happy ever afters.

Sources

For the Tennent family and their marriages see Jonathan Jeffrey Wright, *The 'natural leaders' and their world: politics, culture and society in Belfast, c. 1801–1832* (Liverpool, 2012), chapter 1; *idem*, 'Love, loss, and learning in late Georgian Belfast: the case of Eliza McCracken', in D. W. Hayton and A. R. Holmes (eds), *Ourselves alone? Religion, society and politics in eighteenth- and nineteenth-century*

Ireland: essays presented to S.J. Connolly (Dublin, 2016), 169–91. The account of the Delacherois–Tennent marriage, and its breakdown, draws on *The Manchester Guardian* (30 June 1865, 20 March and 20 September 1866) and the *Belfast News-Letter* (19 November 1869, 1 December 1869, 7 December 1869, 22 December 1869, 6 January 1870 and 27 April 1870). See also, for the Delacherois family's establishment in County Down, John Stevenson, *Two centuries of life in Down, 1600–1800* (Dundonald, 1990), chapter 6.

32

Abductions in eighteenth-
and nineteenth-century Ireland

Maria Luddy

On the night of 4 March 1822 in the townland of Aughrim, near Liscarroll, Co. Cork, twelve well-armed men entered the house of Richard Goold, the son of a prosperous farmer. The abductors were searching for his sister, the eldest daughter of the family. In one of the bedrooms they found a young woman and asked her whether she was the eldest daughter; she said that she wasn't, but the men did not believe her. They ordered her to dress and forcibly took her from the house. The young woman was sixteen-year-old Honora Goold. Forcing her onto a horse ridden by James Brown, the abduction party sped off into the hills of west Limerick and eventually, riding through the night, came to the house of David Leahy, a comfortable farmer who lived with his wife and two sons. James Brown soon realised that they had abducted the wrong daughter but he still proposed marriage to Honora, who refused him. Over the next week Brown repeatedly raped Honora in an attempt to force her to marry him. Eventually David Leahy suggested to Honora that she would be released if she signed a document saying that she was in the house of her own free will. She agreed and when she was finally rescued she was found alone in a cabin 'in a most pitiable condition'. The abduction, deemed a 'barbaric and preeminently atrocious case', was widely reported in the British and Irish press. The youth of the woman and the intense search for her made it a case of great interest.

Once recovered, Honora gave information to the police about her abductors, most of whom were eventually captured. James Brown escaped, and it was thought that he had left the country for America. When the case came to court, Honora, attired in 'mourning dress', gave her testimony 'correct and distinct, interrupted only by those bursts of acute sensibility which the narration of the unparalleled outrage committed upon her caused in the recital of it before the font of justice'. The Leahys claimed that they had been terrorised into supporting the abduction, but they were convicted and sentenced to seven years' transportation. A man named Costello was executed for his involvement in the crime and, in all, eleven other individuals were imprisoned or transported for their participation in the abduction.

The Goold case was one of many hundreds of such abductions that occurred in Ireland in the eighteenth and nineteenth centuries. Essentially, abduction can be described as the practice of carrying off a woman with the purpose of compelling her to marry a particular man, who would then have access to the available dowry of money, land or other property tied to the woman. Abduction was about money and status. Those involved in abductions in the eighteenth century came from the upper levels of society, young men who wanted to marry a 'fortune'. From the late eighteenth century a broader range of social groups were involved in abductions, including servants abducting servants and landless labourers abducting women of little fortune.

Abduction was a noted phenomenon of the eighteenth and nineteenth centuries and, within the context of the history of marriage in Ireland, reflects not only the ability of couples sometimes to overcome parental decisions regarding their marriage partners but also the desire among individuals and families for property and status. Abduction was most often a crime of considerable terror and violence and it is a subject worth exploring for what it says about marriage strategy, attitudes to marriage, consent, parental authority and property, and the value of women in Irish society.

Current figures for abduction reveal that there were at least 200 abductions in the eighteenth century, with at least another 900 between 1800 and 1850. Given the figures we have, it is evident that recorded abductions were at their height in the 1830s and 1840s, and that the first half of the nineteenth century is a much more significant period for abductions than the entire eighteenth century. We must also keep in mind that a number of cases were collusive abductions, where individuals ran away together, thus forcing their families to accept that the couple wished to be married. If the woman was absent from home for any length of time and in the company of men, it was understood that her 'virtue' was compromised; even if she did not marry the abductor her reputation had suffered and it would have been very difficult for her to marry another.

Abductions were a significant way to secure a marriage and hence the 'fortune' that went with the abducted woman. In 1824 a witness to a government commission claimed that the fear of abduction was a factor in early marriages. In his *Local disturbances in Ireland* (1836), Cornwall Lewis claimed that abductions were so common in pre-Famine Ireland that they 'affect[ed] the marrying habits of the population'.

That there was intent to benefit financially from these abductions is without question, and women of lesser fortune also found themselves endangered. Economics remained a primary motivation for abduction in the nineteenth century. Access to land was a vital form of survival for poorer individuals and their families in the eighteenth and early nineteenth centuries. The value of the property associated with an unmarried woman was an enticement for men, and that value was assessed by the status of the father or by rumours of a fortune. One Bridget Grealish was abducted in Galway in 1839, the police noting that she 'had a good fortune'. Even labourers' daughters were not safe from abduction, however. For instance, Bridget Sullivan was the target of an attempted abduction in February 1838. Her father, Patrick Sullivan, held a house and a garden. While the daughters of farmers appear to have been targeted most often, the daughters of shopkeepers and publicans were also abducted. For the eighteenth century Kelly suggests that the victims of abduction were mainly 'young Protestant women of fortune' and that the abductors were 'Catholic men of the lower gentry'. In the nineteenth century the abductions were carried out by men from the farming and labouring classes and, unlike aristocratic abductions, which tended to be between Catholics and Protestants, those of the lower orders were mostly between Catholics.

Abductions were reported in the press and this served a number of functions. It was a way of warning those gentlemen and ladies who read the papers to be solicitous about their daughters' care. It also alerted families to the extent of abductions in the country. In the nineteenth century the press provided greater detail on abductions, and in at least some instances this was a form of entertainment for the reading public. Some of the reports could be read as adventure stories, dramas, tales of resistance and rescue, and of female virtue. For many women abductions were traumatic events and involved their marrying men who had committed violence against them. How, or whether, such marriages survived is an unanswered question.

Further reading

Toby Barnard, *The abduction of a Limerick heiress: social and political relations in mid-eighteenth-century Ireland* (Dublin, 1998).

James Kelly, 'The abduction of women of fortune in eighteenth-century Ireland', *Eighteenth-Century Ireland/Iris an Dá Chultúr* **9** (1994), 7–43.

Thomas P. Power, *Forcibly without her consent: abductions in Ireland, 1700–1850* (New York, 2010).

33

Methodism and the marriages of William Slacke (*c.* 1740–1807) of Kiltubrid, Co. Leitrim

Liam Kelly

The Slackes were a minor landed-gentry family who lived in Kiltubrid parish in County Leitrim. The first in the line was Captain William Slacke, who came from Slack Hall in Wales *c.* 1692 to establish iron-works in Leitrim. Their estate in Kiltubrid parish was small, consisting of little more than 500 acres of mostly poor land. Later generations would practise law in Carrick-on-Shannon to supplement the rental income from their estate.

William Slacke, a grandson of the above-mentioned Captain Slacke, married his sixteen-year-old first cousin, Angel Anna Slacke, *c.* 1764; Kiltubrid House was renamed 'Annadale' in her honour, a name by which the house and the townland are still known today. Angel Anna had spent most of her early years with her uncle, James Wilkinson, who lived near Swords, Co. Dublin; while there, she developed a taste for the high life the city had to offer, and in particular a love for the theatre. The young bride missed the social life of the city when she went to live in the remote, rural north-west of Ireland. To make up for this loss, she returned to Dublin each year to attend the grand balls and the theatre, and it was during one of these visits that she was converted to Methodism. Angel Anna ceased going to the theatre and went instead to Whitefriar Street to hear the Methodist preachers.

This Dublin experience was a life-changing event in Mrs Slacke's life. She began to keep a diary ('this account of my secret feelings') and, when she returned to Annadale, she wrote: 'Sorry I was that I must leave Dublin … I was so attached to them [the Methodists] that could I find them underground I believe I would dig for them'. To the dismay of her husband, she set up a Methodist society at Annadale, consisting mostly of their servants and tenants, and began to invite the travelling preachers into their house for food and lodgings. Andrew Blair was one of the early preachers invited to Annadale and Angel Anna wrote that her husband 'could scarcely be prevailed on to hear him preach … as he believed a lay man [is] not authorised to preach'.

Mrs Slacke continued to invite the lay preachers to Annadale, with 'Mr Slacke sometimes objecting and sometimes allowing it'. That Angel Anna would refer to her husband, in her private diary, as 'Mr Slacke' is evidence of a patriarchal relationship, as is the fact that he had the final say in deciding whether preachers would be welcomed to Annadale or not. Mrs Slacke's new role as leader of the local Methodist society was proving a challenge to that patriarchy, however, and William Slacke was torn between his love for his wife and his conviction that her new-found enthusiasm for Methodism was misguided.

Angel Anna had great affection for the preachers. In a letter to her friend Peg Thompson on 2 May 1793, she expressed the fear that Blakely Dowling, her 'dear brother', would be moved to another circuit, adding that 'this thought chills my fluids, but I must learn to restrain the finer feelings of my heart'. A year later, in a letter to another friend, she wrote of another preacher: 'I love my blessed Brother [Adam] Avrell more and more every day'. It would appear that all the preachers coming and going at Annadale caused some tongues to wag, because Mrs Slacke complained of 'minds whose narrow limits could not conceive the delights of disinterested affection'. Adelia Margery West, a granddaughter of William and Angel Anna Slacke who wrote a memoir in the late 1800s, was very critical of her grandmother, claiming that she neglected her children, preferring instead to mix with people of a 'lower class'. She wrote:

> 'These [Methodist] preachers were good earnest men, but as a rule uneducated and belonging to a very low rank, yet my grandmother preferred them as associates for her children to friends and relatives who were not Methodists'.

William Slacke's opposition to the lay preachers lessened with time and there is no indication of jealousy on his part because of his wife's affection for them; indeed, having seen the good effect that Methodism was having on some of his tenants, he eventually joined the society that his wife had founded. Thus the tensions between husband and wife eased and all the preachers were welcomed to Annadale. John Wesley stayed there in May 1787 and again in May 1789, and John Bredin, another preacher, was present when Angel Anna died suddenly on 15 November 1796. She was 48 years old and was buried in the old cemetery at Kiltubrid, which is situated directly behind Annadale House.

Miss Peg Thompson, who had been a friend of Angel Anna Slacke, was, to the consternation of his family, soon to become William Slacke's second wife. She was a cunning and manipulative woman, and one of her first edicts after moving into Annadale was that she would not receive any Methodist preacher there. The roles were now reversed, with the mistress at Annadale banning the preachers and the master quietly acquiescing. Angel Anna's second son, William, disliked the new mistress most of all. In a deliberate attempt to vex her, he came late to dinner dressed in dirty clothes and shoes, demanded a leg of chicken and tore the flesh off with his teeth, embarrassing her before the friends whom she had invited to dinner and whom she hoped to impress. Adelia Margery West described in her memoir how the next day there was a painful scene between young William and his father 'which ended with him being turned out of the house and which he never again entered while his stepmother was its mistress'.

William Slacke seems to have been the dominant partner in his first marriage but less so in his second. He gave way to the wishes of his second wife when they left Leitrim and went to live at Hollybrook Park in Clontarf, the rest of the family remaining at Annadale. William missed his old life greatly. He had been used to the outdoor life in Leitrim, tending the flowers and riding out for further exercise each afternoon. His health broke after some time in Dublin and he died in 1807. Mrs Slacke refused to let his remains be brought back to Leitrim and he was buried in the vaults of St Andrew's Church in Dublin. Adelia Margery West blamed Angel Anna Slacke's religious fervour for damaging the family:

> 'The worst and most lasting effects of the whole thing was that many old intimacies were broken off ... I cannot but see and regret much injury done by my grandmother to her family ... she was a clever and holy woman but in many ways a mistaken one.'

William Slacke's second wife fractured that family life even more. One hopes that, amid all the tensions and turmoil of their lives, William and his two wives, Angel Anna and Peg, experienced some happiness.

Further reading
Liam Kelly, *The face of time* (Dublin, 1995).
Liam Kelly, 'The growth of Methodism in Cavan and Leitrim 1750–1800', *Breifne* **10** (38) (2002), 454–94.
Unpublished diary and letters of Angel Anna Slacke and unpublished memoir of Adelia Margery West, copies of which are in Leitrim County Library.

Pl. 1—P11310 / NGI.205. *The Marriage of Strongbow and Aoife, c.* 1854.
Artist: Daniel Maclise (1806–70). Oil on canvas. National Gallery of Ireland Collection.
Image © National Gallery of Ireland.

Pl. 2—Exterior view of Castle Leslie, early 1900s. Permission granted by Castle Leslie Estate. With special thanks to Sammy Leslie and Yvonne Murphy, Cultural Heritage Manager, Castle Leslie.

Pl. 3—Aerial view of Castle Leslie and surrounds. Permission granted by Castle Leslie Estate. With special thanks to Sammy Leslie and Yvonne Murphy, Cultural Heritage Manager, Castle Leslie.

Pl. 4—*Skellig Night on the South Mall, Cork*, by James Beale, 1845. © Crawford Art Gallery Collection.

Pl. 5—Howard Helmick (1845–1907), *Candidates for Marriage* or *The Cleric's Interruption* (1881). Oil on canvas. Courtesy of the Booth Family Center for Special Collections, Georgetown University, Washington, DC.

Left Pl. 6—*Divorce is a disease* (1946; 1957 printing). John Henry. CTSI pamphlet cover. © Veritas.

Right Pl. 7—*So we abolished the chaperone* (1946; 1963 printing). George Altendorf. CTSI pamphlet cover. © Veritas.

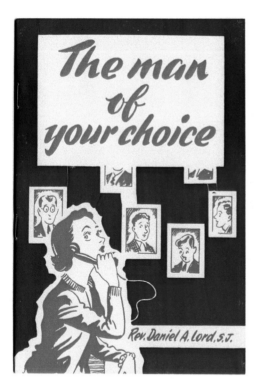

Pl. 8—*The man of your choice* (1955; 1963 printing). John Henry. CTSI pamphlet cover. © Veritas.

Pl. 9—*The girl worth choosing* (1955; 1960 printing). John Henry. CTSI pamphlet cover. © Veritas.

Pl. 10—*Grow up and marry* (1947; 1958 printing). Elgin Studios. CTSI pamphlet cover. © Veritas.

Pl. 11—*What not to do on a date* (1960). W. Kiernan. CTSI pamphlet cover. © Veritas.

THE YOUNG WIFE

Irish Messenger Office, 5 Gt. Denmark St. Dublin

PRICE TWOPENCE

Pl. 12—*The young wife* (Irish Messenger Office pamphlet, 1938). Image courtesy of Ciara Meehan.

WOMAN'S WAY weekly 10d INCLUDING ALL TAX

IRELAND'S LEADING WOMAN'S MAGAZINE

Ireland's Housewife- of-the- year 1967

sponsor McDonnells of Drogheda

Pl. 13—*Woman's Way* cover, 1 December 1967. Image courtesy of Ciara Meehan.

34

A mountainy wedding in 1812

C. J. Woods

One day in the summer of 1810 a much-travelled Presbyterian army surgeon, now rediscovering his native Ulster, was walking through the Antrim mountains, having left Larne with the intention of reaching Ballymena. The walker was John Gamble, whose accounts of his rambles in the north of Ireland afford perceptive, intimate and shrewd insights into local mores. After taking refreshment at a public house (somewhere near what is now the Ballyboley Inn) and having taken leave of the publican, he continued on his way with the intention of reaching his destination by nightfall. The sequel is best told by himself:

About two miles from his house I came to a place where two roads meet. I sat down until some person should come up who could inform me which of them I was to take. Though seated on the ground, I had an extensive prospect; not very fruitful in any part, and as barren as ever Churchill found Scotland in many places. It consisted of reclaimed land and irreclaimable—of scanty grass and barren heath—but not therefore useless—for while sheep grazed on the one, there was plenty of turf on the other. I continued sitting nearly an hour, without hearing a single footstep. I hardly recollect any thing more still; the silence was even oppressive. I gradually fell into a kind of reverie. '*Utrum horum*', I heard from a voice behind me. I looked around, and saw a little man in black, mounted on a horse no larger than a mule. He wore a large grizzled wig and cocked hat. They formed a ludicrous contrast to his jolly face and swollen cheeks, puffed up by good cheer, like a trumpeter's, or Eolus when he gave the winds vent.

'Amn't right', said he, clapping me familiarly on the back, 'haven't you missed your way?'

'No', I said, 'it was to avoid missing it, I remained here'.

'And well you did', said he, 'for I can inform you; come along', taking hold of my coat, 'this is the way'.

'It may be your way', I replied, 'but you will better know mine when I tell you where I am going'.

'*I* can tell you', replied he, 'you are going along with me to a neighbour's house, where you'll get a good dinner and plenty of whiskey into the bargain'.

He then informed me he was priest of the parish, and was going to a parishioner's to marry his daughter to a neighbouring young man. He civilly pressed me to accompany him, apologizing for the freedom with which he had accosted me. I declined the offer; but as our road happened to be for a part of the way the same, we travelled on together. His conversation was as grotesque as his appearance, and was interlarded with scraps of Latin, delivered in a nasal tone, like a Frenchman. He had been educated in France, and had resided there several years.

I asked him how he liked it.

'C'est un pays de Dieu' he replied.

'And Ireland', said I, 'did it not appear strange to you after quitting this Paradise?'

'Ireland is a Paradise', said he; 'I mean will be, when the bugs have left it'.

Who he meant by the bugs I cannot conjecture, nor did I ask him. 'You priests are to be pitied', I said, 'you can go to other people's weddings, but can never go to your own'.

'We don't think of our own', he replied, 'we keep ourselves pure and undefiled vessels of the Lord'.

'You would not be less pure', said I, 'for having good wives—but I suppose you console yourselves with the wives of your neighbours'.

'It is so supposed', said he, 'but I believe wrongfully—for my own part, I bless God, nothing worse ever passed between me and my neighbour's wife than is doing at present'.

'Even if there sometimes had', I said, 'I should forgive you—your situation exposes you to temptation, and *humanum est errare*'.

'*Sed non persistere*', said he. 'When I was a younker at college I was no saint, I warrant you; but since then I was never once either fornicator or adulterer—*Coelum hoc, et conscia sidera testor*'.

We parted at a narrow lane which led down to the house where he was going. I walked slowly forward. Had I suspected what was to follow, I should have gone quicker. I had scarcely got a quarter of a mile, when a man on horseback overtook me. He took off his hat, and hoped I would condescend to eat a mouthful with him. I told him it was impossible, that the evening was advancing, and I should be very late in getting to Ballymena.

'I can get you a bed in a neighbour's house', said he. 'I am sorry I cannot offer you one in my own—it will be so crowded—but if you will demean yourself so far as to make one of us, it will be a great compliment to my daughter and the bridegroom—you travelled better than a mile with the priest, and it wouldn't be reckoned lucky to pass by without taking a *drap* to their healths'.

'A curse on the word', said I; 'I wish it was out of the dictionary—it got me shipwrecked a short time ago, and now it is going to get me into a quarrel—for your feasts, I suppose, generally end in that way'.

'God forbid', said the man, 'there should be any fighting at my bairn's wedding; but even if there were, I am sure you couldn't think any one would forget the respect he owes to a gentleman like you'.

I turned round, and accompanied him back to his house. The lane which led down to it was rocky and uneven—a shallow brook ran along the centre—my companion made me mount his horse, least my feet should get wet. The house was mean-looking enough, but it was cheerly illuminated by the setting sun, impatient, as a poet would say, had it been the wedding of a princess, to hide himself behind the lofty mountain beyond it. No bad emblem, it may be permitted a sober prose writer to remark, of the fugitive sunshine of a married life. I dismounted from my steed with almost as much state as a pope did [...] between two great kings, for the bridegroom held the stirrup, and the priest the bridle. The latter welcomed me with the cordiality of an old acquaintance. '*Salvo multum exoptate*', said he, shaking me heartily by the hand. We then proceeded to the room where the company were assembled. The floor was earthen but clean. A table was decently laid out for dinner. I was introduced to the bride. She was a modest-looking girl about seventeen. She was dressed in a white calico gown and ribands, and had a fan in her hand. The priest now began the ceremony. The evening was close and the room crowded. He soon got into a violent heat, and to cool himself, took his wig off several times, wiped his head, and replaced it. But whatever there might be uncouth in his manner, there was nothing ludicrous either in that of the bride or her parents. The voice of nature will always find its way to the heart, and the tears which streamed down their cheeks bespoke the affection they bore each other.

After the ceremony was over, the whiskey went round, and we then sat down to dinner. It was a very abundant one, not ill dressed, nor, considering the condition of the people, ill served. The priest was grand carver, grand talker too, and grand laugher. I was seated at his right hand, and if I were not comfortable it was not his fault, for no person could be more attentive. The moment dinner was over, the table was removed, and the company began dancing. The music was a fiddle and dulcimer. The dances were reels of three and of four—when one person got tired, another instantly started up in his or her place, and the best dancer was he or she who held out the longest. A singular kind of *pas seul* was performed by a *crack* dancer. A door was taken off the hinges, and laid on the floor, on which he danced in his stocking-soles. He displayed considerable activity, but there was an almost total want of grace. His principal movement consisted in rapidly and alternately raising his feet as high as his waistcoat, and when he succeeded in getting his toes a little way into the pocket, there was a universal burst of applause.

At this point Gamble breaks off his narrative to reflect on the nature of 'ancient Irish dance' and recalls Rinceadh' Fada, which began with 'three persons abreast, each holding the ends of a white handkerchief', the first then moving 'forward a few paces to slow music'. He soon returns to the rambunctious scene in the Antrim mountains of which he was 'so unexpectedly a spectator':

The whiskey was handed frequently about; a few took it mixed with water, but the generality drank it plain. The women scarcely tasted it, nor did the priest. His spirits, indeed, seemed of themselves sufficiently buoyant—he drank plentifully of tea, however, in which I was happy to join him. The company at length got noisy and intoxicated, and I began to find my situation unpleasant—not that I was apprehensive of the slightest danger; but coarseness is oppressive whenever it becomes familiar—vulgarity may be endured when it is modest, which drunkenness seldom is. I was, therefore, agreeably surprised, when the man of the house came and told me a gentleman wanted to speak to me at the door. It was his landlord. The poor man had run up to his house to inform him of me, and to request him to offer me a bed. The gentleman, with great civility, had come down himself, and I gladly consented to accompany him back, to the great annoyance of my friend, the priest, who said, he should now have nobody fit to talk to. I left him singing a French song, which, in the company he was in, could not be very edifying. He had sung one or two in the course of the evening. 'I must give these barbarians', whispered he to me, 'something they don't understand, or they would soon lose all reverence for me'.

John Gamble published his reminiscences of this visit in *A view of society and manners in the north of Ireland in the summer and autumn of 1812* (London, 1813). There is a meticulously elucidated new edition by Breandán Mac Suibhne, to whom we are all indebted.

Further reading
John Gamble, *Society and manners in early nineteenth-century Ireland* (ed. B. Mac Suibhne) (Dublin, 2011).

35

The diplomacy of love:
a trial at the Cork assizes

Barbara McCormack

Breaking an engagement in the early nineteenth century could be a very costly affair, a fact which Major John Vereker of the Limerick Militia came to realise in 1815 when he was forced to pay damages in the amount of £4,000 to his ex-fiancée, Miss Mary Austen of Waterfall in Cork. Just two years previously, the young couple had embarked on a clandestine love affair against the wishes of their parents. Now they were pitted against each other in a dispute that laid bare the private details of their courtship.

During the trial, which was held before the solicitor general and a special jury at the Cork assizes on 1 April 1815, Messrs Quinn and Goold for the plaintiff and Mr Lloyd for the defendant exhibited 'an eloquent display of talent'. This remarkable case captured the public imagination to such an extent that G. Laurent of Marlborough Street, Cork, printed and sold the proceedings for tenpence a copy, no doubt owing to Vereker's position in the upper tiers of Irish society.

John Prendergast Vereker was the eldest son of Colonel Charles Vereker, the 2nd Viscount Gort, and the grand-nephew and presumptive heir of Lord Kiltarton. He was born in the year 1790, the same year in which his father began representing Limerick City in the Irish House of Commons. The elder Vereker was later elected to the British House of Commons for Limerick and served as lord of the treasury from 1807 until 1812 before becoming an Irish representative peer on 30 January 1824, allowing him to sit in the House of Lords.

John Vereker was educated at Harrow in England, returning home in early 1813 to serve as a major in the Limerick Militia. He first met Mary Austen during the summer of that year when he took up lodgings in Blackrock, Co. Cork. Austen's father, Thomas, had sent the family to the small fishing town 'to enjoy the benefits of bathing' while he attended to business in Waterfall. Miss Austen, who was 21 years old at the time and was both educated and accomplished while also possessing 'great personal beauty', soon came to the attention of the Major. The pair met on a daily basis and quickly fell in love, but when news of their courtship reached her father he travelled to Blackrock to determine the Major's intentions. Vereker was open about the attachment but insisted that 'his present circumstances ... forbade him from following its dictates'. This did not, however, deter the young lovers from corresponding in secret for several months, using false names to avert suspicion, through letters of 'ardent love, and eternal constancy'. This correspondence abruptly ended in February 1814 when Vereker yielded 'to filial duty and future prospects' and ended the affair.

During the trial, Austen was described by her legal counsel as a 'young and susceptible female' concerned with vindication rather than financial reparations and hoping for a verdict to rescue her good character. The case itself centred on the following three counts: 'the first, for agreeing to marry at request: the second, a promise to marry within a reasonable time: the third, a general promise to marry'.

Several letters written by Vereker to Austen were presented as evidence in the case. In one letter he exclaims: 'Oh! Mary, what a wonderful passion is love; when it acts upon men of dull souls it makes idiots of them ...'. In another letter, written on 12 January 1814, Vereker mockingly scolds his young lover:

> You will perchance smile at this, but you know right well, you have me in great order. Fortune grant, however, that you may not do after marriage what you have done before it, 'wear the Breeches on the strength of my obedience.'

A change evidently took place in the following weeks, however, and his next letter (dated 1 February 1814) effectively ends the engagement. He writes:

> After some weeks anxious expectation, I have at length received your letter, which is written in such a forced and ambiguous style, as leads me to think your attachment for me is not of so disinterested a nature as I have proved mine to be for you ... I have, in the most solemn manner, since I received it, pledged my honour to my father and lord Kiltarton, that I will yield to their advice.

Charles Vereker was vehemently opposed to the match, threatening his son with disinheritance and banishment from the family estate. This was no doubt a factor in Vereker's decision to reject Austen, effectively breaking his promise of marriage. The Austen v. Vereker trial was not a unique affair in Ireland at this time. A similar trial took place in December 1805, when Eliza Mowlds brought a case against Robert Burke for a breach of marriage contract.

Mr Lloyd for the defendant argued that such cases would reduce the pledges of love to a commercial contract, allowing women to manipulate gullible suitors in what he described as a 'new science, which may be called the diplomacy of love'. Evidently the jury did not agree and, following a short consultation, returned a verdict in favour of Miss Austen, awarding damages to the amount of £4,000.

It seems, however, that both parties eventually found happiness, albeit in the arms of others. Vereker began courting a Miss Daxon from Limerick shortly after his final correspondence with Austen but later married Maria O'Grady, daughter of Standish O'Grady, 1st Viscount Guillamore. He succeeded his father in parliament in 1817 and became the 3rd Viscount Gort on his father's death in 1842. Mary Austen went on to marry Colonel MacMahon of Thomond, Knight of the Royal Military Order of St Louis, in May 1817.

Sources

Cork assizes: Important trial for a breach of promise of marriage, in which Miss Austen, of Waterfall, was plaintiff, and Major Vereker, of the Limerick Militia, Defendant. Printed by G. Laurent, Cork, 1815.

'Marriages of eminent persons', The Gentleman's Magazine: And Historical Chronicle. From January to June, 1817 (Vol. 87, Part 1, 1817), p. 562.

Trial for a breach of marriage contract: Wherein Eliza Mowlds, spinster, was plaintiff, and Robert Burke, Esq. defendant, on the 2d and 3d of December, 1805, before the Right Hon. John, Lord Norbury, Chief Justice. Printed by W. Folds, Dublin, 1806.

36

A clerical error and
the unsettled marriage settlement

Olivia Martin

Marriage settlements in the eighteenth and nineteenth centuries were complex, legally binding contracts, tailor-made by fathers or guardians of both bride and groom. Any necessary adjustments could be managed later through the father or husband's will. The marriage portion to be paid by the family of the bride, as agreed in the marriage settlement, was usually disbursed in instalments and sometimes spread over a number of years.

Reverend Edwin Stock was the eldest son of Joseph Stock, bishop of Killala, author of the *Narrative of the French invasion of Mayo, 1798*. Edwin followed his father into the Church of Ireland and was appointed vicar in the parish of Crossmolina. His father and his prospective father-in-law, Simeon Droz, negotiated the marriage settlement between Edwin and his 28-year-old English bride, Louisa Alicia Droz, dated October 1807, which stipulated that:

> Mr Droz covenants to make over to Edwin Stock, on the day of marriage with his daughter, his Promissory Note for £1000 British payable on demand, his Bond for £2000 payable in five years, & bearing interest of 5 per cent till paid, & a further Bond for £2000, payable after his death & that of his wife Mrs Mary Droz.

A mistake made in the formation of the documentation, which did not represent the intention of the participants, neglected to make provision for children of the marriage but did not come to light until after Louisa's death in 1812, by which time the couple were the parents of two children. The clerical error was rectified on the generous insistence of Louisa's father, who authorised that the £2,000 bond be made over to his grandchildren:

> I wish the amount of my Bond for £2000 to Edwin Stock, as also the amount of the post-obit bond, should be so secured to my grandchildren, Mary and St. George Stock, as that the full benefit thereof may revert to them after their father's decease, he of course enjoying the advantages arising there from during his life time, to defray the expense of their maintenance & education, and to this I conceive Edwin will not have the least objection.

Many marriage settlements designated that specific income be dedicated exclusively to the education and maintenance of children of the marriage. Edwin arranged to have his children educated in London and Eton. It appears that the widowed father relocated to Eton during much of this period, to be close to his children, and arranged for a substitute curate to assume responsibility for his congregation back in Crossmolina.

Edwin left evidence in his letters of his romantic attitude to matrimony during his short marriage to Louisa. His brother Henry seems to have repeatedly ignored his father's attempts to introduce him to potential brides. When he married on 18 August 1810, his father learned of it through a Waterford newspaper, brought to him while he holidayed in England. The bishop requested Henry to bring his 'little bride, to shew her to us, & us to her'. Edwin was delighted; he wrote:

> No one can rejoice more sincerely than I do at your marriage [...] I earnestly pray then that that happiness may long continue to you & your Maria, & increase as you know one another better. This, from your own disposition, & what I know of her character, I am fully persuaded will be the case. I fancy we may then challenge the world to show seven more happy couples in one family than ours has produced within the last three years.

The bishop had ten children, seven of whom married. A letter from the bishop to Henry tells of the decision to proceed with his youngest daughter Emma's wedding at Killala Cathedral, on 17 November 1808, despite the fact that her 'boxes' had not arrived: 'Indeed the bride could hardly have stirred, if my good dame had not stripped herself to fit her out'. In reference to potential delays to another daughter's wedding while the bridegroom sought a curate to take over his parish, the bishop wrote: 'snow melts, you know, under Cupid's fire'.

Unlike his father, who remarried within months of his first wife's death in 1805, Edwin never remarried. At his death in 1826, his will revealed his desire to be buried beside the remains of his 'dear departed wife'. Their daughter, Mary, married Reverend Andrew Jackson in 1827 and her father participated in the marriage settlement negotiations. When complications arose, it was decided that, rather than postpone the nuptials of a young couple eager to marry, the marriage would proceed and negotiations would continue, confidentially, subsequent to the ceremony. Edwin Stock wrote to Henry:

> We have determined, that as the connexion was projected at first on both sides, from very different motives than the quantum of pecuniary attractions, so this apparent alteration of circumstances shall produce no change in our plans [...] we have next resolved to follow the example which was set by my father and father-in-law, in the case of my marriage, viz. we will have the marriage first, and the settlement after [...]. But one thing I have to request dear H, that you will keep this arrangement *a secret*.

Sixteen months later, however, Edwin articulated his concern that the marriage settlement was still not finalised. In his will, Reverend Andrew Jackson left all 'he had to any child of his that might be born'. Only one child was born to him and Mary before Andrew succumbed to mental illness. Their son, George William Jackson, remained dependent on his widowed mother in his adult life because of 'mental infirmity unhappily inherited from his father'. Three of Mary's own uncles had suffered from varying degrees of mental illness, however, a factor *not entirely disclosed* to the Jackson family. In 1873 George was declared a lunatic and was confined to full-time residential medical care.

In conclusion, love was the overriding factor in the marriages of the Stock family, as confirmed by Edwin's communication to his brother:

> I hope, dear H, you enjoy all the happiness which your disposition is so well calculated to feel in the society of an amiable bosom-friend. Now that the honey-moon is over, I may obtain credit when I tell you that feeling will *increase* with every year that goes over your head.

Sources

Stock family papers are held by:
(i) the Manuscript Library, Trinity College, Dublin;
(ii) the Hardiman Library, NUI Galway.

37

'Incompatibility of temper and her conduct towards his children': society divorce in County Tipperary in the early nineteenth century

Denis G. Marnane

On Monday 6 March 1826, after prayers were said, the assembled lords spiritual and temporal (two of the former and 38 of the latter) turned to the business of the day.

Gathered together in the hallowed venue of Westminster Palace, this section of the upper—and at the time dominant—house of the British parliament soon turned its attention to the number of people who occupied (at the same time) a bed in various parts of Italy and, from the state of the bedlinen, what could be presumed about sexual activity by the occupants. Adultery dressed in all its details, unlike the naked pair in the bed, was usually the central act in a divorce drama. This was a time when getting a divorce entailed the expense and difficulty of persuading parliament to grant it. Not surprisingly, in 1826 there were only three such divorce bills passed, and in the entire decade of the 1820s a total of twenty.

Where attention focused on the bed of concupiscence, the maid was always a vital source of information. The maid in this case was Sarah Bean, who in cross-examination confessed that the man spent time in the woman's bedroom. To the question, 'Did you observe any marks as if any persons had been lying in the bed?' she answered 'Yes'. Then came the follow-up question, 'How many persons, according to those marks, did you think had been lying in that bed?', to which the reply was 'Two'. A little later in the cross-examination, the maid described how in Verona she actually saw the man in question in bed with the woman.

The man was the Hon. Richard Bingham, a younger son of the 2nd earl of Lucan, born in 1801 and therefore about 22 when the exploits in Italy took place. He was in Italy because, like many younger sons who were not complete dolts, family connections got him a job in the consular service (incidentally, Bingham's older brother, who became earl in 1839, is famously associated with the Charge of the Light Brigade in the Crimean War). The

Binghams had form in the matter of sleeping with other men's wives. Richard Bingham's father was the guilty party in a famous divorce involving another peer of the realm.

So who was the other erring party in the Italian romance? She was Eleanor Butler, younger daughter of the 17th earl of Ormonde. He died in 1795 and was succeeded, in turn, by Eleanor's two brothers. In 1826, when the House of Lords was examining the evidence of the lady's carnal relations, Eleanor's brother James had recently been elevated to the rank of marquess of Ormonde. The problem for Eleanor was that since 1808 she had been the wife of Cornelius O'Callaghan, 1st Viscount Lismore. When the viscount brought a case against Bingham he won nominal damages, which was a part of the complicated divorce procedure of the period.

From a Gaelic family in County Cork that adjusted to political and religious reality, the viscount's great-grandfather made both reputation and money as a lawyer. Through the purchase of an estate in the 1720s around Clogheen in south Tipperary, the family established themselves so that in time they held around 35,000 acres in the county. The viscount's father was created a baron in 1785 and the viscountcy came their way in 1806. In every respect, except apparently the interpersonal, Eleanor Butler was an idea wife for O'Callaghan. In contrast to O'Callaghan, Eleanor was a member of the most historically distinguished family in Ireland—and she knew it. She allegedly declared that while the house in which she was obliged to live in Tipperary might be good enough for the wife of Lord Lismore, it would not do for the sister of Lord Ormonde. A marriage like this was a business arrangement, and she brought a dowry of £38,000 and a share in a coalmine to his annual income of around £15,000. The union, which lasted until their separation in 1819 and divorce in 1826, produced three sons and a daughter who survived to adulthood. So what went wrong?

The husband's story was that his wife grew increasingly discontented with being shut away in the country. She wanted society and shopping. That meant a house in London. Lord Lismore was anxious to please her but said that he could not afford what she wanted. Her temper grew worse, as did her health, or so her doctor said, claiming that what her ladyship needed was a change of air—preferably Continental, ideally Italian. Evidence from the husband's mother and brother emphasised the lady's 'frequent violence of temper', even striking her husband. Around 1817 Lord Lismore was ready to accommodate his wife but plans had to be cancelled when their son had an accident. Thereafter Lady Lismore was increasingly away from Clogheen, either in England or on the Continent, where (according to her husband, and a necessary part of his divorce claim) she amused herself with Mr Bingham.

Counsel for Lady Lismore argued that she was not in favour of their separation, much less their divorce. From the evidence, Viscount Lismore was determined on separation. The system was weighted against the wife, of course, and even her brother, the earl of Ormonde, admitted that Viscount Lismore, because of 'the unpleasant terms on which they lived', wanted rid of her—an outcome with which the lady's brother agreed. As the number of divorces indicate, this was not an easy option and what appeared to make the case for Lord Lismore was less his wife's alleged adultery than the evidence of his brother, the Hon. George O'Callaghan, that one of her threats was that she would use her influence over her seven-year-old son to turn him against his father.

After the divorce, Lady Lismore reverted to being Lady Eleanor Butler and lived in Italy. Neither she nor her former husband remarried. Not surprisingly, their subsequent relationship was played out among the lawyers and related to her financial affairs, her money usually in arrears. She died at Sorrento near Naples in October 1859, having survived her former husband by some two and a half years.

38

Class, choice and charms in nineteenth-century courtship

Shawn Nichols-Boyle

'I'll tell you what you must do … otherwise I'll not stand it. Give the colleen a chaff [straw] bed, blankets an' all other parts complate, along wid that slip of a pig. If you don't do this, Paddy Donovan, why we'll finish the whisky an' part friends—but it's no match'

—William Carleton, 'Phelim O'Toole's Courtship' (1832).

L ike many later famous Irish literary figures who left their homeland, nineteenth-century author William Carleton fled the close confines of the culture and traditions of his lower-class Catholic upbringing as the youngest of fourteen children on the family farm in County Tyrone but forever found himself returning to these humble beginnings in his stories. Carleton's struggle to simultaneously escape and embrace his modest background makes him uniquely qualified to share his fellow countrymen's challenges in negotiating the seemingly rigid rules of courtship and cleverly (and entertainingly) navigating the duelling influences of passion and practicality, with a little Irish magic and charm thrown in for good measure.

Carleton's intimate familiarity with—and genuine affection for—the Irish peasantry provides sensitive insight missing from most other historical or fictional accounts at the time. He explains that negotiating a marriage was a serious, painstaking business for people balancing precariously on the edge of destitute poverty. In the terse bargaining between the families, disagreement over even a minor possession such as a 'slip of a pig, or a pair of blankets' could immediately halt a potential match: 'These are small matters in themselves, but they are of importance to those who, perhaps, have nothing else on earth with which to begin the world'. The lower your class status, the less choice you had in following your heart over your pocketbook.

In 'Phelim O'Toole's Courtship' (Fig. 3), Phelim's paltry fortune amounted to a half-acre of land, one goat, three hens, the 'chance of a toss up

Fig. 3—Phelim and his potential wife sitting in the potato bin 'talkin' somethin' lovin' to one another' while Phelim drinks whiskey out of his eggshell cup and the families negotiate in the background.

From *Traits and stories of the Irish peasantry*, vol. 2, by William Carleton (Gerrards Cross, 1990), 188. Image reproduced from the 1844 edition.

PHELIM O'TOOLE'S COURTSHIP.

for the cock', two stools, a large pot, and possibly some fresh straw for a bed, as his father already claimed the one family blanket. Phelim slyly jockeys for his best outcome while pretending deep affection for one of his potential wives: 'I don't care a damn about fortune … so long as I get the darlin' herself. But I think there 'ud be no harm in havin' a spare pair o' blankets—an' for that matther, a bedstead, too …'. While Phelim undoubtedly is a profligate, Carleton also paints him as a charming rogue whose disgracefully amusing behaviour in (ultimately unsuccessfully) courting three women at once is partially justified by his dire financial situation.

Carleton meticulously details the characters' material items and property throughout his stories, not just for historical reasons but also because this information dictates their choice of matches and other major life decisions. In 'Shane Fadh's Wedding' (Fig. 4), Mary Finigan, with her 60 guineas, thirteen head of cattle, two feather and two chaff [straw] beds with sheeting, quilts and blankets, three pieces of bleached linen and a flock of geese, can safely spurn the advances of the less fortunate Dick Cuillenan:

'You ought to know, Dick Cuillenan, who you spake to, before you make the freedom you do … that'll be apt to get you a broken mouth, some time … stop yourself, Cuillenan—single your freedom, and double your distance, if you plase; I'll cut my coat off no such cloth.'

Mary's parents also have the luxury of supporting their daughter in her spirited response and encouraging her independence. When Dick appeals to Mary's mother to intercede on his behalf, her reply reflects her daughter's boldness:

> 'Now if she married you, Dick, where's the farm to bring her to? … when you want a wife, go to them that you might have a right to expect, and not to a girl like Mary Finigan, that could lay down guineas where you could hardly find shillings.'

Mary's eventual choice also shows that the path to marriage need not be so transactional; cultural insiders know the open secrets to negotiating the strict traditions. Mary follows her heart in selecting Shane Fadh without her father's approval and engages in a 'runaway match', where the couple abscond to a relative's house for several days. Her family are forced to accept the pairing and to enter into the formal wedding preparations because it would be more scandalous to reject the couple after they have spent several nights sleeping together—and certainly they have ruined any other potential matches.

Thus does true love find a narrow but possible path through the morass of unwritten regulations and beliefs surrounding courtship for the nineteenth-century Irish peasant. Irish Catholics were long used to a system rigged against them, and in a time when secret societies like the Ribbonmen and the Whiteboys were omnipresent they also found ways to subtly resist and manipulate other established practices against their self-interest, such as the rules surrounding courtship. Where outsiders see liars and deceitful cheats, Carleton frequently celebrates the witty Irish tricksters and their powers of evasion.

In 'Rose Moan, the Irish Midwife', readers cannot mistake Carleton's admiration of the midwife's artful playing upon her clients' superstitions and belief in magic to persuade or dissuade them from potential suitors. The midwife performs an elaborate ritual for those seeking to know whether their passion is reciprocal: she suspends the Bible from a string passed through a key, reads romantic verses from the Book of Ruth, which the supplicant repeats, and sees whether the Bible then turns. A turning Bible means mutual affection and marriage, while a stationary one means no attraction on the other side. Of course, Carleton describes the midwife's real genius in surreptitiously visiting the object of desire ahead of time and discovering their intentions,

Fig. 4—'Shane Fadh's Wedding': Shane and Mary celebrating their wedding with friends and family.

From *Traits and stories of the Irish peasantry*, vol. 1, by William Carleton (with a foreword by Barbara Hayley) (Gerrards Cross, 1990), 51.

SHANE FADH'S WEDDING.

and then bending the Bible to her will. He is reasonably sceptical of other charms, which range from grinding a dormouse to a powder and slipping it into the drink of the object of your affection to induce love for you (for those of lesser means) to tucking a special coin into your breeches for nine days to ward off 'pishthrogues' (evil charms) against your chosen match (for those with more disposable income).

Carleton clearly delights in the inventiveness and creativity of his fellow Irishmen's beliefs, even if he does not necessarily still share them. Shane Fadh's description of how he wins Mary over is pure poetry: 'I whispered the soft nonsense, Nancy, into poor Mary's ear, until I put my *comedher* [come hither; old love-charm] on her, and she couldn't live at all without me'. Similarly, when the willing recipient of this *comedher* evades her father's wishes and meets Shane to plot their runaway match, these are the words of someone who understands that true love is worth the risk and subterfuge:

'I'm going to trust myself with you for ever—for ever, Shane, avourneen … I can bear poverty and distress, sickness and want with you, but I can't bear to think that you should ever forget to love me as you do now; or that your heart should ever cool to me: but I'm sure … you'll never forget this night, and the solemn promises you made me, before God and the blessed skies above us.'

Carleton shows us that passion can overcome practicality, transcending class concerns with determination, wit and possibly a bit of magic.

Further reading

William Carleton, 'Phelim O'Toole's Courtship' and 'Shane Fadh's Wedding', in *Traits and stories of the Irish peasantry*, Vols 1 (1830) and 2 (1832) (reprint, Gerrards Cross, 1990).

William Carleton, 'Mary Murray, the Irish Match-Maker' and 'Rose Moan, the Irish Midwife', in *Tales and sketches, illustrating the character, usages, traditions, sports and pastimes of the Irish peasantry* (Dublin, 1845).

39

Couple-beggars

Katie Barclay

Some years ago an excommunicated priest became an inmate of a Dublin gaol, and married all that went to him who had the means of paying the fees. He was familiarly known by the *sobriquet* of 'The Couple-beggar'. He proposed three questions to all applicants, to which they were expected to reply in the affirmative; or, to speak more correctly, which he answered himself:—"You are come to be married? and to be sure you have. You have got your friend's consent? and to be sure you have." The third question, and by far the most important one to the interrogator, was "You have got the money to pay the priest?" and holding out his hand, "to be sure you have" (*Drogheda Journal*, 25 August 1835).

James Woods of Smithfield, Dublin, the 'celebrated couple-beggar', died unexpectedly in August 1829, aged 65. Just as the inquest was about to begin a woman appeared, claiming to be his wife, and demanded that his property be given to her. The peace officer removed her, but she had scarcely left when, perhaps fittingly, a second claimant, a 'remarkably ugly woman', disrupted proceedings! The coroner determined that there had been no foul play in his death, despite a rather curious life. Woods had been a curate in Galway twenty years earlier, when he was prosecuted for criminal conversation and sent to prison. As discussed by Diane Urquhart elsewhere in this volume, 'crim con' was the suit by which wronged husbands sought reparation from the men who had committed adultery with their wives—actions very unbecoming in a minister. Whilst in prison, Woods began performing private marriage ceremonies to supplement his income, and continued in that profession once he left. Perhaps one of the most famous couple-beggars of the 1820s, his name was a regular feature in court cases arising from bigamy and irregular marriage disputes. It was said that in sixteen years he married 'no less than five thousand couples'. Eight years before his death he got married himself, but later separated from his wife and was ordered by the court to allow her a weekly allowance of half a guinea.

The couple-beggar (or 'buckle-beggar') was a marriage celebrant who worked outside the boundaries of the established church and sometimes the law, providing marriage services—and occasionally divorce—for a fee. They can be found across Europe but were common in areas, like Ireland, where different religious groups lived alongside each other and where the established church had a legal monopoly. They were present in many Irish towns in the early nineteenth century, and were particularly notable in Dublin and in areas with a large Presbyterian presence.

Many 'couple-beggars' were simply ministers of non-established churches who provided services for their congregations, but the most famous were those men who offered weddings and certificates without asking any questions of the bride and groom. Such men were often 'defrocked' ministers of the established church but could also be ministers of other denominations, respectable or not, looking to earn an extra income. In Ireland, Roman Catholic priests were often criticised for performing this role, but the evidence suggests that they were mainly concerned with marrying their own population; 'notorious' celebrants tended to be Protestant. The legality of the marriages they performed varied; 'irregular' marriage, outside the prescriptions of the Church of Ireland, did not annul a marriage in most circumstances, but certain marriages—involving under-age heiresses, or mixed marriages performed by Catholics, for example—were invalid. The men themselves were at risk of prosecution.

Despite this, couple-beggars were remarkably popular. The claim that Woods married over 5,000 couples may seem high, but the surviving register of Dr Schulze, a well-known couple-beggar and the 'German' or 'Dutch' minister of the Lutheran Church in Poolbeg Street, Dublin, evidenced that he married over 6,000 couples between 1806 and 1837, a number that far outstripped his legitimate congregation. Most days he married at least one couple, and on occasion sixteen. The Revd James M'Guire, who performed marriages in the 1840s from the same house in Smithfield that had been occupied by Woods, testified in court that he had married 500 couples in two years.

The key advantage for many couples was that they were not required to call the banns in a church before the marriage, alerting the congregation—and perhaps their family—to the forthcoming nuptials, and they did not have to pay for an expensive licence to avoid calling the banns. Couple-beggars were very popular with couples who wanted to elope, with those unable to afford a divorce but wishing to remarry, and with those who simply desired

137

a private ceremony out of the public eye. The cost of a service varied, often reflecting what couple-beggars judged that the couple could afford. The privacy and secrecy led such marriages to be associated with scandal—couples who wished to avoid their parents' disapproval, bigamists and men wishing to seduce women, hoping the marriage would not 'stick'. The couple-beggar Mr Sandes was described in the *Dublin Evening Mail* in 1842 as exercising 'a degrading office, scouted by all but profligates and runaways, and entailing ruin and misery on many families'. Daniel O'Connell argued in the House of Commons in 1831 that such men 'did a deal of mischief'. From the 1780s, both the Armagh and Dublin Roman Catholic diocesans performed investigations into the state of the problem, which was of particular concern as they still accepted irregular marriages as valid.

While many were disturbed by this phenomenon, it operated with some community regulation. Couple-beggars were often well-known figures, like Schulze and Woods, located in particular areas. Woods's death was marked by the press and, a few weeks later, the Revd Stennet or Stenson not only took on his business but did so from the same address as Woods, with Mrs Jane Woods as his assistant. Mrs Woods testified in a bigamy case that Mr Stennet was her lodger. A year later, the Stennet–Woods partnership had broken up and Stennet summoned Jane for 'illegally detaining a door label bearing his name', which he alleged was his property. He now operated his business from Brunswick Street, but Jane continued to carry on business, passing off another man as the Revd Stennet to unsuspecting parties. Possibly the most interesting part of this exchange is the way that Stennet used both the magistrate's court and the court journalist, who reported proceedings in the local paper, not only to legitimise his operations but also to advertise his change of address. The couple-beggar may have provided a private service but his was a big and well-advertised business.

Further reading

Seán J. Connolly, *Priests and people in pre-Famine Ireland, 1780–1845* (Dublin, 2001).

John Gamble, *Society and manners in early nineteenth-century Ireland* (ed. B. Mac Suibhne) (Dublin, 2011).

40

Popular divorce

Katie Barclay

For most people unable to afford an English act of parliament or later access to the English courts, a legal divorce was unavailable in nineteenth-century Ireland. Lack of legal access to divorce did not stop unhappy marriages or families from breaking down, however, and so Irish communities came up with a range of strategies to enable spouses to uncouple. For the middle and upper classes this might have been a formal legal separation drawn up by a lawyer, but for those in the lower ranks more creative routes were needed. Two common options that emerge through bigamy cases and reports from the lower courts were informal agreements made between couples but reinforced through community-endorsed rituals, and a rather unconventional use of the local magistrate and police courts.

Unsurprisingly, many marriages ended through private agreements between spouses and, as long as both agreed, the surrounding community tended to turn a blind eye. Patrick Byrne testified during his bigamy arraignment that he had been married by Mr Schultze five years ago, but that he and his wife 'came to a mutual understanding that they should each be free to marry again as they did not well agree'. He had remarried, and his first wife had bought wedding clothes to marry another man, when he was arrested. Byrne was found guilty and transported for seven years, but he declared that he would return to 'live in splendour with the second wife'. Elizabeth Corsain plead guilty to bigamy, but during testimony it emerged that her first husband had paid her second husband £100 to marry her and had bought the ring for the second marriage, and that all three lived together after the remarriage, the second husband sharing a bed with the first during her confinement. In contrast, when a group of poor women in Dublin learned that a local joiner had sold his wife to a bricklayer for two guineas and ten pots of porter, *without* her permission, they seized the two men, 'hoisted them upon a pole and colted them about the streets, hooting

139

them as objects of ridicule and contempt'. Other men threatened to sell their wives during arguments.

As marriage was commonly proved through the production of the marriage certificate, destroying the certificate was an important symbol of its dissolution. As a result, for some ruining a certificate could end a marriage. This was the case in 1838 when John Arnold, a cordcutter, decided after a few days of marriage that he wanted a divorce, to which his wife agreed on the condition that he remain single for the remainder of his life. He returned with his bride to the couple-beggar Revd Schultze, who pronounced a divorce by tearing the certificate. The case only came to light when Arnold remarried in front of a Catholic clergyman, in breach of his agreement with his ex-wife, and she prosecuted him for bigamy. Similarly, when sixteen-year-old Jack Nicholson married fourteen-year-old Catherine Hamilton without his parents' consent, he 'tore [the certificate] sure enough, when I was aggravated' by the couple's aggrieved parents. He later changed his mind and wished to adhere to the marriage; perhaps if he had not the divorce would have been final. Returning to the couple-beggar for divorce or performing rituals around the tearing of the marriage certificate symbolically validated the decision to part amongst the lower classes. In Northern Ireland there are also examples of couples claiming to have been divorced by their priests and who then thought themselves free to remarry.

While couple-beggars, irregular marriage and divorce, and community justice continued to play a key role in popular divorce, the formalisation of the system of police courts and petty sessions in the first decades of the nineteenth century shaped the regulation of lower-class life. The informal nature of magistrate courts, which allowed couples and families to air their grievances and receive guidance and judgement, made them popular forums for dispute resolution within families. Magistrates often found themselves playing the role of marriage counsellor and mediator. Moreover, one of their functions was to order alimony payments for deserted spouses, protecting Poor Law boards from the burden of their support. An unexpected outcome of these dual functions was that magistrates could find themselves in the position of regulating separation and divorce amongst the poor.

In 1833, for example, the Dublin magistrates negotiated a settlement of 5s. a week for a woman who was obliged to leave her husband owing to his violence, perhaps seeing this as akin to enforcing social order. They could be squeamish, however, about authorising splits that had not yet happened, recognising that legal separations were not in their jurisdiction. In 1838, when Anne Lube charged her husband with assault, she asked the court to forego punishment but to induce her husband to provide her with financial support. The magistrates asked her husband what he would allow his wife and he agreed on 6s., out of his guinea a week salary, and to take his son to live with him—clearly anticipating that such an agreement was a prelude to a separation. This unsettled the magistrates, who, before allowing the consent to the alimony payment to be signed, noted to Mrs Lube that 'And mind, Mrs Lube, you must live in the one house together for it is not our wish that you should separate more particularly as he may yet reform and drop his evil habits'.

Belfast magistrates appear to have been more active in negotiating separations in violent relationships, perhaps reflecting their Presbyterian heritage in which marriage was not a sacrament and so divorce less problematic. In 1846 the magistrates attempted to negotiate a separation with alimony between the Addisons, using the threat of a £5 fine and imprisonment to get Addison to agree. He would not give more than 2s. 6d a week, which the court thought too little. Thomas King's lawyer asked, when he was charged with stabbing his wife repeatedly with a sword, whether, instead of prosecution, they could agree a separation. In this case, which was particularly violent, the magistrates sent him to trial.

Such separations were not a legal divorce but they did allow couples to part. Moreover, as the evidence from bigamy suits suggests, many couples believed, or claimed to believe, that their separations allowed them to rebuild their lives with new partners. Given that many bigamy cases only came to light when an original spouse protested, or even more commonly when a woman became indigent and the Poor Law board wished to find her financial support, it may be that for Irish lower-class couples who happily separated popular divorce was divorce enough.

Further reading

David Fitzpatrick, 'Divorce and separation in modern Irish history', *Past and Present* **114** (1987), 172–96.

Diane Urquhart, 'Irish divorce and domestic violence, 1857–1922', *Women's History Review* **22** (5) (2013), 820–37.

41

A runaway romance: Sydney, 1848

Kiera Lindsey

One wet autumn evening in 1848, fifteen-year-old Mary Ann Gill climbed out of her bedroom window on the third floor of her parents' Sydney hotel, then shimmied down an unstable drainpipe to elope with James Butler Kinchela, a man who was not only twenty years her senior but also the youngest son of a previous attorney general of New South Wales. An 'intimacy' had developed in late summer while Kinchela had been residing at Gill's Hotel. When, however, the gentleman settler had asked the publican for his daughter's hand in marriage he had received a 'flat no' before being told to settle his hotel bill and leave.

Undeterred, Kilkenny-born Kinchela came up with the idea of a runaway romance. Two nights before Mary Ann took to the drainpipe, the gentleman settler stood on the street below her bedroom and shared his strategy. Once she had escaped her father's house, she would take a coach to the Parramatta Racecourse, then known as the 'Australian Gretna Green', where the errant couple would be married by special licence. Having cautioned Kinchela that her father would kill them both 'if he took me from my father's house and did not marry me', Mary Ann agreed to this plan. The next day she stole a carpet-bag from her mother and filled it with possessions worthy of her new life as the wife of a gentleman settler. Then, on the night in question, Mary Ann made her way down the drainpipe and through Sydney's darkened and dangerous streets to the coach that was to carry her to her future.

As is so often the case the course of love did not run smoothly. While waiting at their appointed rendezvous, Kinchela decided to warm his 'cold feet' with 'several jugs of something strong', and when he learned that Martin Gill, an emancipated convict from Dublin, was in hot pursuit of his daughter, the country squire decided to make a discreet exit. Before he did so, he warned Mary Ann of her father's imminent arrival and begged her 'to come again' the following morning, so that the matter could be concluded to their mutual satisfaction.

No sooner had Mary Ann's slippery suitor vanished than her furious father arrived. Retrieving his daughter, he took her home, gave her a horse-whipping and went to bed. The following morning, however, when Gill went to his daughter's room he found a curtain dancing in the breeze of the open window and discovered that Mary Ann had yet again fled.

The legal depositions that detail what happened next describe how those who were breakfasting with Kinchela at the well-to-do hotel near the racecourse were excited by the appearance of a figure on a large brown mount galloping through the early dawn mist. The rider looked 'either drunk or mad', one report noted, and was bouncing about 'bareback ... still in his nightshirt, with both boots unlaced'. Bringing his horse to an abrupt halt outside the establishment where Kinchela was dining, the enraged publican bounded up the hotel steps, pushed his way through the crowd and presented two pistols at the gentleman settler. 'Will I give you time, sir?', he growled, before aiming one of his weapons directly at Kinchela's head.

Two shots were fired that morning but both missed their mark. Eventually Martin Gill was wrestled to the ground and his guns confiscated, and he was charged with 'shooting with intent'. If found guilty, Mary Ann's father faced the death penalty or perhaps even worse—the rest of his life in a remote penal outpost. But that is not what happened. Despite the fact that multiple witnesses testified to Gill's wrathful vengeance, and a blacksmith even confirmed that powder had been discharged from both of his pistols, a jury acquitted the ambitious colonist of all charges. The popular publican then commenced proceedings against Kinchela, who was promptly convicted of abduction and sentenced to nine months in Darlinghurst Gaol.

There are many questions surrounding this curious colonial episode. As Kinchela's defence barrister asked the court, 'Why should a father of Mr Gill's position oppose his daughter's union with such a gentleman?' After all, Mary Ann was the daughter of two Roman Catholic emancipists who had been transported for petty theft in the 1820s, while James Butler was part of the Protestant élite. Such a match promised social mobility to both Mary Ann and her parents. Gill's fierce opposition to this union may have had something to do with the bitter sectarian tensions which shaped Irish relations during this period, while another part of the answer can be traced to the various ways in which abduction was perceived within both Irish and colonial society at that time.

The act of taking a woman without parental consent was subject to some attention within Ireland's ancient legal texts. These draw a clear distinction between coercive abductions, where a woman was taken by force in an act of war or lust, and other instances in which a woman feigned her elopement to look like an abduction so that she could avoid an overt act of filial defiance. Over the centuries rituals evolved around both practices, and by the eighteenth century abduction was so ingrained within Irish society that it was often referred to as something of 'a national pastime'.

Nevertheless, as Protestant authorities became increasingly oppressive towards the Roman Catholic population of Ireland during the eighteenth century, abduction came to acquire more sinister elements. Many disenchanted Irishmen formed 'Abduction Clubs', kidnapping and sometimes also assaulting and raping Protestant heiresses so that they could force these women into marriage as a way of resolving their financial woes and restoring their confiscated lands. By the early eighteenth century these 'forced marriages' posed such a threat to the dynastic wealth of Protestant Ireland that abduction was made a capital offence in 1707 and remained so until 1842. Thanks to this legislation, thousands of men, as well as some women, were convicted of abduction. Hundreds were imprisoned, many executed, and at least 150 transported to Australia for stealing neither a handkerchief nor a loaf of bread but a woman.

At the same time an elopement ritual also became popular throughout Irish rural society because it offered couples whose marital ambitions ran contrary to social and parental conventions a way of negotiating their kinship obligations. Each Lent, a man could 'abduct' his intended bride from her home, and as long as the woman sat before her abductor on a horse it was assumed that their union was consensual. Many local priests were prepared to solemnise such unions 'for a decent price', and consequently each Lent there was a veritable exodus of couples making their way on horseback to their 'illicit' nuptials.

It is highly likely that both Gill and Kinchela were familiar with these Irish customs and aware that the law also stipulated, as Irish lawyer Roger Terry insisted while presiding over a colonial case in 1851, that 'it mattered not if the woman was willing or otherwise … legally, she had no rights'. A man must secure the consent of her parents or guardians; otherwise he had engaged in an act of property theft that carried 'grave consequences'. Kinchela had grown up in Kilkenny, where he would have witnessed these runaway romances enliven the Lenten season. He probably perceived his actions as 'harmless' fun. Indeed, that was the word he used when he first proposed the idea to Mary Ann and also how he described it to the court. But for Gill, the Dublin street urchin made good, Kinchela had not only engaged in property theft but had also violated the paternal rights of a man who had worked hard to secure a respectable place for himself within colonial society.

While abductors who faced the Irish courts in the early nineteenth century could hope to be acquitted by indulgent juries who may have dabbled in such romantic folly themselves, things were very different in New South Wales, particularly by 1848. Once scorned and ridiculed for its convict origins and ruled by agricultural oligarchs, the colony had only recently abandoned transportation in 1840. This had encouraged mass immigration of free British settlers, who recognised that their new home was likely to grant them greater influence than they might ever enjoy 'back home' but only if they could wrest control from the established autocrats. The year 1848 was also an election year in New South Wales, and men like Martin Gill and these recent immigrants saw this election as their first real opportunity to extend the franchise, advance the cause of self-government and get their hands on the reins of the colony's future. To achieve this, however, these men needed to prove that the colony was 'fit for government'. And so, for a society previously condemned as 'a colony of concubines', where the stabilising institutions of marriage and family had become crucial to their political future, Kinchela's romantic risk-taking threatened not only the reputation of the colony but also its future.

Over 100,000 words were written in the colonial newspapers about this thwarted elopement, ensuring that it soon became the colonial *cause célèbre* of 1848. Throughout that year, reports of the trial ran alongside articles about the election and the two repeated similar sentiments. After all, here was a member of the so-called idle classes 'taking' the daughter of a hardworking emancipist, violating not only this respectable man's role as the head of that family but also the institution of marriage itself. Perhaps, then, it is not surprising that Kinchela was convicted and jailed on polling day, the very day that middle-class men like Martin Gill enjoyed a decisive political victory, which future premier Henry Parkes would soon declare 'the birthplace of Australian democracy'. Once an act of rustic romance that was celebrated in Ireland as 'gentleman's sport', abduction had suddenly become a metaphor for the great change in social attitudes that was shaping the Victorian era.

Nonetheless, while the course of love did not run smoothly for Mary Ann and her beau, it did eventually hold true. After Kinchela served his prison term, the pair fled to the Californian gold-fields. And there in 1852, as the chaos of the gold-rush swirled about them, the couple were finally married in the aptly named St Mary's Roman Catholic Cathedral.

Further reading

James Kelly, 'The abduction of women of fortune in eighteenth-century Ireland', *Eighteenth Century Ireland* **9** (1994), 7–43.

Kiera Lindsey, 'So much recklessness: abduction in the colony of New South Wales', *Australian Historical Studies* **44** (3) (2013), 438–56.

Kiera Lindsey, *The convict's daughter: the scandal that shocked a colony* (Sydney, 2016).

42

The courtship, marriage and honeymoon of a Church of Ireland rector in post-Famine Ireland

Ciarán Reilly

According to the Register-General of Marriages in Ireland, just over 60,000 marriages were registered during the years of the Great Famine, 1845–51. Remarkably, more marriages took place in 1846, during a time of great distress, than in 1851, when the blight had almost vanished. The statistics for these years are somewhat misleading, however, given that Roman Catholics were exempt from the provisions of the act. Of these weddings we know very little, save a handful of newspaper accounts of high-society ceremonies. The latter were usually lavish affairs, such as that of Lord Carbery and Harriet Shuldham in August 1852. We are told that the bride, accompanied by twelve bridesmaids, wore a dress trimmed with orange blossoms and silver shamrocks. The newly married couple departed for Castle Freke, Lord Carbery's home, after a *déjeuner* at the Imperial Hotel, Cork, where all the delicacies of the season were enjoyed by those present. We know little, however, about the courtship or the honeymoon enjoyed by the wedded couple. That kind of information was not often made public, and we rely solely on personal diaries for such intimate details.

In May 1852 a sketch of 'Cupid and an arrow' drawn in the diary of John Plunket Joly, the son of the rector of the parish of Clonsast in King's County (Offaly), indicated that he had found a potential wife. By now the worst years of the Famine were over, and Joly's impending marriage to Julia Armit (1827–86), daughter of Count Lusi, was reflected in the number of parties and balls which were held in their honour as the couple prepared for their wedding. The engagement, however, coincided with the death of Joly's father, Revd Henry (1784–1852). Remarking on these conflicting emotions, Joly recorded in his diary: 'so ends the month of June 1852, a month of memorable incidence to me. The early part deeply clouded by the death of my poor dear father, my first and best friend—the remainder growing gradually brighter.'

The courting of Julia lasted several months, with Joly making regular trips to Dublin, where he was introduced to members of the Armit family. The parties were lavish affairs for which no expense was spared. At one such gathering in the Armits' home the guests enjoyed 'tea, coffee, dancing, supper, courting, talking and fun kept up till 2am'. Another party hosted by the Armits, attended by 41 people, was described as being 'very gay', and a number of musicians entertained the guests. His uncle, Charles Joly, also hosted a 'grand ball' at which 65 guests were treated to a 'violin band, dancing, singing, courting and all kinds of pleasantry'. Afterwards, and as an opportunity to spend time together, Joly and the young countess enjoyed a 'romantic drive in a covered car'.

By December 1851 Joly had replaced his ageing and increasingly infirm father as rector of Clonsast, having being ordained two years earlier in Chester, England. The position came with an annual salary of £460, which allowed for the complete renovation of the family home, Hollywood House, coinciding with Joly's engagement. This was a necessary prerequisite for a newly married couple who wished to decorate the house to their own tastes and style, and it mattered little that Hollywood had only recently undergone renovations in 1847. In preparing for the marriage, Joly also made a number of purchases which were necessary for the ceremony and for the house. These included a watch and chain valued at £21, an enamelled diamond ring for £4 4s. and a grand piano costing £42. Other purchases included frock coats, gloves, socks, a handkerchief and a collection of miscellaneous books and sheet music.

On 4 June 1853 Joly married Julia in a ceremony conducted by his cousin Augustus West, chancellor of Kildare. Afterwards, and having obtained permission from the archbishop to take a leave of absence from his parish, the newly married couple, accompanied by their housemaid, Martha Pattison, travelled to Kerry on their honeymoon. Staying in the Victoria Hotel, Killarney, the couple spent more than a week visiting a variety of landmarks: Muckross Abbey, Innisfallen, O'Donahue's cascade, the Gap of Dunloe and Ross's Castle. They also took time to row around the middle lake, then frequented by newly married couples. Returning to the family home near Bracknagh some days later, the newly-weds were greeted by a large gathering of tenants and neighbours. Throughout the night there was 'great dancing around a bonfire', for which members of the local band, which Joly had formed some years previously, provided music and other entertainment. Settling in to her new life in the King's County countryside, Julia revelled in the hospitality afforded to her as she visited the neighbouring country houses in the north-east of the county. The couple were popular amongst their tenantry, lending large sums of money on loan to those who wished to improve their holdings.

Their marriage, however, was short-lived. By 1857 Joly was in declining health. Despite receiving advice from several doctors to undertake a trip to Egypt or France for health reasons, he chose to remain in Ireland for the winter of 1857 and died the following March. Soon after, his widow left Hollywood House and moved to Dublin. This short marriage produced four children, including John (1857–1933), their fourth, who was later educated at Rathmines School under the direction of Dr Benson. His academic ability was evident at a young age and at sixteen he had experimented with the construction of a thermometer, a microscope and a deep-sea sounding apparatus. Later, as a physicist, geologist and engineer, he was a professor at Trinity College Dublin and was described by many as 'Ireland's most eminent man of science in modern times'.

Further reading

Ciarán Reilly, *John Plunkett Joly and the Great Famine in King's County* (Dublin, 2012).

43

A high-society wedding in Cavan (1853)

Jonathan A. Smyth

The following account describes the double wedding of two sisters from County Cavan in 1853. The extravagance of the undoubtedly happy occasion was in sharp contrast to the fate of many in the county who had survived the Famine.

On 16 August 1853, the community of the Church of Ireland parish of Drung gathered to watch the arrival of gentry from across Cavan and beyond as they pulled up at the local Church of Ireland church. Both brides-to-be were daughters of the archdeacon of Ardagh and vicar of Drung and Larah parish, Marcus Gervais Beresford. The archdeacon resided with his family at the local vicarage, known as Corravahan House. The Beresfords were a prominent and respected Anglo-Irish family, whose forebears included the 1st earl of Tyrone and the 1st marquis of Waterford. Although not particularly wealthy, Marcus Gervais Beresford was considered pre-eminent when it came to charity. Five years later, having ascended to the bishopric of Kilmore, Elphin and Ardagh, it was noted that he made a donation towards the cost of building the new cathedral at Kilmore.

An account of the Beresford girls' double wedding was provided courtesy of the local newspaper, *The Anglo-Celt*, their reporter having obtained a personal invitation. The first of the couples to tie the knot that day were Captain Thomas Heywood, serving in the 16th Lancers, of Hopend, Herefordshire, and Mary Emily, youngest daughter of the archdeacon. When their nuptial blessing was complete, the archdeacon's eldest daughter, Charlotte Henrietta, took centre stage and married Henry B. W. Milner, son of Sir William Mordaunt Milner, baronet, of Nunappleton Hall, Yorkshire. The Milners possessed an estate in Yorkshire.

The unnamed journalist noted in his report, dated 25 August 1853, that there had been a trend of late for the young brides of the upper classes 'to have a great number of beautiful girls, their relatives and friends, to attend upon them as bridesmaids at the altar; twenty-four were invited to grace the nuptials of the Misses Beresford', which, it was said, required 'no small amount of good taste, of time, and of trouble, to invent and provide, and fit a becoming uniform upon some twenty or four-and-twenty bridesmaids.' With regard to the style worn by the bridesmaids, it was reported:

> let us isolate her, and contemplate her requirements. Look at her tiny foot glistening in white satin; smooth as an onion boiled in butter; look at the wreath of blush roses, forming two-thirds of a circle, that bounds that loveable little face 'brightening all over' at the role it is about to act; then the gown, so deeply plicate at hip and waist; expanding as it descends in an ample rotundity, and bespeaking an enormous profusion of nether involucra. The bonnet, that pet of a bonnet, artfully constructed to conceal the cervical vertebrae and large portion of the occipital bone; and the veil, and the gloves, and the sash, brought into a neat point at the anterior termination of the corset from whence two 'streamers float upon the breeze'. We say nothing here of the jewellery, nor of the showers of pins that are scattered from the trembling hand of the eloquent ladies' maid; and which, subsequently, become the undisputed property of the house-maid, through whom they are destined to flow down to, and irrigate, if we may use the term, the entire household; nor of the bouquet of flowers; nor of the pocket handkerchief; that acre of lace surrounding a palms breadth of cambric. No, the millinery arts have triumphed; and we are lost in the wondrous perfection they have achieved.

Afterwards, the wedding party, consisting of 86 guests, including Lady Farnham and the Burrowes and Clements families, were invited to Corravahan House to enjoy the hospitality of the Beresfords.

The banquet consisted of mouth-watering sirloins of beef, 'saddles of mutton' and, to top the menu, a 'haunch of venison, the growth of a seven years' buck'. Food for the feast was shipped in from across Ireland and Britain. Hams came from Limerick, Wicklow, Belfast and 'Westphalia'. Turkey pouts were imported from Norfolk, and a supply of salmon had come from Ballyshannon. The tables, although specially constructed—or, rather, reinforced—were said to 'have absolutely groaned beneath the task imposed upon them'.

Champagne, according to *The Anglo-Celt*, was a 'favourite beverage of all ages and sexes', as 'the corks popped out accordingly with a very cheerful sound'. The reporter added: 'for our own part, if our opinion in drinkables of this nature be held to be worth anything, we would advise ... if the weather be very warm and the thirst very great ... a tumbler or two of sparkling Saint Peray ... bien moussence ... it cools the tongue and palate a merveille'. The wedding cakes were described as resembling an upper and lower millstone in shape.

The party had remained indoors owing to the rain. By evening, however, the damp weather cleared and all visitors to Corravahan were able to return home. Later that night the journalist called to see Fr Tom Brady, the Catholic parish priest at Drung. Knowing that his friend would visit, Fr Brady had invited some 'choice spirits' to greet his caller. The reporter wrote that 'on our entrance we were greeted with nine times nine, and one cheer more ... what happened between that time and day-light may probably furnish an article on some future occasion'. One imagines that they had plenty of interesting things to discuss, especially when one considers the conditions lately endured by people in the locality. In particular, the bountiful feast on offer at the Beresford girls' sumptuous wedding was in sharp contrast to the recent Famine.

Sources

John Charles Coombe, *St Fethlimidh's Cathedral, Kilmore: a short history* (1992).
Raymond Refaussé, 'Marcus Gervais Beresford (1801–1885)', in *Dictionary of Irish biography: from the earliest times to the year 2002*, vol. i (Cambridge, 2009), 469–70.

44

'Far from Ireland's green shores': marriage and the Irish emigrant

Gerard Moran

Throughout the nineteenth century Ireland's greatest export was her people, with an estimated eight million leaving for destinations as near as Britain and as far away as Australia, New Zealand, North America and Argentina. While the records for most of the century are fragmentary and unreliable, what is clear is that as many women as men left after 1876, which meant that, unlike other European countries, the Irish were able to marry partners from their own country and, as the evidence will show, often from the same parish back home. While many families left during the Great Famine and through assisted emigration such as the Peter Robinson scheme from the North Blackwater region of Munster between 1823 and 1825 and the James Hack Tuke schemes from Mayo and Connemara in the early 1880s, the main group of emigrants after 1850 came from the 16–24 age cohort and were single. While some girls left to earn the dowry that would enable them to return to Ireland and secure a marriage partner, the emigrants who remained turned to their fellow countrymen and women for marriage.

In Ireland an unmarried person had few rights as regards inheritance, so that emigration was a liberating experience for many, allowing them not only to be independent and wealthy but also to choose their marriage partners. In Ireland most marriages were arranged by the parents, with the bride and groom having little involvement, but emigrants did not face the same constraints and enjoyed greater flexibility in their choice. Whereas back home a couple seldom married outside their social class, outside Ireland the main criterion for a marriage partner was that they were Irish rather than from the strong farmer or labouring classes. While marriage opportunities for women in Ireland were dependent on having a dowry, this was not the most important consideration in the foreign destinations where the Irish settled. In Ireland, the principal criterion was that the bride should bring a dowry appropriate to the status of the family from which she came. As a result, land was an important determinant in the choice of a marriage partner, especially after the Great Famine, and it influenced the value of the dowry that the bride brought with her. Prior to 1845, the farm enabled marriages to take place at an early age, as the land was divided between all of the sons, while after the Great Famine only the eldest son could marry, as he inherited the farm; for the remaining males, without the requisite financial security, emigration was the only alternative, not only for financial independence but also for marriage opportunities. This was at a time when the age of marriage in Ireland was being delayed. By the end of the nineteenth century, Irish men were not marrying until their late thirties or even older, but emigration offered both men and women the possibility of marrying earlier.

The church records in those countries where the Irish settled provide a good indication of the marriage patterns of the Irish emigrants. By the early 1850s one third of New York's population were Irish-born or first-generation Irish, and they settled in the poorest parts of the city, such as Five Points. By 1860, 55% of the population of Five Points were Irish. The marriage records for the Church of the Transfiguration from 1853 to 1855 provide an indication of where they came from, where they lived in the parish and their ages when they married. A total of 257 marriages are recorded for this period; 442 (86% of the total getting married) were from Ireland, with the highest number from County Sligo (87). After that, 44 were from Cork and 40 from Kerry, but there were also strong representations from Tipperary (39), Galway (31) and Mayo (21). The Irish were more likely to take partners from Ireland, with only fourteen cases of marriages with non-Irish partners. Even then the tendency was to take partners who were English-speaking, mainly English-, American- and Canadian-born.

Although the Irish may have left Ireland, a strong bond with home remained, evident in the fact that there were 120 marriages in which both parties were from the same county. In 37 cases, both the bride and the groom came from County Sligo, as with Dan O'Connell from Cliffony and Ellen Garvey from Drumcliffe, who married on 28 December 1853, and Thomas Boylan from Templeboy and Catherine Begley from Screen, who married on 3 January 1854. Among the other areas where both parties came from the same county were Cork (14) and Kerry (13). An even closer relationship can be observed in the fact that many of the marriages involved couples who were from the same parish in Ireland. Five were from Drumcliffe, Co. Sligo, as in the case of Thomas Gilroy and Bridget Garvey, who married on 26 June 1851. In four cases both came from Tousist, Co. Kerry, and four from Ahamlish, Co. Sligo.

Living close to other Irish immigrants also allowed people to choose partners from home. Ten of the marriages at the Church of the Transfiguration involved people who not only came from the same parish in Ireland but also lived in the same tenements in Five Points, as with Pat Scalon and Bridget Byrne, both originally from Lismore, Co. Waterford, who lived at 31 White Corner, Orange Street. A feature of Irish life before the Great Famine was that people married young, girls in their late teens and men in their early twenties. In Five Points, 43% of the men who married were under 25 years of age, the youngest being Peter Boland from Ballisodare, Co. Sligo, who was eighteen. One third of the women who married were under twenty, Mary Corkery from Kenmare, Co. Kerry, being the youngest at sixteen. Another 42% were in the 21–25 age cohort.

In conclusion, leaving Ireland often allowed emigrants the opportunity simply to marry, something which may not have been possible at home. Furthermore, marriage patterns in places like Five Points indicate that emigrants were more likely to wed a partner who was Irish rather than from other immigrant groups.

Further reading

Tyler Anbinder, *Five Points: the nineteenth-century New York City neighbourhood that invented tap dance, stole elections and became the world's most notorious slum* (New York, 2002).

Art Cosgrove (ed.), *Marriage in Ireland* (Dublin, 1985).

45

Single-shaming: Chalk Sunday, Pus Monday, Cock Tuesday, tarry men and the Skellig Lists

Clodagh Tait

The prime season for marriages in nineteenth- and early twentieth-century Ireland was Shrove (also called Seraft or, in Irish, *Inid*), the period between Little Christmas and the start of Lent. Most parish registers show a pattern of intensive marriage activity in February or very early March, with Shrove Tuesday being the last day for weddings until the end of Lent. In many places the days before Ash Wednesday were marked by customs that mocked local spinsters and bachelors, of whom communities might have many examples, given the pattern of late marriage evident by the end of the 1800s.

In the west and midlands, young people chalked the coats of those showing no sign of imminent marriage on 'Chalk Sunday', the Sunday before Ash Wednesday; ashes or more indelible substances might also be used. In parts of Connacht and Munster, salt was thrown on 'old maids' on 'Salting Tuesday', 'to preserve them for another year'. In various places it was claimed that unbetrothed women went around with disconsolate faces on 'Pus Monday', '*Domhnach na nDeóirín* [Sunday of the little tears]' or '*Domhnach na Smúit* [Sunday of the scowls]', while men who remained unmarried after 'Cock Tuesday' would be asked 'Did you let the cock crow on you again?'

Those left single by nightfall on Shrove Tuesday might be further persecuted by their neighbours. In parts of County Limerick, 'tolls' were demanded of the unmarried by bands of young men and the proceeds spent on drink; Charlotte Wilson reported that in 1930s Adare 'sometimes they meet with a very hostile reception'. Figures were drawn with paint or tar on the gateposts of bachelors and spinsters in east Cork and west Waterford: my father remembers 'tarry men' on a gatepost at Ballybranigan, Co. Cork, in the 1950s. In parts of County Westmeath, unmarried 'boys and girls' (Kevin Danaher writes about unmarried adults being spoken of—and treated—as if they were children) were 'tied with chains and put on a slide' and dragged around. In the areas of Macroom, Rockchapel and Midleton, Co. Cork, singletons might likewise be 'rounded up' by young men with ropes, and even be dunked in water or made to stand in ponds.

These raucous Cork customs were part of 'Skellig Night', which was also widely observed in County Kerry. James Beale's lively 1845 painting of Cork city centre, 'Skellig Night on the South Mall' (Pl. 4), shows a carnivalesque torchlit scene of women and men being manhandled, pulled around on sledges and otherwise teased. An 1832 letter to Thomas Crofton Croker described 500 men in the streets of Cork on Skellig Night, 'blowing horns, firing, ringing the bells of houses, breaking lamps etc., and all on the occasion of the Skellig Lists'. In Bantry 100 years later noisy processions formed in the town, with youngsters dragging ropes with cans tied to them and shouting 'Come to the Skelligs'. Based on the conceit that the Skellig Islands still operated on an older calendar, and that Ash Wednesday therefore arrived later there than elsewhere in Ireland, the idea was that a trip to the rock would give obstinate spinsters and bachelors a last chance at marriage.

This was the theme of 'Skellig Lists', ballads produced annually throughout southern Cork and Kerry that conjured up incongruous pairings to accompany one another on the pilgrimage. Those satirised came from all sections of society, and both Catholics and Protestants appeared in and wrote them. The lists' descriptions of the supposed pilgrims' personal characteristics and family circumstances were regularly hilariously (to the listeners) uncomplimentary. For example, one twentieth-century Kerry list described a potential husband and father-in-law thus:

> Oh what a boy, and oh what a cad
> Is 'Seán a scuab' and his little one lad.
> Do you think, 'shy Seán', that the offer made
> Is enough to satisfy 'Molly the maid'?

The poem ended in mock exasperation:

> Oh God help us what a flock
> Must brave the elements and face 'the rock' ...
> They've tried, they've failed, the shelf must hold
> For another year unless too old
> This motley clan of apes and asses.
> Oinseachs [fools], swanks that go as lassies.

157

The lists mostly circulated orally and in manuscript, and a large number of manuscript versions are preserved in the National Folklore Archive. By the 1830s, however, Cork city's flourishing printing trade meant that large numbers were also being published: Croker estimated that about 30,000 were sold in 1836. His collection of 29 broadsides from that year is now part of the Bradshaw Collection in Cambridge, which contains at least 50 further printed Skellig Lists dating from before the early 1840s. Printing of the lists continued into the later nineteenth century, though their ephemeral nature means that few survive; the exceptions include four in UCC library dating from about 1871/2.

Several proclamations against the sale of Skellig Lists in Cork city and surrounding towns from the 1850s ordered the police to seize any they found. Cork's mayor and corporation were concerned with both the damage to the reputations of respectable people and the potential for assault by aggrieved subjects. In Queenstown (Cobh) in February 1870, for example, William Beatty attacked Cornelius Condon, a ballad-singer hawking Skellig Lists in which Beatty was mentioned, put a rope around his neck and attempted to drown him. The magistrates were unsympathetic to Condon, and though Beatty pleaded guilty to assault he was only fined one penny. In the same month, a Cork 'urchin' selling lists 'of a particularly personal and offensive character' was apprehended and 200 copies were seized. The printers fought back: the *Scorpion Skellig List* of 1871 mocked two policemen, described the RIC as the 'Rich I.C.' and ended:

Now ragged urchins hear my prayer,
If the *alligators* catch you,
Go at once to our good Lord Mayor,
Who's bound to mind and watch you.

Skellig Lists were still being published in Cork in 1884, when a young seller assaulted and abused a policeman (whom he claimed had kicked him first) and was given fourteen days in jail or a fine of £1. The combination of official disapproval and the decline of the Cork print trade meant that Skellig Lists moved back into oral and manuscript circulation. By the 1930s, 'single-shaming' Shrove customs were in decline, with some informants of the Schools Folklore collection already placing their heyday far in the past.

Sources

A catalogue of the Bradshaw Collection of Irish books in the University Library, Cambridge, vol. 3 (Cambridge, 1916).

Thomas Crofton Croker, *Popular songs of Ireland* (London, 1839).

Maura Cronin, 'Provincial publishing', in J.H. Murphy (ed.), *The Oxford history of the Irish book: the Irish book in English, 1800–1899* (Oxford, 2011).

Kevin Danaher, *The year in Ireland: Irish calendar customs* (Cork, 1972).

Kevin Danaher, 'Marriage in Irish folk tradition', in A. Cosgrave (ed.), *Marriage in Ireland* (Dublin, 1985).

Irish Folklore Commission archive, www.duchas.ie.

46

Lizzie and William's
Continental honeymoon, 1859

Angela Byrne

At 2pm on 14 March 1859, a pair of newly-weds made the crossing from Kingstown (Dún Laoghaire) to Holyhead, leaving, in the
groom's words, 'a disconsolate party cutting up wedding cake to
distribute amongst our many friends'. Elizabeth Olivia Darley (*c.* 1829–1907)
and William Hartigan Barrington (1815–72) had married earlier that day in
St Peter's Church, Dublin. William was some fourteen years older than his wife,
had studied law at Cambridge and had travelled in Germany, North Africa,
Russia, Scandinavia and Spain. Little is known about Elizabeth, save that she
was the daughter of Henry Darley and Maria Louisa West of Wingfield, Co.
Wicklow, and that she had previously spent some time in France.

The concept of the honeymoon as the period of bliss following a wedding
dates back to the late sixteenth century, but the post-wedding holiday now
known as the honeymoon emerged, for the European upper and upper middle
classes, in the late eighteenth century. This particular wedding journey, made in
March–May 1859 and taking in London, Paris, Marseilles, Nice, Geneva, Milan,
Venice, Trent, Stuttgart, Baden and Strasbourg, is recorded in a small leather-
bound diary held in the National Library of Ireland (MS 34,390/5). The diary
was authored by William, with Elizabeth making minor contributions in the
form of brief notes on expenditure and an inventory of clothing.

The wedding journey is, by definition, characterised by firsts. The first
stop on their journey was at the George Hotel in Bangor, Wales, where they
had their 'first tête à tête dinner'. After resting in Bangor for the night, they
proceeded to London, where they spent three days visiting and being visited,
and seeing the city. They then sailed from Folkestone across the Strait of
Dover—'a lovely passage of little more than 2 Hours'—and travelled on to
Paris by rail, arriving at the Louvre Hotel, Paris, at 11pm on 19 March. The
following day being Sunday, the pair attended a church service and, despite
the 'wearying sermon', they 'remained for sacrament first time both together'.

From Paris they travelled to Lyons and Marseilles by rail, and thence via Nice to Geneva, where they met 'an attentive waiter who won Lizzie's heart with flowers'. The pair enjoyed small kindnesses and good wishes from several people they met *en route*, particularly locals. In Bangor the hotel landlady had welcomed them with teacakes, and in Turin a gardener presented Elizabeth with a bouquet of camellias. This special treatment signals Elizabeth's signified but unspoken status as a newly married woman. While William logged some of the 'firsts' they enjoyed on their wedding journey, like the dinner in Bangor and receiving the sacrament in Paris, the privacy of the diary was not secure enough to allow the recording of other, more delicate matters. The only hint at physical intimacy in a journal that was by definition an intimate object occurs when William records that *en route* from Venice to Trent he hired three places in the chaise, 'so as to have the Cabriolet to ourselves'. The pair's closeness as a newly married couple is revealed only in William's persistent use of the diminutive 'Lizzie' (rather than Elizabeth or Mrs Barrington) in reference to his new wife.

Elizabeth had apparently lived in France seven years before her marriage and enjoyed rediscovering familiar places on the wedding journey. Despite knowing that she had travelled to France at least once before, William noted that the journey from Folkestone to Paris was 'a good days [*sic*] work which to my surprise did not tire Lizzie much'. William continued to frame Elizabeth's experiences as new by emphasising her wonder at the changes that had taken place in the city in the seven years since she had last been there. William, speaking for both travellers, emphasised the newness of Elizabeth's experiences because she was now seeing France differently, through the eyes of a married woman. The wedding journey was his gift to her and he enjoyed seeing her savour its details. This tone changes only slightly when they reached the 'singular & most interesting city' of Venice, where they were both so engaged with sightseeing that William neglected his journal for the first four of the six days they spent there. Venice appears as the centre point of the journey and they were 'quite sorry to leave indeed'.

The couple's itinerary was a safe option and a common choice for newly married Victorians, emulating the classic 'grand tour' that had epitomised genteel travel in the eighteenth century. William had some adventures in North Africa and in Russia as a younger man, but with his new wife he made a tamer journey. They experienced mere glimpses of danger—or, more accurately, lack of safety—by roaming around Venice's narrow streets without a guide or map, finding their way only 'by the aid of the bits of white marble in the pavement' that alert the pedestrian to the canal edge. William was also thrilled about the risk of impending war in Italy—the Second Italian War of Independence in April–July 1859. The pair had shared a rail carriage with an English consul who informed them that war was 'inevitable' and imminent, leading them to cut their journey short.

In all, the diary physically embodies the union of two individuals and the erasure of Elizabeth's individuality. Her prior experiences are barely acknowledged. William is the voice of the tour, the guide, the well-travelled older man displaying Europe to his passenger. He takes pleasure in observing her reactions to new sights, as well as sights that she had seen before as a single woman. Their itinerary was typically Victorian and appropriate to their social position as landowners, as were the roles they assumed on the journey. In William's univocal record, Elizabeth's happiness was always considered in material terms. We cannot know what more she desired from her honeymoon, leaving as she did only the lightest of footprints during her Continental wedding journey.

Further reading
Angela Byrne, 'A gentlemanly tour on the fringes of Europe: William Hartigan Barrington in Scandinavia and Russia, 1837', *Irish Economic and Social History* **40** (2013), 31–47.

47

Four Victorian weddings and a funeral

Patrick Comerford

our weddings and a funeral in one family circle provide telling stories of how Irish society was changing at the end of the Victorian and Edwardian eras, in the decades immediately before World War I and the Easter Rising in 1916.

The first wedding took place secretly in 1870, when Lady Blanche Noel (1845–81) married her music teacher, the Irish-born Thomas Murphy. She was born Lady Blanche Elizabeth Mary Annunciata Noel at Exton Hall in Rutland on 25 March 1845, and Queen Victoria was her godmother at her baptism.

Her baptismal names illustrate how deeply her parents were influenced by the Tractarian movement. Her father, Charles Noel (1818–81), second earl of Gainsborough, was a prominent Whig politician who embraced Roman Catholicism in a very public conversion in 1850. Her mother, the former Lady Ida Hay, was a cousin of Queen Victoria and one of her bridesmaids; and her grandmother, Lady Elizabeth FitzClarence, was an illegitimate daughter of King William IV.

Lady Blanche and her sister, Lady Constance, were received into the Catholic Church by Pope Pius IX on New Year's Day 1850. As a child, Blanche was schooled privately, learning Italian, French, German and Spanish, and some Latin and Greek, and travelling through Italy and Germany. After her mother's death she was left to her own teenage ways at the family home, Exton Hall. She sang in the choir in the family's private chapel, and had daily music and singing lessons from Thomas Murphy, the tall, handsome and well-educated young organist in the chapel who was also the private music tutor to the Noel sisters.

In their hours together in the chapel after Matins and Vespers, Blanche and Thomas fell in love. Lord Gainsborough was aware of nothing until a visiting friend noticed their intimacy. In his indignant disapproval, one story says, he allowed the marriage to take place in his private chapel; another account says that the couple eloped to London, where they married, and that Blanche was disowned and disinherited by her father.

It is likely that Gainsborough objected not because Murphy was Irish but because he was a commoner who brought no titles or estates into the family. Whatever his objections, Blanche and Thomas were married in the chapel at Exton on 6 March 1870. One of Gainsborough's conditions, however, for consenting to the wedding in his chapel was that the couple should immediately leave England. The love-struck pair sailed for America and Blanche never saw her family again. There is little truth to the story that they travelled in the steerage compartment, and that when they arrived 'she and Murphy bummed around New York. They had no money and hadn't eaten for 24 hours. She sold her earrings for a loaf of bread and said it was the best meal she ever had.'

The couple settled in Bartlett, New Hampshire, where Murphy taught music and French at a boys' school and was the organist in a local church, while Blanche earned a reputation as a writer with magazine essays, short stories and travel logs. Gainsborough appears eventually to have had regrets about the way he treated his daughter. In 1874 he provided her with an annuity of £60 and invited her back to Exton Hall—if she left her husband.

Blanche accepted the annuity but refused her father's conditions for her return to Exton. She was not present for a second family wedding in the same chapel in 1874, when her sister Lady Constance (1847–91) married a more acceptable Irishman, Sir Henry Bellingham (1846–1921). The Bellinghams were once a powerful and influential family in County Louth, and for over 100 years, without interruption, a Bellingham sat in the Irish House of Commons as MP for the county. At Oxford Sir Henry, who became the fourth baronet, became a friend of Cardinal Newman and Cardinal Manning, and while he was still in his twenties he made a very public conversion to Roman Catholicism in 1873, a year before his marriage.

Nor was Blanche present at a third family wedding in 1880, this time in Ireland. Her widowed brother, Charles Francis Noel (1856–1926), by then known as Viscount Campden, married Mary Elizabeth Dease in Coole, near Castlepollard, Co. Westmeath. Unlike Blanche and her Irish husband, Charles and his Irish bride returned to live at Exton.

In New Hampshire Blanche had a reputation for feeding and clothing local poor children. The couple had no children of their own. Blanche died just four days short of her 36th birthday after four days' illness; she had remained a fervent Catholic all her life. Her funeral took place on 24 March 1881 in the Catholic Cathedral in Portland, Maine, and she was buried temporarily in a vault in the Calvary Cemetery before her body was brought back to England and buried beside her mother in the Noel crypt at Exton.

Gainsborough, who had remained a widower, died at the age of 62 on 13 August 1881, a few days after Blanche had been reburied in the family crypt. On his deathbed he agreed that Thomas should continue to receive Blanche's small annuity. He was buried beside his wife in the crypt. His titles and estates passed to his eldest son, Charles, who had married Mary Dease the previous year.

Thomas Murphy moved first into a boarding house and then to Boston, where he died on 11 October 1890. He was buried alone at Calvary Cemetery. His younger sister-in-law, Lady Ida Noel, who had become a nun as Mother Mary Emmanuel, also died that year. His other sister-in-law, Lady Constance Bellingham, died at Bellingham Castle a year later in 1891.

In 1895 Henry Bellingham married his second wife, another prominent English Catholic, Lelgarde Harry Florence Clifton. He still mourned Lady Constance, however, and in 1902, when a 200-year-old great royal oak at the castle gates fell in a storm, he had it carved for the Calvary erected in her memory at the gates of Bellingham Castle.

The fourth society wedding in the family circle was celebrated in 1905, when Henry's younger daughter, Augusta, married John Crichton-Stuart, fourth marquess of Bute, then said to be the wealthiest man on these islands. The *Princess Maud*, a chartered steamer, took the guests across the Irish Sea to the harbour at Annagassan, Co. Louth, for the wedding at Bellingham Castle.

But when the wedding party and guests departed as they had arrived, by steamer from Annagassan, the Edwardian world they left behind was falling apart, never to be put together again. Within a decade World War I had broken out, and the events were already in train that would lead to the Battle of the Somme and the Easter Rising in 1916.

Exton Hall remains the home of the Noel family; the chapel where Lady Blanche and Lady Constance married their Irish husbands occupies a unique Catholic niche in the country house wedding market in England. Bellingham Castle is now a romantic wedding venue and hotel between Drogheda and Dundalk, and the nineteen luxury bedrooms include the sumptuous Bute Suite that recalls one of those four society weddings over a century ago.

48

Shotgun wedding?

Linda-May Ballard

Marriage, while being of central significance to the couple involved, is also of broader social concern, involving the disruption of two families and the establishment of a new unit. This broader social relevance is particularly reflected in the exchange of gifts and food, and is strongly symbolised by the custom of sending out pieces of wedding cake to those who were unable to be present for the occasion. The event of a wedding is also marked by behaviour which may be disruptive, specifically nowadays in the form of hen and stag parties. Similar disruption was also typical in the past in Ireland; while some forms of disruptive behaviour were highly localised, others were very widespread, with related forms of several customs being known in other countries.

The right of the community to be involved in an event of wider relevance is perhaps most clearly expressed by the arrival of the strawboys at a wedding party. Until relatively recently most of these parties took place in the bride's family home. In many areas the party might suddenly be interrupted by the unannounced appearance of the strawboys in their distinctive straw costumes and conical masks. A strawboy's mask covered the entire head, ensuring anonymity while not impeding the wearer's sight. The lead strawboy would expect to dance with the bride, the others with bridesmaids or other unmarried female guests. They would also expect to be treated hospitably, and the wisest choice was to ensure this. Strawboys who were well treated would unmask, revealing their identities, and a bonfire would be built in the yard outside the house on which their costumes were burned while everyone danced round the fire. The disruption of the strawboys symbolised the social disruption brought about by the wedding. Their unmasking and the destruction of their costumes symbolised reintegration and the acceptance of the new couple as a distinct family unit. The implications of this were more clearly expressed by the consequences of failing to treat the strawboys hospitably.

Fig. 5—L3249/5. Group of men from County Antrim, *c.* 1960, assembled with shotguns to give a traditional salute to a bridegroom as he travelled to his wedding. Photograph © National Museums NI Collection. Ulster Folk and Transport Museum.

Instead of symbolising reintegration and success for the new couple, the actions of the strawboys then carried a much more sinister meaning. The costumes would be removed after they had left the party, the identities of the participants thus remaining concealed. Thrown into high trees at the boundary of the bride's home place, the costumes would be left to rot.

Among the many customs that might be described in association with Irish weddings is another which was not without risk. In some areas there was a tradition of discharging shotguns to provide a salute honouring either bride or groom as they left their respective homes to travel to the wedding ceremony. On some occasions the shots would be fired in honour of the couple after the wedding (Fig. 5). While these salutes seem usually to have passed off without incident, there were occasional unfortunate and even tragic results of injury or fatality.

Frequently, barriers would be placed along the route to be taken by either bride or groom to the church, and the custom was to pay to have these barriers removed. In some areas the groom scattered money before entering the church for the ceremony, and in others the couple did so after the wedding had occurred. This symbolically invited everyone to join in the celebrations and perhaps helped to prevent a degree of disruptive behaviour.

In some areas races were held from the church to the home of the bride after the wedding ceremony. These might be either on foot or on horseback, in which case women often rode pillion. The winner might expect to be rewarded with broth in some cases or with whiskey in others, and occasionally with a garter worn by the bride. If a bottle of whiskey was the prize, this would be shared with other guests and the empty bottle then given to the bride to smash. A shattered bottle would bode well for the fertility of the new couple.

While the festivities generally took place in the bride's parental home, the parental home of the groom was usually where the new couple would live. The journey made by the couple between the two homes was usually known as the 'drag home'. Instead of harnessing a horse to pull a vehicle, friends would assist in drawing or 'dragging' the couple. At the new home, the bride's mother-in-law might hand her either the tongs from the fireplace or a plate from the dresser. The fire strongly symbolised the centre of the household, and control of the fireplace meant domestic oversight of the home. In cases where a couple set up home in a newly built house, the fire would be kindled by carrying a brand from an existing blaze, and great care was taken to ensure that domestic fires remained alight at all times. If the bride received a plate, she would be expected to smash it. This, too, was strongly symbolic, as the dresser was an important symbol of domesticity. The symbolism here suggested that the bride now had control of the home, but in reality this might be more difficult to secure and the symbolism might be a closer reflection of her new role in looking after her husband's parents. This is also reflected by the fact that in several areas she would observe a 'month's mind'. She would remain in her new home for a month, especially without visiting her own parents, as she became accustomed to her new role.

The 'drag home' ensured that several friends were on hand when the couple arrived in their new home. The bridal bed then became a focus for pranks, for example with briars or frogs being placed between the sheets, or Epsom salts in the chamber pot. A sentry judiciously positioned outside a window could generally be relied on to report the outcome. Once again, the wider community asserted its right to be involved in the establishment of the new family unit.

Further reading

Linda-May Ballard, *Forgetting frolic: marriage traditions in Ireland* (Belfast, 1998).

49

Murder at the wedding: Knocknamuckly, 1888

Raymond Gillespie

Weddings are usually happy affairs, but occasionally they have the effect of drawing together families whose disputes and grievances run deep and, fuelled by the merrymaking, they burst out in brawling or worse. Such was the case in one of the most celebrated Irish murders of the late nineteenth century. Just before ten o'clock on the morning of Friday 2 March 1888, the daughter of the sexton of Knocknamuckly parish church, four miles south-east of Portadown in County Armagh, opened the building for a wedding. Shortly after that, the wedding party arrived at the church in one carriage from Gilford. It was comprised of three couples: Thomas Thompson (the groom), aged 25 or 30 and a spinner at McMaster's mill in nearby Gilford, and Mary Ann Moffett, a sister of the bride; Frances Jane Moffett (the bride), daughter of a 'respectable' farmer from Lisnamuntry, and William Coulter; and finally Margaret Dilworth and Joseph Twinem, who were to act as witnesses.

When they entered the church, two people were already there: Revd Richard Oates, the rector, who had come to the parish ten years before from Liverpool, and, sitting on the fourth seat from the door on the left-hand side, a man who was later identified as one William Thompson, a small shopkeeper from Gilford whose late sister had been married to Thomas Thompson, the groom. The bridal party walked up the aisle toward the altar, and as they passed William Thompson, who all later agreed was smiling, he rose and shot the groom in the back at close range, the bullet piercing his right lung. He had bought the gun the previous day in a hardware store in Portadown. In the mayhem that followed, William Thompson made no effort to escape but went out into the churchyard, where he remained until 11.30am when he was arrested and taken, with the injured man, to Portadown. Thomas died about 10.30pm that evening.

The inquest was summoned for Saturday and found that Thomas had, indeed, been murdered by William. Then events took a strange turn. On

6 March, two days after the murder, the police arrested Elizabeth Thompson, William's mother, and they began dragging the canal opposite Gilford station looking for a dagger or a sword that was supposed to have been thrown in the previous Sunday. Some sort of implement was found, supposedly purchased by William Thompson, the murderer, and said to have been thrown into the canal by Elizabeth's daughter. The main case against Elizabeth was founded on an alleged conspiracy with two of her sons on the day of the murder to kill Thomas Thompson. Elizabeth was remanded in custody but eventually released.

There was no shortage of explanations for the events of 2 March. One theory was that William was drunk, but the daughter of the sexton was clear that he 'appeared to be sober'. A second possibility was that he was mad and, within a week, rumours were circulating that William had been in an asylum. The coroner's jury raised this possibility but were assured that there was no truth to it. Some jurors refused to believe the assurances but nevertheless returned that there was no evidence that William was of unsound mind. At his trial William would vehemently deny that he was mentally unbalanced, but claimed that he had been profoundly affected by the treatment of his sister by his brother-in-law, Thomas—he committed the murder, as he later put it, 'in passion'.

It appears that the murder revolved around a family dispute that may have gone back some years. It was claimed that Elizabeth Thompson had told William that 'if she had been in his clothes she would have put a bullet into Thomas Thompson long ago', and the Moffetts did not escape criticism either, for they were 'a bad clan'. The immediate problem, however, was the earlier wedding of William's sister and Thomas Thompson. According to the crime report, when Thomas had married in 1883:

> on the wedding day there was a general quarrel among the members of the family and the deceased [Thomas] refused to take his wife home alleging that she was illegitimate. Since that date he and the accused [William] had never spoken and the latter alleged that his sister ... was badly treated by her husband. When the accused heard of the intended second marriage he expressed his sorrow that his sister's child should have a stepmother and his ill feeling against the deceased appeared greatly intensified.

Indeed, William was heard to say 'his poor first wife' before being arrested, and medical evidence was called during his examination by the magistrates on the profound impact that his sister's death had had on him.

After an initial examination by a magistrate on 9 March, William was taken to Armagh gaol, where he remained until his trial in July 1888. It took the jury ten minutes to reach the verdict of guilty, and William Thompson was sentenced to death for the murder of Thomas Thompson, his last words from the dock being 'Good bye boys, God save the queen'. There was a belief, however, that the sentence should not be carried out, since he had acted in a fit of depression after the death of his sister when, in the words of one contemporary report, 'he became depressed in spirits and his mind became so weakened that those who knew him best asserted that he was not responsible for his acts'. A memorial signed by the jurors in the case, as well as by a number of clergy, doctors and local landlords, was sent to the lord lieutenant, asking that his sentence be commuted. This was done and on 4 August he was transported to Dublin to be imprisoned in the Dundrum Criminal Lunatic Asylum.

Here events took another strange turn, for within a few months he had escaped and disappeared. Nothing was heard of him until four o'clock on the morning of Monday 10 September 1906, when he walked into Markethill police barracks in Armagh to give himself up. He had visited his sister's grave at Mullabrack the previous day. He was quickly rearrested and returned to Dundrum to serve the remainder of his sentence. It seems that he had spent the intervening years in the army, serving first in India and then in the Boer War.

Marriage is about forming new families and supporting older ones, but sometimes that process can go radically awry, often at weddings themselves, with disastrous consequences. As the *Belfast News Letter* commented of the Knocknamuckly murder on 5 March 1888: 'the whole affair is more like what one would read in some sensational novel than what would happen in real life', yet truth is often stranger than fiction in matters relating to families and their disputes.

Sources

According to the contemporary indices, two files on the case in the Convict Reference Files series once existed, but these are no longer in the National Archives of Ireland. A short return does, however, exist in the Irish Crime reports, return of Outrages for 1888. The case attracted considerable newspaper coverage at the time but the most important reports are of the inquest, magisterial examinations and trial of William Thompson in the *Belfast News Letter* of 5 March 1888, 10 March 1888 and 11 July 1888.

50

Mixed marriages in
pre-independence Ireland

Oliver P. Rafferty

The Council of Trent, in its marriage legislation enacted by the decree *Tametsi* in November 1563, stipulated that for a marriage to be valid it had to be conducted in the presence of a bishop or pastor, or a priest designated for the purpose of witnessing the marriage. There must also be two other witnesses to the marriage. Trent ruled that all marriages, irrespective of religious adherence, had to be conducted in this manner. Given the circumstances of Europe in the sixteenth century, the decree was only to apply where it had been promulgated in individual parishes.

In Ireland the Protestant state never legislated for marriages between Catholics. By 1726, however, Catholic priests were forbidden to assist at mixed marriages under pain of death. By 1746 mixed marriages were declared invalid. This was repealed in 1778, but the prohibition on conducting mixed marriages was removed only in 1871, although the death penalty for this offence had been abolished in 1833.

The problem for the Catholic authorities in Ireland was the status of *Tametsi*. Synods in the seventeenth century determined that conditions in Ireland were such that *Tametsi* could not be implemented. Gradually, in places, the regulations of *Tametsi* were deemed to obtain, but there was considerable uncertainty, and as late as 1786 John Thomas Troy, archbishop of Dublin, determined that he would not publish *Tametsi* unless the Holy See ruled that the decree did not apply to marriages where one or both of the partners were Protestant.

Already in 1780 Archbishop James Butler of Cashel had taken the view that mixed marriages were always regarded as valid, even when conducted by a Protestant minister. This was given support by the ruling of Pope Pius VII in 1800 that Maria Fitzherbert's marriage in 1785 to the future George IV was valid, although it had been conducted by an Anglican clergyman. A custom grew up in such marriages that boys would follow the religion of the father and girls the religion of the mother. This continued to obtain into the early years of the twentieth century, as witnessed by the census returns for 1911, which also showed that Catholic/Protestant mixed marriages accounted for only about 1% of all Irish marriages.

This Irish custom concerning the religious upbringing of children flew in the face of papal legislation on the matter, however. In 1748 Pope Benedict XIV issued the encyclical *Magnae Nobis*, aimed at the situation in Poland. Adverting to rulings by his predecessors Urban VIII and Clement XI, he reiterated the point that Catholics were forbidden to marry heretics. His own earlier decree of November 1741, addressed to Catholics in the Netherlands, had repudiated 'base love' and 'detestable marriage'. The validity of such marriages was not, however, determined by the presence of a Catholic priest. In his subsequent ruling, Benedict decided that marriage with a non-Catholic was permissible only in situations where the Protestant partner 'abjured' heresy and gave a solemn undertaking to rear the children of such a marriage as Catholics.

In 1785 the Holy Office ruled that Pope Benedict's decree of 1741 would now apply to Ireland, and by 1827 it was judged that *Tametsi* applied to the whole country. When Paul Cullen returned to Ireland from Rome in 1850 to become archbishop of Armagh, he introduced the practice of the nuptial Mass. One of his motivations was that he thought that this would discourage mixed marriages, of which he heartily disapproved and was convinced that this was the strict teaching of the church. The marriage legislation of the Synod of Thurles, 1850, over which Cullen presided as papal legate, reflects this antipathy. It was laid down that a papal dispensation was required for such marriages and, in addition, the Catholic partner had to sign a declaration that the children would be raised as Catholics. It is clear that these rulings were widely ignored. Indeed, Thomas Grant, the Catholic bishop of Southwark, could complain in 1857 that English Catholics who wanted to get married to a Protestant would frequently go to Ireland for the marriage ceremony, since many Irish priests did not demand the promise to raise the children as Catholics. In 1852 the First Provincial of Westminster ruled that a papal dispensation was not needed for mixed marriages. This was confirmed by the Holy See in the following year and some Irish clergy decided to follow the English practice in the matter.

In 1908 the Holy See issued the decree *Ne Temere*, stipulating, among other matters, that marriages between Catholics and non-Catholics were governed by the Tridentine marriage legislation. Further, the decree asserted, unlike *Tametsi*, that non-Catholics who contract marriages with each other cannot be bound by Catholic marriage regulations. As far as interfaith marriage was concerned, however, an appropriate dispensation was necessary. Furthermore, marriages not performed before a Catholic priest where one or both parties were Catholic were declared invalid. This gave rise to the notorious McCann case in Belfast. Alexander McCann married a Presbyterian after Easter 1908 in her church. McCann's priest persuaded him that the marriage was invalid, since his wife would not repeat the ceremony before the priest. McCann abandoned his wife and took their children to America. The case became a *cause célèbre*, questions were asked in parliament, and Joe Devlin, the Catholic MP for West Belfast, declared that *Ne Temere* was a gift to Orange propagandists and that Agnes McCann was the greatest Tory asset since William III.

Ne Temere aroused Protestant fury and confirmed for Unionists in the context of the Home Rule crisis that Home Rule really would be Rome Rule. The Home Rule Act of 1912 stipulated that the Irish parliament could not legislate to make any religious belief or ceremony a condition for the validity of marriage. This was reiterated by the Government of Ireland Act 1920. Despite what is often said, *Ne Temere* makes no ruling about the religion of the children of mixed marriages. This was regulated definitively by the Code of Canon Law of 1917. Under its terms, non-Catholics had to give a written undertaking safeguarding the children's Catholicism.

Further reading

Linda-May Ballard, *Forgetting frolic: marriage traditions in Ireland* (Belfast, 1998).
Art Cosgrove (ed.), *Marriage in Ireland* (Dublin, 1985).
Alan Fernihough *et al.*, 'Intermarriage in a divided society: Ireland a century ago', *Explorations in Economic History* **56** (2015), 1–14.

51

'The lady … God intends for my wife': letter from M[ichael] J. Murphy [to Dr Edward Thomas O'Dwyer, bishop of Limerick (1886–1917)] on 'mixed marriage'

David Bracken

Among the collected papers of Dr Edward Thomas O'Dwyer, held in Limerick Diocesan Archives, is the enclosed forthright letter from Michael Murphy, a clerk in the civil service, regarding his prospective marriage to his Protestant fiancée, Madeline Beasley, and the conditions for any dispensation in respect of same. In conscience, as a 'Protestant lady of spirit', Miss Beasley cannot comply with the conditions of the dispensation, which 'are calculated to revolt all her instincts as a mother, and her faith as a Christian'. The conditions, which Murphy describes as 'stringent', are not made explicit in the surviving letter. It is probably safe to assume, however, that O'Dwyer was insisting that any children born to the couple would be raised as Catholics, and possibly that the ceremony would take place in a Catholic church. For Murphy's part, the question of conscience is also central: he will not ruin his fiancée by withdrawing his offer of marriage, even if he has to seek the aid of her church. In the event, the couple were married in St Peter's Church of Ireland church, Dublin, in November 1895.[1] From the remove of the 21st century the letter is interesting, illustrating that compliance with the dictates of the Church was far from universal. Murphy himself questions whether the laws of the Church in respect of marriage 'were ever complied with *in toto* even by the most faithful Roman Catholic'. His letter is evidence that individuals in relatively modest situations were capable of speaking their truth to the ecclesiastical power. He concludes: 'Miss B. has no fortune but she is the lady whom I believe God intends for my wife'.

---

1 Michael Murphy, civil service clerk, 25 Whitworth Road, Drumcondra, and Madeline Beasley, 4 Warburton Terrace, Bray, were married in St Peter's (Church of Ireland), Dublin, on 5 November 1895 (Civil Records of Births, Marriages and Deaths available at: Irish Genealogy.ie, https://civilrecords.irish-genealogy.ie/churchrecords/images/marriage_returns/marriages_1895/10545/5841040.pdf).

23 Rutland Sq[ua]r[e], Dublin

21ˢᵗ Oct[obe]r [18]95

Very Rev. Dear Sir,

I notice by the dates on y[ou]r letter of the 19ᵗʰ inst[ant] that it reached here yesterday, and regret that I did not receive it until today.

As I promised you in mine of the 18ᵗʰ, I communicated with Miss [Madeline] Beasley as regards the conditions of dispensation and the result was what I expected: she could not conscientiously comply with them. And I may here express it as my opinion that no Protestant lady of spirit would comply with them: for they are calculated to revolt all her instincts as a mother, and her faith as a Christian differing in some points of doctrine from the R.C. church. The dispensations, as per cutting, are evidently the laws of the church, but it is a question whether they were ever complied with *in toto* even by the most faithful Roman Catholic. I am sure that in many instances, where mixed marriages have taken place, the sacrament has been administered and the ceremony performed in the R.C. and Protestant (or o[the]r) churches respectively, and that the issue of the marriage have been brought up, partly in the Roman Catholic church and partly in the church of the non-Catholic parent. But whether, as regards the latter part of the foregoing statement, the conditions of dispensation were violated after the marriage had taken place, I cannot tell. As regards the other assertion, *viz* that some marriages have taken place in both churches, it may have been in cases where the marriage was first performed in the Protestant or o[the]r church, and that after confession etc., the R.C. church sanctioned the union by a second marriage. But I am certain that you will agree with me when I say such cases have occurred.

As you will be anxious to know my present attitude in the matter of my approaching marriage, I may state it simply by saying that I intend to marry Miss Beasley on the less stringent conditions and if my own church does not come to my aid, I have no alternative but to seek the aid of hers. It is entirely a conscientious matter with me and I have calculated the event in all its bearings, with the result that I am convinced it is better for me to take this step than ruin Miss Beasley and myself by withdrawing. You will do me an injustice if you suppose that I am actuated by worldly motives in this decision, for I may tell you that Miss B. has no fortune but she is the lady whom I believe God intends for my wife.

Yours faithfully.

M[ichael] J. Murphy

Source

Limerick Diocesan Archives (LDA)/BI/ET/F.

52

The making of a match in north-west Donegal, 1906

Frank Sweeney

In the scattered bogland farms of north-west Donegal at the end of the nineteenth century, marriage was a planned and considered event for the sustainability and well-being of all concerned. Parents were ensuring their own security as well as that of the couple getting married. Their holdings could only produce enough for six months of the year. The balance was ensured by seasonal emigration to the farms of central and lowland Scotland, where the men went to work and sent enough money back home to sustain the family during the lean periods. Marriage could not have any random components in such a society. Every stage had to be planned in detail to ensure that all the families concerned had sufficient security and support when problems arose or when the men were away in Scotland. Relatives and in-laws were crucial components in this arrangement. Into this vital consideration came Frank Sweeney in 1906.

Mickey Neddy's eldest son Frank, who was born in 1877, was now almost 30 years of age and, after periods of hire as a boy, he was back and forth to Scotland, where he did seasonal work on the farms around Dalkeith, not far from Edinburgh. When he arrived home in November 1906 thoughts turned to marriage. It was time for him to find a woman and get married. January and February were the months when the vast majority of weddings occurred in north-west Donegal—the period before Lent, when no weddings could take place. After Easter the men would be gone to Scotland and would not return until November. So those who were thinking of marriage had only a short period to get all the arrangements made.

Peggy and Mickey Sweeney, being people of the world with a strong sense of property, possessions and security, no doubt considered all the options from around the area, and finally they sent Frank to select one of Johnny Doherty's daughters, who lived less than a mile from them. This was a prudent decision, for a daughter of that house would come with a good dowry and a chance to get a good start in life. The Doherty family were known as decent upstanding people, sober, sensible, with a good area of land, and it was also known that, with such a large number of daughters to be settled, they would be anxious for suitors to come calling.

Frank had set his eye on Mary, the second daughter, who was reputed to be very beautiful (though thoughts of marrying someone for beauty would astound most local people of that time), and it was well known that he fancied Mary and was going to ask for her. After much discussion and consideration with his parents, for these decisions were not taken lightly, he eventually went to the Doherty home late at night, in case he would be seen, and asked for Mary. Johnny took umbrage at his request immediately and refused him right away, telling him that he should know well that he could not walk into a home and make *broc* of his family (i.e. take one out of turn; *broc* = crumbs). Asking for the second girl would imply that the oldest girl had something wrong with her. Johnny told him that he had belittled the family and the Doherty name. He then asked Frank to leave.

It was the custom that the girls in a family were married in order of seniority. As Biddy was the eldest, she would have to be taken first. Frank went back home and told his parents about the events of the night and they sat up till morning discussing the problem. Late the next night, Mickey and Peggy Sweeney crossed the mountain to the Doherty home. They apologised for Frank's behaviour the previous night. Peace was made. Johnny said that Frank could have the oldest girl if he liked but no other.

The Sweeneys returned home and the proposition was discussed with Frank. He had no other choice, really, so he agreed to accept Biddy.

Some days afterwards, Mickey and Peggy again crossed the mountain to the Doherty home in Meenbanad. The purpose of their visit was to discuss the financial arrangements and the dowry that would come with Biddy, as well as the post-marriage settlement of where they would live and settle down. The negotiations, which were conducted in Irish throughout, were long and the bargaining was tough, without much progress as the hours passed. Eventually, Johnny looked in desperation at Mickey and asked him what he considered to be a fair dowry for his son to receive. Mickey, never one to miss an opportunity to maximise a situation, replied: '*An méid a chlúdódh an teach ceann tuí seo le giníocha nó an t-urlár seo le nótaí chúig phuint*' ('The amount that would cover the thatched roof of this house with guineas or the floor with five pound notes'). The Doherty's house was very long, as it had a byre attached.

Johnny eventually conceded and agreed to the dowry. Two milch cows and two dozen hens would be Biddy's dowry, as well as some guineas to start life on nine acres of mountain land belonging to the Dohertys that would be given to them, situated midway between the two families. Handshakes took place to seal the deal. When the Sweeneys had gone home, Johnny's wife, Máire, berated him for not standing up to Mickey and Peggy and accused him of being too soft in the deal. She ranted that they had given away far too much.

It was customary that once the deal was done the wedding would take place within a very short time. The marriage record shows as follows:

Roman Catholic Church of St Columba, Burtonport.
No. 110. 12th February 1907. Francis Sweeney, full age, bachelor, farmer, residing in Cruckakeehan, son of Mick Sweeney, farmer,

married

Brigid Doherty, aged 19 years, spinster, no occupation, residing in Meenbanid, daughter of John Doherty, farmer.

The wedding breakfast was held in the bride's home, as was the custom; it would have consisted of the traditional meal of bowls of chicken soup, with chicken, potatoes and some vegetables washed down with bowls of milk. A glass or more of whiskey would then be shared by the men, while the women would drink tea. It was customary for the men to go to the pub for a number of drinks in the evening, while the women stayed at home. It was in the loft above the cows that Biddy and Frank went to bed that first night. Biddy's younger sisters, Annie and Maggie, cried because Biddy had to go to bed with a strange man that night.

An important consideration in the making of marriages in north-west Donegal at that time was proximity to both families. When the men were in Scotland for seven months each year, the wife needed help from her own family and from members of her husband's family. Proximity would ensure that Frank would be available to help the Doherty family in the cutting of turf, delving the land, saving and putting in crops at a time when the *meitheal* (a group of neighbours helping each other) or communal group system of help was very important. For the woman, such proximity to the parental home was important when she had to go shopping, work in the field, travel long distances with her knitting, or when she was having children. The new homestead was also quite convenient to the old Sweeney home in Griall, where Frank would help his parents and share various things with them.

As indicated, an important element in such location was the proximity of relatives who would provide milk when the cow ran dry, so that there was always a plentiful supply for children and adults, milk being one of the staples of the daily diet. A husband's absence for six months each year could leave his wife in a precarious situation were it not for the security of family and kin. History had taught the local people that marriage to a stranger left a woman very vulnerable.

Frank and Biddy had five children. They lived together into old age and seem to have had a very happy life. The arrangement worked well for both families, who shared many of their assets. Even Frank's children spent long periods living in their grandparents' homes, herding cows and doing messages and jobs about the house. From that point of view, the marriage had been a complete success.

53

The poultry instructress and the papal count

Carol Maddock

I hate weddings, but the Poole Photographic Collection in the National Library of Ireland allows me to indulge an ironic guilty pleasure—poring over old wedding photographs. I can scrutinise and critique the uncomfortable yet fantastic fashions of the late nineteenth and early twentieth centuries. I can wonder about all those long-ago hopes and dreams, family alliances and *mésalliances*, and enjoy them all from the comfort of home, thanks to a hefty digitisation programme at the National Library. And there's an additional on-line pleasure for nosy people like me. If you could afford a professional photographer at your wedding back then, you were 'well-to-do'. This meant that there was a good chance that your wedding was reported in local, and even national, newspapers. So I can find out much more from on-line newspaper archives about the *dramatis personae* in these black-and-white wedding photos, and a wealth of detail about the nuptial arrangements and accoutrements, right down to the material used in wedding dresses or the colour of wedding flowers. Don't judge me—it's a harmless hobby!

I love one of the Poole Collection photos especially, that of the wedding of Kathleen Murphy and Thomas O'Loughlin (Fig. 6). It took place in Kilkenny on Wednesday 27 September 1911—a sunny day (thank you, *Kilkenny People* newspaper, for that detail). There was a spectacular amount of hoo-ha around this wedding, and the *Kilkenny People* milked it for all it was worth in the following Saturday's edition. The entire front page and an article on page 7 were given over to the extravaganza. And what an extravaganza it was—all because of the groom, Thomas O'Loughlin of Killarney Villa, Ballarat, Australia.

Thomas was originally from Kilkenny but had lived in Australia for years. When his Uncle Martin died, Thomas inherited a huge fortune amassed from gold-fields, land, hotels and racehorses. Thomas was a generous benefactor of the Catholic Church in Australia. Closer to his old home, he donated £40,000

Fig. 6—Chevalier O'Loughlin wedding, large family group. POOLE WP 2350a. The Poole Photographic Collection. © National Library of Ireland.

to build a church in Kilkenny. That's where this wedding took place—in the modestly named O'Loughlin Memorial Church. Thomas had received a papal honour some years earlier and was thereafter known as Chevalier O'Loughlin, no less. Moreover, on his wedding day Thomas was made a papal count by Pope Pius X. The marriage ceremony was performed by the bishop of Ossory, Abraham Brownrigg, with 30 priests alongside, some of whom had travelled from Australia. See what I mean about hoo-ha?

I find the bride intriguing. Before her wedding, Kilkenny woman Kathleen Murphy had been working in Fermanagh as a poultry instructress. In his toast to Kathleen at the wedding feast, the bishop managed to get in a good dig at the rest of young Irish womankind. He held that Kathleen did not, 'like a great many of our country women, give herself up to a life of ease and indolence, but she struck out boldly and vigorously into the world, resolved to work her career through life and earn for herself an honest and honourable livelihood'. I look at her in this wedding photo and wonder how she ended up marrying Thomas O'Loughlin. Did they know each other from his visits back to Kilkenny? Was there genuine affection between them, or was it initially a sort of arranged marriage? According to the *Kilkenny People*, Thomas had the whole world to choose from, but there was unbridled local joy that he had returned to his 'native county to select from the honoured class from which he himself has sprung a suitable partner in life'.

Anyhow, the marriage ceremony took place at eight o'clock in the morning, and was followed by a 'sumptuous déjeuner' at 9.30am in the nearby Club House Hotel, where this photo was taken. Again, the *Kilkenny People* supplies all the delicious details. Here's what was on the menu:

> Lamb kidneys, cutlets à la St. Clair, kidney sauté, turkey galatines, chickens à la Milanaise, partridge, spiced beef, chickens in aspic, lobster salad, chickens à la Bechamel, tongue, game pies, salad à la Russe, trifles, mergingues [*sic*], Maraschino jellies, Charlotte Russes, peach creams, chocolate creams, fruit jellies, pear condé, gateaux, gelée à la surprise, pineapples, peaches, grapes, pears, plums, apples.

The champagnes on offer were 'an exceptionally high class brand', and the wedding cake, sourced from Miss Edwards of Cavendish Row in Dublin, was blessed by Bishop Brownrigg before being cut by Kathleen 'amidst loud applause'.

The *Kilkenny People* did not print a photograph, but I could put together the 'who's who' from snippets and details in the lengthy article. Kathleen and Thomas are in the centre of the front row, flanked by Kathleen's sisters and bridesmaids, Daisy and Sheela. The women in the back row are almost certainly her sisters too (Kathleen was the fifth daughter). I believe, from shape of nose and mouth, that the young man on the left in the back row is Kathleen's brother. The man in the middle of the back row is Charles P. Close of Limerick, Thomas's best man, and the elderly gentleman is the father of the bride, James Murphy of Ballybur Castle, a widower.

Now to the really important element—the clothes! The bridesmaids, Daisy and Sheela, wore silk dresses and hats of St Patrick's blue and their bouquets were pink carnations, supplied by Thornton's of Grafton Street, Dublin. Kathleen was in white satin with a crepon overdress, and wore 'rare and costly diamonds'. Her bouquet was orchids, white heather and carnations. The diamonds and her bouquet were 'the gift of the bridegroom'. And speaking of gifts, the *Kilkenny People* gave over a whole column to listing the wedding presents and who gave what. There was more silver, lace and linen than you could shake a 'silver-mounted walking stick' at (from Revd John Cahill of Clara)! See why I love the union of old photos and newspapers? For nosy armchair time-travellers like me, they're the wedding gift that just keeps on giving.

54

The aristocrat and the actress

Terence Dooley

In 1913 May Etheridge was a very beautiful young chorus girl working with a dance troupe at London's famous Gaiety Theatre. The daughter of a salesman, she got her first stage role in *The New Aladdin* at the age of thirteen. She quickly became a stage celebrity; one newspaper reporter later described her as 'a pronounced brunette with sparkling eyes, an expression most demure, even when she smiled, and a figure which most men found pleasant to look at. Everybody predicted a great future for her. She had youth and talent, health and good looks.' It was while on stage that she was first spotted by Lord Edward FitzGerald (1892–1976), brother of the 6th duke of Leinster (Fig. 7). Edward was the son of Hermione, 5th duchess of Leinster, from her extramarital affair with Hugo Charteris, then styled Lord Elcho. When Hermione and her husband Gerald, 4th duke of Leinster, were reconciled following her affair, Edward was taken back to the family home at Carton in County Kildare. By the time Edward was only three years old both Hermione and Gerald had died prematurely. Without parental guidance, he developed a reckless and dissolute personality.

Edward was immediately attracted to the 'pink pyjama girl', as May was popularly known in gaiety circles (Fig. 8). He was simply another aristocrat smitten with an actress, part of a trend since the late-Victorian era, when gaiety halls became the favourite haunt of young male aristocrats. In fact, by 1914 seventeen peers had married gaiety girls or actresses, and countless others had well-documented affairs. In Ireland the marriage of Geoffrey Taylour, later 4th marquess of Headford, to Rosie Boote in 1901 had become a *cause célèbre*; he was subsequently forced to resign his commission in the Irish Guards, and the young couple were socially ostracised by their peers for years. Such romantic alliances were widely scorned in aristocratic circles. In her 1914 memoirs, Lady Warwick quoted one *grande dame* who epitomised aristocratic mores; having discovered the picture of an aristocrat's chorus girl fiancée in the same newspaper as her niece, the old lady pronounced: 'I found a portrait of my niece on one page, and opposite to her was the chorus girl whom that fool — is going to marry! Why should one rub shoulders with a creature like that, even in a weekly paper? What are we coming to?' But the emerging popular press all over the western world loved headlines such as: 'The peer and the chorus girl'; 'Stage charms more potent than millions'; 'Girls of the Gaiety choruses doff pink tights … to reign in homes of wealth and name'.

One newspaper article would later claim that on a holiday trip home to the north of England May Etheridge and a group of friends pulled into a gypsy encampment to have their fortunes told. The fortune-teller told May: 'I see love and riches and strawberry leaves and they're all for you, my child. You're going to be a duchess and have as wealthy and handsome a husband as any girl could wish.' She eventually became a duchess but 'love and riches' were no more than tea leaves in a cup.

On 12 June 1913, barely a month after his coming of age, the press reported May's marriage to Lord Edward FitzGerald in a private civil ceremony at Wandsworth Registry Office. The young actress believed that her

Above Fig. 7—Lord Edward FitzGerald.

Right Fig. 8—May Etheridge, the 'pink pyjama girl'.

dreams had all come true. In an interview with the *Daily Mirror*, she told the reporter: 'We became acquainted and gradually got to be very good friends, and—oh, well—then we just became engaged. I suppose it is really rather romantic.' Edward's infatuation, however, was fleeting. He later wrote:

> I was twenty, easily impressed and ready to enjoy the company of any pretty girl. May was more than pretty. She was tiny, dark and looked like an angel. Other people envied my being with her, and that pleased my vanity. I saw her again and again, I was fond of her, she liked me. Her interest flattered me. She was gay, too, and adorable. But I was not in love with her.

The young bride arrived dressed in a powder-blue coat and skirt and a hat 'with a big osprey in it'. Edward was dressed in 'a lounge suit and a straw hat'. The registry office was located beside a busy polling station on the day of a by-election in Wandsworth, and so the fancy car and the fashionable style of the couple attracted a crowd of curious onlookers. After the ceremony, the couple exited by a back entrance of the registry office, 'escaped into the scullery of an adjoining restaurant, thence into the restaurant proper, ran past the astonished diners and eventually reached the street and a taxi cab'.

There was no romantic honeymoon for May. Edward made the excuse that he could not afford to pay for rooms at the Cavendish Hotel, so he went to a house in Belgrave Square while May went to her home at 76 Amesbury Avenue. For the next two days he did not contact her, and when she tried to contact him she was fobbed off by the butler at Belgrave Square. Within a short time, Edward made it clear that he regretted his decision to marry a gaiety girl. May had naively thought that she would be brought to Buckingham Palace to be presented to the royal family; Edward callously told her that he had made 'sufficient fool' of himself by marrying her without presenting her at court. His behaviour towards May became increasingly objectionable, but not before she had become pregnant with a son, who was born on 27 May 1914 and christened Gerald.

Edward deserted both mother and infant almost immediately after the birth, and May was forced to bring Gerald back to the impoverished surroundings of her mother's flat at Baron's Court in London. He was dressed in clothes made by May's grandmother in Brixton and May could only afford to pay his medical bills by pawning the presents given to her by Edward. Not being able to afford a nanny, May had often to take her young son to the club where she worked at night.

Meanwhile, Edward's eldest brother, Maurice, was a patient in an asylum in Edinburgh. He was never going to marry or have an heir. Their other brother, Desmond, had been killed in the Great War in 1916. Edward's uncle, Lord Frederick, the family patriarch, may have been disgusted with Edward's marriage but he now had to face the reality that his child with May was a future duke of Leinster. Thus in 1914 Lord Frederick began a four-year legal wrangle which eventually resulted in Gerald being made a ward of court. In 1918 the little boy was allegedly dragged screaming from the arms of his distraught mother and brought back to Ireland, where he was reared by his great-aunt at Johnstown Castle in Wexford. May was forbidden to see her child except on specified occasions.

In 1926 Edward began divorce proceedings against May on the grounds of alleged adultery with a professional footballer, George Newal. She was living in 'a very small and humble' cottage 'in one of the poorer parts' of Bournemouth. She vowed she would 'fight to the last ditch' but the odds were stacked against her: Edward was the aristocrat, she the lowly actress. The courts granted the divorce in 1930. Five years later May committed suicide, after at least one previous failed attempt. The heartbroken 'pink pyjama girl' died in penury after long years of depression and separation from her son. Had she lived, she would have seen Gerald become the 8th duke of Leinster.

55

'What they have been in all times':
marriage in World War I Ireland

Fionnuala Walsh

My husband's in Salonika
And I wonder if he's dead,
I wonder if he knows he has
A kid with a foxy head . . .

There's lino in the parlour
And in the kitchen too,
A glass-backed chevonier
That we got from Dicky Glue . . .

These verses are from a song popular in Cork during World War I. It is told from the perspective of the 'separation woman'—the soldier's wife in receipt of a separation allowance from the British government to compensate her for the absence of her husband. As the song suggests, many women did not miss their men and, indeed, found compensations in their absence. Some were glad to be rid of an abusive or neglectful husband, especially when monetary compensation was provided. Working-class women were accused of drinking away the separation allowances and of betraying the soldiers at the front by their behaviour, but recent research suggests that incidences of public drunkenness in fact declined sharply during the war. The majority of women, of course, greatly missed their husbands and grieved their deaths and absences.

Marriage took on increasing importance in wartime. The newspapers for August and September 1914 are full of wedding announcements for soldiers and war brides. The number of marriages in 1914 and 1915 increased in Ireland owing to the emotional upheaval caused by the war and the desire of soldiers to ensure that their wives would be looked after by the state through separation allowances and widows' pensions. Some of these marriages were short-lived. Olive Pakenham Mahon of County Roscommon married Captain Edward Stafford-King-Harman in July 1914. Edward was immediately sent to Belgium, where he was killed in action in November 1914, leaving Olive a widow aged twenty and expecting a child.

The service of an estimated 210,000 Irishmen in the armed forces affected the marital chances of the women left behind. The number of marriages declined after 1915, with the 1917 number the lowest since 1900. Concern was expressed in the press about the impact of the high military death rate on the marriage prospects of young women. The *Lady of the House*, a Dublin magazine, lamented in January 1918 that marriage and motherhood— 'that great joy and duty'—would not be possible for 'hundreds of girls now approaching womanhood' owing to the loss of so many men in the war. The gender disparity in the 1921 British census was widely publicised. Mrs Mary Hartnett of Sandymount, Dublin, commented on the census figures in the *Lady of the House*, observing that 'one must conclude that marriage for all is an impossibility' and that women must consequently become 'the competitor of men' in the workforce.

The sense of the loss of a whole generation is evident from accounts of the Irish landed gentry. David Fitzpatrick describes the 'lopsided community' among county families, 'overstocked with women, the very young and very old'. Of the 109 Irish peers who served in the war, 29 were killed or died of wounds sustained on active service. Elizabeth Bowen represents the post-war anxiety and sense of inevitable decline among the landed gentry in her novel *The last September* (1929). There is a shortage of men in the novel and a noticeable lack of children, perhaps representing the lost generation and the wartime losses of heirs for the 'Big Houses'. The narrator notes at one point that 'children seem in every sense of the word to be inconceivable'.

Nevertheless, the idea of the 'superfluous women' was greatly exaggerated. The demobilisation of soldiers following the November 1918 Armistice resulted in increased numbers of marriages in Ireland in 1919 and 1920. Females made up almost exactly 50% of the population in both the 1911 and 1926 censuses (including both the Free State and Northern Ireland), indicating no post-war 'surplus' of women. The very significant decline in the numbers of men and women emigrating from Ireland during the war years counteracted the loss of men on military service. Indeed, the numbers married in 1926 were slightly higher (+1.7%) than in 1911, particularly among the age group most likely to have been affected by the war, indicating an increased focus on marriage and reproduction following years of conflict. A significant number of those widowed in the war married again. Indeed, the *Lady of the*

House warned in 1916 that war widows were 'dangerous rivals' in the marriage market. Each widow received a state dowry equal to one year's pension when they remarried. Olive Pakenham Mahon married again in 1921 and had three more children. Significant numbers of Irishwomen never married but this was not unique to the immediate post-war period. Early twentieth-century Ireland had a particularly low marriage rate. Despite the promotion of marriage and motherhood, such goals were not possible for much of the Irish female population.

As the war drew to a close, the *Lady of the House* debated the potential impact of the war and the achievement of suffrage on the post-war marital life in Ireland. One commentator, Mrs Fitzroy Stewart, believed that marriages would be different after the war. Women would be their husband's equal and ideally 'his friend and comrade'. Another woman interviewed at the same time, the novelist Madame Albanesi, had a more conservative outlook. She predicted that thousands of women would 'drop back into the placid atmosphere of the home life' and not concern themselves with suffrage or using their vote. She suggested that the domestic sphere would still be central for the large majority of women, who would remain 'what they have been in all times—women who find their greatest happiness and their most necessary tasks in the love for their husbands and children, and in the care of their homes'.

Madame Albanesi was correct in her predictions. It seems somewhat parodoxical, but the loss of so many lives in the war brought renewed emphasis on domesticity, marriage and motherhood after the war's end. Despite women's wartime role in the workforce, the Victorian idea of the 'angel in the house' persisted, and the roles of wife and mother remained elevated above other positions available to women at the time.

Further reading

Ian F.W. Beckett, *The Great War 1914–1918* (Harlow, 2007).

Elizabeth Bowen, *The last September* (London, 1929).

David Fitzpatrick, *Politics and Irish life, 1913–1921: provincial experience of war and revolution* (Cork, 1998).

W.E.Vaughan and A.J. Fitzpatrick, *Irish historical statistics 1821–1971* (Dublin, 1978).

56

Here comes the bride: the Irish wedding dress

Jean Mary Walker

Wedding celebrations in Ireland follow a form deeply embedded in western culture that has changed little over the generations, and at the centre of it all is the bride. In Irish tradition, wedding preparations were largely the province of the bride's family, who were 'giving away' their daughter, and the wedding feast, or wedding breakfast, displayed the largesse of the bride's family.

As befitted her central role, the wedding apparel of the bride was invested with huge importance, and was calculated to reflect the standing of the bride's family and to enhance the chaste beauty of the bride. The wearing of a veil was replete with even more symbolism and, like the dress itself, the veil has endured more for its effect as a theatrical reveal than as an intrinsic part of the marriage service.

The Irish, as a race who appreciate the grand gesture, were as style-conscious as any other people and, following fashion, adopted the white wedding dress almost as soon as Queen Victoria established the trend at her wedding in 1840. Through the centuries since, whether the gown was bought, borrowed or home-sewn over months of evenings, getting the bride ready to walk up the aisle involved the concerted efforts of women in the family—mother, aunts and friends.

From the early nineteenth century skilled wedding-dressmakers were at a premium. By the middle of that century every large market town and all the major department stores had bridal departments, and a considerable home industry grew out of the lacemaking initiative of charitable foundations intent on finding work for women; handmade Limerick and Carrickmacross lace became very desirable when flamboyant and luxurious fabrics were in style.

In the twentieth century the upheaval caused by two world wars, revolution and economic depression dictated the style of wedding fashion. During the First World War the majority of brides wore simple dresses,

Fig. 9—An inauspicious year for
a wedding: this couple married in
Ireland in 1919. Image courtesy
of Ms Sandra Clarke, Co. Meath.

'teagowns' or suits suitable for their 'going away', even if the couple's honeymoon was limited to the day of their wedding. Between the wars, in spite
of the turbulent times, Irish brides were quite as stylish as their counterparts
across Europe, and many followed the trend for wearing dresses of blue beige
or cream, while movies and fashion magazines also had a huge influence on
bridal fashion.

Pity the poor brides who were married in those years of war and revolution! In 1914 Kate Smith of Meath came home from America to be married,
bringing her crisp, white broderie anglaise dress with her. Shortly after the
birth of her child in 1915, Kate died of peritonitis. At this time Kate's husband William, a sergeant in the Royal Irish Fusiliers, was a prisoner of war in
Germany. He died on his way home in 1917, leaving their small daughter to
be raised by family.

Weddings were taking place in Dublin on Easter Monday of 1916—the
first day of celebration after the abstentions of the Lenten season—and while
most ceremonies would have been well over by midday, when the first gunshots signified the beginning of the end of normality, one happy bride dashed
out of the Pro-Cathedral on her new husband's arm to find her waiting car
being eyed up by Seán MacEntee in his frantic bid to get out of the city before
the first gunshots were fired.

Margaret Byrne and Richard Clarke were married in 1919 and, like
other couples, were beginning their newly-wed life in a world that was war-
weary, ravaged by conflict, revolution and, most ignominiously, by the 'flu

epidemic that followed (Fig. 9). In spite of the inauspicious times, weddings by their nature are full of optimism for the future, even if celebrations were restrained, and many brides wore 'going-away outfits' rather than wedding lace on their bridal day, a pattern that was later replicated in the years of World War II, the so-called 'Emergency'.

During those austere days of shortage and rationing, many were the bolts of fabric smuggled across the border from the Free State, wrapped around the slim waists of young women and disguised by voluminous overcoats, to find their destiny as neatly tailored suits with sharp collars and emphatically padded shoulders in the utility style worn by brides of the day.

The heyday of the white-gowned bride was to begin after World War II, when shortages finally ended in Britain and Europe, and Dior unveiled 'the New Look'. Now brides and their families were determined to indulge their bridal fashion fantasies, especially as innovative acrylic lace fabrics became available in the Irish stores. Thereafter, film stars and royalty again dictated the style of wedding dress most favoured: Princess Elizabeth (as she was then), Princess Grace of Monaco, Jacqueline Kennedy (American royalty) and Princess Diana. Their nationality was not important but their style certainly was.

The goal of hosting the perfect wedding continued unabated, especially as the number of couples having elaborate weddings increased from the 1950s onwards. In some areas wedding ceremonies were held on only one day a week, with wedding groups waiting their turn for the church (Fig. 10).

Where an entire household might be preoccupied for many weeks—if not months or years—in the planning of this most auspicious event in a girl's life (and often that of her mother too), it was not unreasonable to expect that occasionally the smooth planning might go awry. Stories of wedding dress fiascos are often recalled by women whose wedding day is long past, but the memory of any mishap remains fresh as the day it happened; that in itself is testament to the importance of the event, and the smallest of details can live long in the memory.

Of course, not all Irish brides were living in Ireland before their wedding; many young women were living in England or further afield, yet it remained important for brides to come home to be married in their home place. Many couples only got home shortly before the big day, having relied on family and friends to do the advance organisation. When they did come home, like Kate Smith in 1914, many brides brought their wedding dresses with them, while others experienced the horror of going to the dressmaker for a 'final fitting' on their return home, only to discover that more than a few alterations needed to be made to their wedding gown.

Fig. 10—Peggy Clarke (left) was married after Anne Clarke-Brannigan in Duleek church in 1963. Image courtesy of the Farnan family.

A County Meath bride bought her most expensive shoes ever in London and brought them home for her wedding; more than 50 years later, it still disappoints her that the photographer failed to capture even a glimpse of them in the wedding photos. The apocryphal story of the girl who, having left her newly bought wedding shoes on a train, resorted to clip-clopping up the aisle in her friend's shoes might also be far truer than we imagine.

The old rhyme 'something old, something new, something borrowed, something blue' could be invoked to justify wearing borrowed or 'pre-loved' dresses, something that was far more common than might be admitted; the rhyme elevated the practice to the status of a long-venerable tradition. Customs such as sewing the last stich into the wedding dress and the wearing of a lace garter have also endured, making it clear that, anachronistic as it may seem in the 21st-century Ireland of equality, the vision of the bride gliding up the aisle in her wedding gown seems set to remain part of our culture for some time to come.

Acknowledgements
With thanks to contributors to the 1916–1966 Wedding Photograph Project, Ballivor Community Library, Ballivor, Co. Meath.

57

A peer's daughter marries a Catholic doctor: the Hon. Beryl O'Brien and Pat Gallagher, 9 April 1929

Maeve O'Riordan

The daughters of the peerage in Ireland consistently married men who were less wealthy than their fathers. There were, of course, exceptions: those who had no brothers and who would inherit their fathers' estates, and those who attracted wealthy and solvent men for more romantic reasons. Still, it was common for the daughters of peers to marry clergymen, soldiers, lawyers and small landowners. Advice columns, and even novels, encouraged women from wealthy backgrounds not to be too proud to refuse a proposal of marriage from men who could never give them the wealth enjoyed by their mothers. There was some awareness that the world was changing for women, but for the daughters of peers it was still expected that they would live out their lives on unearned inherited income received in the form of quarterly payments. Marriage, preferably a financially advantageous marriage, was the only viable career choice for all but the most defiant and creative daughters of this class right into the twentieth century.

It was unusual, however, for daughters of Protestant landowners to marry Catholic men. On 9 April 1929, the 15th Baron Inchiquin's eldest daughter, Beryl, married John Francis Patrick (Pat) Gallagher of Ardlougher House in the Glenties, Co. Donegal. This marriage was evidence of the significant power shift within Ireland from the Protestant landed élite to the rising Catholic middle class, which had been happening since the 1880s. Beryl's paternal family lived at Dromoland Castle, Co. Clare, and claimed their descent from Brian Boru, high king of Ireland, while her mother, Ethel (née Foster), was an extravagantly wealthy English heiress with an estate in Shropshire. Pat Gallagher, on the other hand, was a trained medical doctor whose father, while a Justice of the Peace, was also a grocer and publican (*Donegal News*).

The wedding was widely publicised in the papers. These articles followed the standard formula of reporting on society weddings; describing the expensive lace and style of the dress, as well as the decorations used in the church, and naming the prestigious guests hosted by the bride's mother at her fashionable London residence of 43 Portland Place. The couple were to go on a typical upper-class honeymoon to visit the Italian lakes before moving to Kenya, where the groom had a practice.

This showy white wedding complemented the mercenary nature of the marriage settlements that were as much part of these society weddings as the lilac and lace used to beautify the participants. Both parties were to have their property placed in trust, and the €6,500 which Beryl would inherit on her mother's death was not to be used by her husband (though he would inherit half the sum if Beryl predeceased him). The cost of buying a home and practice were to come out of his income.

Exactly one year after the wedding, Beryl wrote to her mother to inform her that she was 'about again and feeling very fit' after the birth of her first child, Maeve. She reported that Pat was disappointed that the baby was not a boy, but Beryl professed to prefer little girls as 'they are daintier and nicer to dress'. Living in Nanyuki at the base of Mount Kenya and 200 kilometres north of Nairobi, Beryl, as a white woman of the ruling élite, may well have held racist views towards the local population. She hoped to get a (presumably white) nurse from Nairobi when the monthly nurse completed her brief tenure, but if she failed she intended to look after the baby herself and had 'already bathed and dressed her twice to learn'. She planned on breastfeeding the baby for at least three months.

The next surviving letter from Beryl to her mother in 1932 saw the Gallagher family living on the island of Jersey. Beryl opened the letter with the line: 'I am afraid this letter will annoy you very much, but it is better to get it off my mind now. I have decided to become a Catholic.' Ethel angrily annotated the letter with a large 'R' before the word 'Catholic' to denote 'Roman Catholic'. The reaction to this letter, and the subsequent conversations, illustrate the importance of the married state for mother and daughter, as well as the deep-seated prejudice against the Catholic faith within the ascendancy class in 1932. Beryl was not the first daughter of an Inchiquin to marry a Catholic. Her father's half-sister Beatrice had married the celebrity Italian inventor Guglielmo Marconi in 1905. This marriage had provided gossip fodder when it emerged that the families had controversially agreed on the possibility of a divorce in advance of the wedding if it proved unhappy. It finally ended in an annulment in 1927 to allow the Catholic Marconi to remarry. Ethel feared that the legitimacy of her daughter's marriage might be called into question by her conversion, but Beryl promised her that her own marriage was nothing like her aunt's 'farce' of a union.

Ethel sought advice from both her sister Bee and the Church of Ireland archbishop of Dublin on how best to counter her daughter's arguments for conversion. The consensus was that Beryl could not be swayed in her (misguided) conviction, and in any case it was assumed that Beryl would eventually convert, as she was 'surrounded with the pressures and influences of his Church', though no one thought that she would have held such a conviction if she had not married a Catholic. Beryl elaborated on her belief in an eighteen-page letter (with appendices) which she asked her mother to share with the wider family. This discussed questions such as heresy and the origin of the mission of St Patrick. She commended the Church's stance against divorce and birth control.

Catholicism was, of course, linked to nationalism and republicanism in Ireland, and Beryl was careful to distance herself from Sinn Féin and even from Éamon de Valera. Her religious conviction might be Catholic but her political outlook remained conservative, despite her Irish priest in Jersey preaching of the past injustices carried out against that church.

The Hon. Beryl Gallagher's final address was in Stillorgan, Dublin, where she died in 1972 after seventeen years of widowhood; the house was a far remove from the sprawling Dromoland Castle of her youth. Beryl had been assimilated into the Catholic upper middle class through her marriage to a practising doctor and her conversion to his faith. She excelled at her hobby of bridge and their children made middle-class marriages. While the conversion outraged her mother, it allowed Beryl to fit the ideal of wifehood as she saw it, as she could be in agreement with her husband in matters of faith. While she had refused to be 'bullied' by him and had been strong-minded in demanding that they marry in the Church of England in 1929, by 1932 she was committed to Catholicism and looked forward to attending Mass each Sunday. The importance of shared faith was held by a number of her relatives. Beryl's maternal aunt Bee believed that the conversion would lead to a happier marriage, as did Beryl's Catholic sister-in-law, who had prayed every day for her to enter the Catholic Church.

Sources

The letters discussed in this chapter can be consulted in the Inchiquin Collection in the National Library of Ireland. Newspaper reports were taken from the *Irish Independent*.

58

Marriage and the introduction of children's allowances

Sarah-Anne Buckley

From 1939, the issue of a family allowance was regularly being addressed in the lower and upper houses of the Irish parliament, the Dáil and Seanad respectively. The reasons for this are complex, but most scholars agree that the allowances were initially discussed in response to the extreme poverty in many larger families and, later, the impact of the Beveridge Report published in 1942 in Britain. Yet some of the most contentious and long-lasting issues relate to gender roles within marriage and the emerging welfare state.

Beginning in 1944, the children's allowance in Ireland was introduced earlier than in many other European countries. Unlike other states, however, there were three key differences in the allowance's implementation. Firstly, the allowance would be given to fathers, not mothers; secondly, it would be paid from the third child upwards; finally, the allowance would be known as the children's allowance and not the family allowance.

Scholars differ in their interpretation of the allowance's introduction, with some pointing to debates being couched in concerns about British initiatives and others focusing on the alleviation of poverty. Others argue that pro-natalist views were intrinsic, although it appears from the departmental files that the primary concern was the alleviation of poverty in larger families rather than social engineering. Concerns surrounding the social and health conditions of poor families had been raised by voluntary and charitable organisations during the Second World War period and before, forcing the State to take a more interventionist role in child protection and family support. In 1942 the Inter-departmental Committee set up to investigate the allowance acknowledged that there was significant poverty in large families for which the allowance could offer some assistance.

Proposals driven in the Dáil by Seán Lemass and Éamon de Valera nevertheless received much opposition, as an examination of the parliamentary debates shows. This opposition primarily related to concerns surrounding the role of the male breadwinner, traditional gender roles and the 'sanctity of the family'. Seán MacEntee was the most vocal opponent, claiming that the allowances would undermine the role of the father as the provider in the family and would therefore amount to State interference in the family unit. The Department of Local Government had a number of concerns, most surrounding the interference of the State in the family (which could appear socialist), while the Department of Finance pointed to the 'numerous charitable institutions and organisations which through voluntary effort and subscription of money cater most efficiently for the poor and the sick'. Even those who were in favour of the allowances were hesitant about the sum that would be paid and the parent to whom it would be administered. The payment to fathers was a result of anxiety over the viability of the family and the need to protect preconceived gender roles. That a single unmarried mother could not collect the allowance—and that this was the case until 1974—is particularly revealing.

Although the debates from 1939 to 1944 are significant, a study of the provisions of the 1944 act reveals the principal concerns. Again, that the head of the household (effectively fathers) would receive the payment until 1974 is significant, as it represented gender inequality in welfare provision and the endorsement of the male-breadwinner family model. While many fathers nominated mothers as recipients of the allowance, this does not take away from the State's choice to award the allowances to married fathers. The naming of the allowances in this instance is also significant, as 'children's allowances' did not signify a replacement of the family wage in the way that 'family allowances' did. That the payments were a 'paltry sum' shows that the government was careful not to make it appear that the allowances would supplant family initiative, particularly in the face of possible criticism from the Catholic hierarchy. Finally, that the allowances were initially given only from the third child onwards demonstrates an official endorsement of larger families, but most importantly the existence and recognition of poverty in large families.

Although the provisions in the 1944 act did balance the Church/State boat sufficiently, the introduction of the allowances also signalled the beginning of the Irish welfare state. While there would be numerous battles fought between the Church, the State and groups campaigning for welfare for poor families and children over the coming decades, the State had finally begun to realign the dependency on charity with regard to the care of vulnerable families. They were also becoming actively involved in the relationships of husbands and wives. To this day, campaigners against the means testing of the allowance argue that it is the only income for many women whose husbands are withholding financial support. Its universality therefore offers equality, acknowledging the need to support all types of families.

Changes to the allowances after their introduction also reflected changes in Irish society. In 1952 the allowances were extended to families with two or more children (albeit at a lower rate) and in 1963 to one or more children. Over time the sum was also increased. For mothers and fathers the allowance became an important part of the family budget, especially for those experiencing poverty. That marriage and gender were central to many aspects of the debates is especially significant—and in many respects remains so today.

Further reading

Caitríona Clear, *Women of the house: women's household work in Ireland 1922–1961: discourses, experiences, memories* (Dublin, 2000).

Mel Cousins, 'The introduction of children's allowances in Ireland, 1939–1944', *Irish Economic and Social History* **27** (1999), 35–55.

Lindsey Earner-Byrne, *Mother and child: maternity and child welfare in Dublin, 1922–1960* (Manchester, 2007).

Finola Kennedy, *Cottage to crèche: family change in Ireland* (Dublin, 2001).

59

Marriage and migration

Jennifer Redmond

The Irish have always migrated and so, too, have they married. In fact, the issue of marriage and the loss of families from Ireland arose frequently and controversially over the last two centuries. The shift from early to delayed marriage, with the consequent permanent celibacy and singlehood of many in Ireland, was a feature of life after the Famine. But did migrants recreate marriage patterns like those at home in their new lands, or did they create new life trajectories for themselves? Did modern maidens really revile marriage, as was a common accusation? And if they did marry, whom did they wed?

As Ireland gained independence in the 1920s, the high rates of migration—particularly of young single women who otherwise should or could have been marrying at home—worried some, both in terms of the potential for moral trouble and the loss of the future mothers of Ireland. The Catholic newspaper *The Standard* quoted the late Arthur Griffith: 'If you can do nothing else for your country … get married', positing marriage as a nationalist act and a personal, intimate expression of patriotism. This kind of discourse almost always focused on women rather than men, as if marriage was a female preoccupation. Following on from this, women who migrated were often cast as deserting their traditional roles at home for modern ones abroad, an accusation often levelled with a somewhat bitter tone.

Many left as young, single people, often unskilled and looking for opportunities in America, Canada, Australia, New Zealand and, most frequently, Britain. These opportunities included marriage, much to the chagrin of commentators, including the Catholic bishops of Ireland. In 1947 they privately contacted the taoiseach, Éamon de Valera, to express the following: 'The Bishops view with great alarm the continuous drain on the womanhood and future motherhood of the country as the result of the present wave of emigration', referring to the fact that once wartime restrictions on women's migration to Britain were lifted in 1946 women flocked there. In the 1950s, reflecting on the centenary of the Famine, some feared that the 'Irish will virtually disappear as a nation and will be found only as an enervated remnant in a land occupied by foreigners'. This rather dramatic prediction thankfully did not come to pass, but the lingering unease with the lack of marriages and the consequent loss of families to Ireland because of migration persisted.

What do we know of migrant marriage patterns? Evidence of people's lives once they migrate from Ireland can often be fragmentary, and how they navigated relationships was never tracked with the diligence that historians would prefer. Nevertheless, we get glimpses now and then of their marriage trends. The 1951 census in Britain reported that 18% of 20–24-year-olds born in the Republic were counted as married, the proportion rising steadily as the age groups increased, with two-thirds of 30–34-year-olds also being married. While these rates were lower than their counterparts born in England and Wales, they still show a significant interest in marriage amongst the Irish in Britain. It was also found that the Irish preferred to marry their own. In an analysis of 37 parishes within the Westminster Diocese for the period 1948–54, 71% of Irish-born Catholics married fellow Catholics. Many migrants reported meeting partners at ceilidhs, parish dances, County Association functions and traditional Irish dance halls.

Singledom, however, was the choice for most young Irish migrants in Britain in the 1950s. In 1959 it was reported that Irish single emigrants outnumbered married ones by 3:1 in most areas of Britain. Higher rates of single Irish people, both men and women, could be found in London; it had a 5:1 ratio of single versus married emigrants. This suggests that some were focused more on career than on marriage, although it could also be that London was most attractive to the young and newly arrived Irish migrant. As time wore on, greater mixing between the Irish and others seems to have occurred. In 1971 the British census detected that of the almost two million Irish living in Britain over half of the men (56.6%) and women (50.4%) had British-born spouses. Irish women also showed more variety than their male counterparts, being twice as likely to marry European men and three times as likely to marry men from the Commonwealth.

We also know that the remittances sent back by migrants allowed others in their family to marry and begin families. The scale of remittances in 1942, for example, was found to total over £1 million, rising to over £2 million in 1942 as the war workers sent back large proportions of their wages. Such was the scale of the money sent home by migrants that from 1936 to 1942 total postal and money orders received in the Free State amounted to £8,019,950!

By the 1950s net remittances contributed £12 million of Ireland's Gross National Product, going into keeping farms within families and allowing new generations to prosper. So the Irish abroad may have been reluctant to commit at young ages, but their wages helped families at home to prosper and multiply.

Sources

Department of Industry and Commerce Memorandum, 'Remittances from Great Britain and Northern Ireland', Department of the Taoiseach files, National Archives, S12865, June 1942.

Memorandum from the Irish Bishops to the Taoiseach, Department of the Taoiseach files, S13598A, NA.

The Standard, 8 February 1930, p. 10.

Further reading

Mary J. Hickman and Bronwen Walter, *Discrimination and the Irish community in Britain: a report of research undertaken for the Commission for Racial Equality* (London, 1997).

Mary Lennon, Marie McAdam and Joanne O'Brien, *Across the water: Irish women's lives in Britain* (London, 1988).

John A. O'Brien (ed.), *The vanishing Irish: the enigma of the modern world* (London, 1955).

A.E.C.W. Spencer, *Arrangements for the integration of Irish immigrants in England and Wales* (ed. Mary Daly) (Dublin, 2012).

60

'Happy is the corpse that the rain falls on. And far happier is the bride that the sun shines on': marriage superstitions in Irish folklore

Barbara McCormack

Many of us have heard the traditional rhyme about a bride wearing something old, something new, something borrowed and something blue on her wedding day. Less well known, however, is the tradition of cutting a cake over the bride's head as she stands on the threshold of her new home. Indeed, how many excited couples know that marrying in harvest time signifies a life of constant gathering and poverty, or that Saturday is an unlucky day for a wedding? How many brides are aware of the dangers associated with marrying a 'beardless boy', an act which not only brings bad luck but also signifies the death of her mother or father? These are just some of the superstitions or folk beliefs captured in the Irish Folklore Collection at University College Dublin, a unique repository of material relating to Irish culture, history and customs gathered by folklore collectors from the 1930s onwards.

Superstitions, omens and prophecies are plentiful in Irish folklore, and this is certainly the case when it comes to marriage. Many of these traditions are associated with nature and the changing of the seasons, while others are connected to the calendar and days of the week. Some appear to have local resonance while others are common throughout Ireland. Most have clear meanings (breaking an egg and finding two yolks is a sign of a wedding) while others are more ambiguous (for some reason sneezing three times on a Monday is a lucky omen for marriage). Others are strikingly practical, such as the tradition of paying the marriage dowry a week before the wedding (when the ring was being purchased). Rain on a wedding day is not only bad for outdoor photographs, it's also a sign of very bad luck. Likewise, seeing seven magpies immediately before a wedding ceremony means poverty and misfortune. If a cow has a bull calf soon after the wedding, however, this is a very good omen.

We are all aware that timing is important when it comes to marriage, and according to some Irish superstitions there are certain days and months to be avoided. It is very unlucky to marry on a Saturday or a Monday, for instance, while Sunday and Wednesday are lucky days for matrimony. It is also very unlucky to get married during the month of August or, indeed, at any stage in autumn, because 'what is bound that season is loosened in spring'. January, April, June and November are much safer months for weddings.

Superstitions for predicting or prophesying marriage are also common in Irish folklore. A cuckoo heard before dawn (particularly during the month of May) is a marriage omen, and a frog coming to the door of the house signifies a wedding in the family. A woman's apron catching fire is a sign of marriage and dreaming of a christening is another marriage omen (on the other hand, dreaming of marriage is a sign of death). Two spoons or knives presented in a single cup means an invitation to a wedding, and it is said that if a man or woman falls off a chair they will be married within a year!

In order to ensure a happy and prosperous marriage there are certain measures that can be taken. A girl wishing to marry a particular man, for example, should sleep in his unwashed nightshirt. A bride should be accompanied to the church by her mother or another woman with children in order to ensure the fruitfulness of her own marriage; it is also important for another married woman to attend the wedding ceremony. A two-shilling coin should be carried in the pocket for luck, and the bride and groom should borrow something from a neighbour to wear on their wedding day. Throwing an old shoe after the bride on her way to the church is another way to ensure good luck, as is throwing a broom out after a couple on their way to be married (conversely, it is very bad luck to sweep out the house on the morning of a wedding).

Some other things to avoid include breaking a glass on the night of the wedding or dropping a ring during the ceremony, both of which are seen as very bad omens. A bride should never wear pearls on her wedding day, and a 'courting couple' should never leave a house through the same door by which they entered. In some places it was considered very unlucky for a pregnant woman to attend the wedding ceremony. One account in the National Folklore Collection records how a woman in the 1920s was not allowed to attend the wedding of her brother-in-law because she was pregnant. If a wedding party meets a funeral procession they should immediately turn back and let the funeral pass. An old saying in this regard is:

'Happy is the corpse that the rain falls on. And far happier is the bride
that the sun shines on'.

Other superstitions relate to the period immediately after the wedding. In certain parts of Galway a new bride couldn't visit her home until the 'month's visit', which took place on the fourth Sunday after her wedding day. A girl or woman should never be the first person to welcome a new bride (as she will have no luck herself), and it is said that a woman who keeps her maiden name after marriage can cure whooping cough.

Acknowledgements
Published with thanks to the Director of the National Folklore Collection, UCD.

Sources
The Irish Folklore Collection is an invaluable archive of manuscripts, sound recordings, books, videos and photographs covering all aspects of Irish life. Seán Ó Súilleabháin's seminal work *A handbook of Irish folklore*, first published in 1942, is an essential guide to this collection and is now available as an e-book published by Comhairle Bhéaloideas Éireann: the Folklore of Ireland Council.

61

Marriage divination

Jenny Butler

In Irish tradition, bound up as it is with a Roman Catholic value system, marriage is viewed as a social expectation and, historically, more so as a duty. Married men and women had a higher social status than those who were unmarried; indeed, the older, unwed members of the community were often regarded with pity, scorn or even ridicule. Since so much rested on marriage in traditional Irish society, some people attempted to obtain knowledge of their marriage prospects by way of magical practices. Various forms of divination were employed and many were specifically associated with certain dates and festivals.

Samhain or Hallowe'en (31 October), which traditionally marks the start of winter, can be conceptualised as a crack in time when the otherworld or spirit realm is closer to the everyday human world—or, as some describe it, 'when the veil between the living and the dead becomes thin'. Mirrors are often associated with the practice of witchcraft and symbolically represent a parallel world. As such, they are associated with marriage divination at *Samhain*; for example, a girl might peel an apple while staring into the mirror and perchance spy her future husband behind her, his placement perhaps representing the future in relation to the mirror, a foreshadowing of his being in the future. Another divinatory custom was for girls to spread a nightdress or other item of clothing before the fire, or boys their shirts, then hide and keep watch to see whether an apparition of their future partner would come to turn the articles of clothing during the night.

Dreams of marriage were also significant. A young woman might eat a salted herring in three bites to bring on a dream in which the husband-to-be offers her a glass of water. A marriage-related dream could also be induced by a young woman placing the first and last spoonful of colcannon (a traditional dish of potato, cabbage and onion) into her left stocking and putting this beneath her pillow. The concealed ring in the fruit 'cake' called *bairín breac* (barmbrack) on Hallowe'en has continued to the present day to be a sign of impending marriage for the one who gets it in his or her slice. Historically, other items were placed in the brack along with the ring: a button in one's slice meant bachelorhood, a thimble spinsterhood, a chip of wood foretold that the unfortunate recipient would be beaten by a future spouse, and a religious medal indicated that the finder would enter a convent or seminary and therefore not marry. Such significations reflect the values and social norms of the time.

While getting married during the month of May is popularly viewed as unlucky in Ireland, May Eve is associated with marriage divination. Like *Samhain*, this liminal period from May Eve to dawn on May morning (1 May) is understood as a crack in time when charms and magical practices might be more efficacious. As with the magical practices that took place at *Samhain*, mirrors were significant during *Bealtaine* (the May festival). For instance; a girl who gazed upon the reflection of the 'young May moon' in her mirror might glimpse her future husband peering over her shoulder. The water in wells was credited with special powers during *Bealtaine* and the image of a girl's husband-to-be might magically form as she looked at her own reflection in the water.

Cork-born folklorist Thomas Crofton Croker, in his three-volume collection *Fairy legends and traditions of the south of Ireland* (compiled between 1825 and 1828), recorded an account of the *druchtín* (Anglicised as 'drutheen'), a small white slug used in marriage divination. On May morning one could sprinkle flour on a piece of slate and place the slug upon it, and its movements would be interpreted as forming the initials of one's true love and future spouse. Lady Wilde referred to a similar divinatory custom involving gastropods in her book *Ancient cures, charms and usages of Ireland* (1890), where she describes the fetching of a snail—which should be the first one encountered—before dawn (this being a transitory and hence liminal time) on May morning and the placement of the creature on a plate that has been lightly sprinkled with flour; a cabbage leaf is then placed over the snail and the configuration is left thus until after sunrise. On removal of the cabbage leaf, the initials of the true love's name would be revealed. Actions of the snail could be further interpreted in relation to marriage prospects: if the snail was within his shell on removal of the leaf, the future husband would be rich; if the snail was stretched out of the shell, the future husband would be poor and likely without a house of his own.

Lady Wilde also references a divinatory method connected with thresholds, which hold magical significance as liminal spaces. It was customary to sweep the threshold clean on May Eve and this ritual cleansing might be interrupted by the sprinkling of ashes over the threshold area. If a footprint was discovered in this area in the morning, it was deemed to be a sign of a marriage in the household if the footprint pointed inward toward the house, but was a death omen for that household if pointing the other way; this perhaps represents the symbolic arrival of a suitor for someone in the house and, conversely, the coffin being carried out in the case of a death.

On St Brigid's Day or the festival of *Imbolc*, which marks the first day of spring, people would make various items from rushes, including St Brigid's crosses, imitation ladders and spinning wheels, the latter two exchanged as 'love tokens' between young people. On the night of 1 February, young women and men might sleep with a spinning wheel or ladder of rushes under their pillow in the hopes of seeing their future spouse spinning or climbing up a ladder respectively. A couple might agree to place these items under their pillows as a test to see whether they would dream of each other; if they did, they were sure to marry before the next St Brigid's Day.

Since marriage was forbidden during Lent by Catholic Church authorities, Shrove Tuesday was a very common time for weddings to take place. It is also known as 'Pancake Day' and some divinatory customs are connected with the pancakes themselves. If a young person, man or woman, but especially the eldest daughter of the house, flipped the pancake without creasing it, that person was in with a very good chance of a marriage proposal in the coming year; if the pancake crinkled up or fell on the ground, however, this was an indication of remaining single. Sometimes the mother in the household would put her wedding ring into the batter, and the person who got the pancake containing this was viewed as in luck for a forthcoming proposal.

Midsummer fires on 23 June, the eve of the feast of St John the Baptist, were also utilised for divination. Young girls would wait for the fire to burn low before jumping over it or skipping through the embers in the hopes of finding good husbands, while couples held hands and jumped over fires together and onlookers tried to interpret the flames' flickering as signs of marriage between particular pairings. Yarrow was also gathered close to St John's feast-day and used in charms for marriage, and girls would place the plant under their pillow to induce a dream of their potential partner.

The end of harvest also yielded an opportunity for marriage divination. The treatment of the last sheaf of corn cut in an area (or *cailleach*, as it is known) had regional variations in interpretation; in some places it was said that the man who cut or bound it would die a bachelor, while in County

Carlow the girl who could fell it with one blow of a reaping-hook would be married within the year.

On New Year's Eve, girls would place a sprig of mistletoe or some holly and ivy leaves together under their pillows while saying the following charm: 'Oh, ivy green and holly red, tell me, tell me whom I shall wed!' There are many symbolic interconnections between the annual cycle of festival celebrations or 'ritual year', dreams, magic and the foretelling of marriage, which in Irish tradition is always an important and propitious event.

Further reading

Thomas Crofton Croker, *Fairy legends and traditions of the south of Ireland* (London, 1835).

Kevin Danaher, *The year in Ireland: Irish calendar customs* (Cork, 1972).

J.F. Wilde, *Ancient cures, charms and usages of Ireland* (London, 1890).

62

Marriage in twentieth-century Ireland

Caitriona Clear

'Every day there's one of them would say,
She'll agree now, you'll see now … '
—Percy French, 'The Darling Girl from Clare' (*c.* 1900).

The exuberant competition of the farmer's son, the shopkeeper's son and others for Kate Flynn in this ballad gives us one view of matrimony in Ireland in the century or so after the Famine. A different one is given in Maura Laverty's autobiographical novel *Never no more*, set in Kildare around 1910–22, in which Miss Derrigan, who works in a drapery shop in Ballyderrig (a fictionalised Rathangan), 'walks out' with an insurance agent for fifteen years. Halfway through their courtship she buys a second-hand pram, oiling and polishing it regularly. When they get married they leave Ballyderrig for a neighbouring town, with the pram strapped onto the sidecar beside them. The next time that Ballyderrig sees the pram it is being wheeled by the rag-and-bone woman. Its owner has died in childbirth with a stillborn child.

Both fictions—the cheerful Clare one and the chilling Kildare one—are rooted in some kind of truth. Marriage rates fell in Ireland between the Famine and the 1960s, and the average age at marriage increased, but not always and not everywhere. Even parts of the country with high proportions of bachelors or spinsters had plenty of young life in them, because those who married usually had large families. This meant that many of those growing up in Ireland in the early twentieth century had a large number of childless elders interested in them. The persistent interference in their nieces' lives of Kate O'Brien's beloved aunts, Presentation nuns in Limerick city in the early twentieth century, caused petulant and angry exchanges in the convent parlour. The single aunt or uncle living with the family had even more opportunities for cross-generational intervention. Such over-parenting (however well meant) cannot but have caused risk aversion and timidity among the young, which in turn played its part in delaying or stopping marriage into the next generation. Property was not the only obstacle to matrimony, but people with the fewest expectations of a higher standard of living had higher marriage rates. Peig Sayers, from one of the westernmost parishes in Kerry, a domestic servant from the age of ten, was nineteen when she married a small farmer/fisherman in 1892 and moved out to the Great Blasket Island. Lillie Reynolds, a Protestant domestic servant from Wicklow, was 22 when she married James Connolly in 1890. In 1911 the highest proportions of middle-aged single people were in the fertile farming areas of Leinster and Ulster and in the Rathdown/Kingstown borough of Dublin.

Complicated family obligations could also postpone the forming of new ties. In Wexford in 1934 the death of their co-resident aunt enabled Bessie Bolger (41) and her brother Wat (37) to marry their long-time sweethearts. But older relatives were not an insuperable barrier to marriage; the vertically extended family was as common in close-knit communities in Britain and on the Continent as it was in Ireland, right up to the 1970s. From the mid-twentieth century, however, the horizontally extended family was coming to be seen as particularly problematic, especially if the unmarried third party was female. The agony aunt on *Woman's Way* in 1963 breezily advised the worried fiancée of a man in a long-term sibling household that his sister should certainly move out after they were married, but she did not specify what the brother's obligations should be to someone who had kept house for him for 25 years.

Literature and social commentary in the 1940s and 1950s blamed Irish men for low marriage rates and late marriage. In this era, however, women rather than men delayed or refused marriage. Waiting a decade or so to tie the knot made sense to people who were obliged to surrender paid work on marriage. Kilkenny domestic servant Maura Loughman was 30 in 1942 when she married Ned Healy, who was a carpenter. Dubliner Phil O'Keeffe enjoyed hopping from one office job to another so much that she had nine years' working life behind her when she married in 1954. 'Mental nurses' who gave evidence to a government commission in 1939–40 accepted pragmatically that many female nurses did not get married until they had at least twenty years' service behind them, and most female National School teachers delayed marriage until their late twenties at least. Single women in Ireland in the post-Emergency era had freedom and money unknown to previous generations. When Bishop Lucey of Cork warned darkly in 1956 that townswomen were too fond of amusement and diversion to settle down he might have been on to something. Urban single women formed the backbone of organisations like the Legion of Mary, the Gaelic League and amateur drama, but increasingly their rural counterparts had Muintir na Tíre, Macra na Feirme and the Irish Countrywomen's Assocation. It was generally recognised that giving all this up meant real sacrifice, and the *Limerick Rural Survey* in the early 1960s was not alone in arguing that no woman should be expected to marry onto a farm without some social outlets, including regular transport to the nearest town.

Letter-writers to Irish magazines in the 1960s were adamant that marriage should be companionate and kind: farmers' sons who inquired about dowries were laughed to scorn, but husbands who brought tea in the morning and helped with the children were appreciated and thanked. At this stage all religious and secular authorities were insisting on something that reasonable people had always known: marriage was hard work but it need not be unpleasant. One very appreciative husband was Cúil Aodha man Seán Eoin O Súilleabháin (1882–1968), who wrote the sprightly and sedate song *Mise 'gus Máire* ('Máire and I') about his lovely wife, *an stáidbhean mhodh mhaisiúil* ('the steady, modest, elegant woman'). We can only hope that Máire was as happy as he was.

Further reading

Angela Burke, *Maeve Brennan; homesick at the* New Yorker (New York 2004).
Timothy Guinnane, *The vanishing Irish: households, migration and the rural economy in Ireland, 1850–1914* (Princeton, NJ, 1997).
Mary Healy, *For the poor and for the gentry: Mary Healy remembers her life* (Dublin, 1989).
Maura Laverty, *Never no more: the story of a lost village* (London, 1942).
Kate O'Brien, *Presentation parlour* (London, 1963).
Phil O'Keefe, *Standing at the crossroads* (Dingle, 1997).

63

Brides' Aid: a marriage of principles in Dublin's Jewish community

Natalie Wynn

Marriage is regarded in Judaism as the ideal human state. The instruction to 'be fruitful and multiply' (Gen. 1: 28) is classed as the first of the 613 commandments (*mitzvot*) that are set out in the Torah (from the Book of Genesis to the Book of Deuteronomy inclusive) and are eternally binding for Jews. The importance of marriage as a partnership is emphasised in the second version of the creation story, where God states: 'It is not good that man should be alone; I will make him a helper corresponding to him' (Gen. 2: 18). The family holds a central place in Jewish culture; important rites such as the ushering in and out of *Shabbat* (the sabbath) and the Passover *seder* take place in the home, and the home is seen as playing a key role in the transmission of the Jewish belief and practice upon which the very continuity of the Jewish people depends.

The Hebrew word for charity, *tsedakah*, literally means 'righteousness'. This reflects the principle that it is the obligation and duty of the better-off in society to support those less fortunate than themselves. Regular *tsedakah* is incumbent on all who can afford to give, according to their means. Assistance is seen as the right of the needy, with no negative connotations attached. Discretion in attending to need is paramount, in line with the teachings of the celebrated scholar Maimonides (1135–1204), who emphasised the importance of respecting the personal dignity of the recipient. Since the Middle Ages, formal and semi-formal charitable infrastructures have formed an integral element of Jewish communal life, in line with the size and financial means of a given community. These structures provide for a range of needs, including food, accommodation, education and health care. Although nowadays Jewish charitable relief aspires to reflect the highest ideals of *tsedakah*, in the past the reality has often fallen short—sometimes far short—of its values. In the nineteenth and early twentieth centuries, Jewish charity and philanthropy in the western world were deeply influenced by external thought, most notably

Fig. 11—Bessie Gertrude Noyek, founder of Brides' Aid, in 1959. Courtesy of Natalie Wynn.

the notions of 'deserving' and 'undeserving' poor that were fashionable at the time. Charity has been used as a means of social control and manipulation within Jewish communities the world over, while discretion has frequently fallen by the wayside. In Dublin, the extant records suggest that an inclination towards social control was more aspirational than actual; as a small community where everyone knew each other, it was far more prone to fail on the part of discretion.

No written records survive from Brides' Aid, which operated from 1926 until the 1980s or 1990s. It has received little attention in the formal historical record, despite what it has to tell us about attitudes towards marriage, charity and communal solidarity during an important phase of Jewish communal life in Dublin. The organisation reflected the significance of marriage and the family in Jewish culture; the highest aims of *tsedakah*; and a growing self-confidence among Dublin's immigrant community that allowed them to focus on traditional models for charity and relief as opposed to the judgemental approaches that were prevalent in non-Jewish society. Brides' Aid was just one of a range of Jewish charities, benevolent organisations and self-help initiatives that operated in Dublin during the first half of the twentieth century, notwithstanding the relatively modest circumstances of the community as a whole at this time. Its founder, Bessie Gertrude Noyek (1880–1961) (Fig. 11), was in many ways representative of her peers. She

215

was among the first generation of Jews to be born in Dublin during the foundation period of the current community. Bessie Gertrude was a strong and resilient character, having been left to bring up her five children over a nine-year period while her husband attempted unsuccessfully to establish himself in South Africa, a separation that was characteristic of the Jewish migrant experience at this time.

Brides' Aid was established to enable needy women—often new immigrants—to get married with joy and dignity. The organisation provided grants for wedding dresses, basic trousseaux and receptions. Its beneficiaries were allowed complete freedom in choosing their outfits, which were made up by the society's volunteer dressmakers. This assistance was treated nominally as a loan, with no preconditions attached. The recipient simply had the option of repaying the society at any time, should she wish—or be in a position—to do so. The activities of Brides' Aid were funded by a combination of regular subscriptions and donations, collected by volunteers. The society operated so discreetly that even the bride's in-laws would not necessarily be aware that she had received assistance, and tactful approaches were made to those felt to be too embarrassed actively to seek its help.

Because of the 'veil of secrecy' that surrounded the workings of Brides' Aid, few of the details are known to the relatives of those involved in the society. They stress, however, the integrity and scrupulousness of its operations. Elaine Brown, whose mother Maie Goldwater was a dressmaker who volunteered with Brides' Aid, sums up the aim of the society as the aspiration to make everyone's wedding as happy an occasion as possible. She and Marleen Wynn, granddaughter of Bessie Gertrude, emphasise the importance of discretion in Brides' Aid, and its marked sensitivity towards the dignity of its beneficiaries. Volunteer collector Lilian Hardy believes that the society made it possible for many women to marry who might not otherwise have had the means to do so, and feels that it played an important role in helping new and needy immigrants to adjust to life in Dublin.

In the 1980s, when its services were no longer required in Dublin, Brides' Aid turned to assisting new immigrants to Israel by funding weddings and forwarding used dresses from the Dublin community. By then it had been integrated into another female-led relief organisation, the Dublin Jewish Ladies' Charitable Society, now itself defunct. Given the depleted numbers and improved economic circumstances of today's community, the Dublin Jewish Board of Guardians is all that remains of the city's formerly rich and multifaceted Jewish philanthropic infrastructure.

Further reading

Natalie Wynn, 'The history and internal politics of Ireland's Jewish community in their international Jewish context (1881–1914)' (unpublished Ph.D thesis, Trinity College Dublin, 2015).

64

Marriage and the pamphlet covers of the Catholic Truth Society of Ireland

Lir Mac Cárthaigh

The archives of the Catholic Truth Society of Ireland (CTSI) provide a unique visual record of twentieth-century Ireland through the work of some of the country's finest commercial artists. From 1899, when the society was founded, to the 1960s, when its publishing focus changed, the CTSI produced several thousand pamphlets that strove to wrest the public's attention away from the burgeoning mass media and towards matters of faith. In order to meet this challenge, the society insisted that their pamphlets be 'bright', 'cheerful' and 'use modern methods of production, display and salesmanship'.

The pamphlet cover artists, such as George Altendorf, Seán Best and John Henry, were stalwarts of newspaper advertising, and employed the bold visual language of the movie poster, the comic strip and the sales card. They recognised the imperative to make the pamphlet covers as striking as possible; Henry told the CTSI that every cover 'should be a miniature poster'—design advice that is just as applicable today. Their arresting graphic idiom was particularly suited to the declamatory titles of Fr Daniel A. Lord, the American Jesuit who helped draft the Hays Code for movie production. John Henry's cover for Lord's *Divorce is a disease* (1946) (Pl. 6) is a miniature masterpiece in which lettering, expression, line thickness, light and shade come together to create maximum impact.

The CTSI and its artists used the visual conventions of different genres to stratify its publications. Some of the more dramatic pamphlets adopted the chiaroscuro of the pulp novel jacket, while other, more jocular titles employed the negative space and unadorned lines of the newspaper cartoon. Many of the pamphlets that focus on marriage and relationships, including *So we abolished the chaperone* (1946) (Pl. 7), *The man of your choice* (Pl. 8) and *The girl worth choosing* (Pl. 9) (both 1955), make use of a visual language familiar from fashion plates and romance comics, perhaps suggesting an intended readership that was predominantly female.

The occasional direct depictions of domestic life, such as *The Christian family* (1945), seem closer to American advertisements of the 1940s than to the realities of post-war Ireland. Nevertheless, if the vision of the country set down by the CTSI's artists does not tally with the literal facts of the period, the pamphlet covers give us a clear indication of how themes such as marriage, relationships and the family took shape in the nation's collective imagination (Pls 10 and 11).

Further reading

CTSI, *Catholic Truth Society of Ireland: first fifty years, 1899–1949* (Dublin, 1949).

David J. Endres, 'Dan Lord, Hollywood priest', *America: The Jesuit Review* **12** (December 2005), https://www.americamagazine.org/issue/554/faith-focus/dan-lord-hollywood-priest, accessed 21 February 2019.

Lir Mac Cárthaigh (ed.), *Vintage values: classic pamphlet cover design from twentieth-century Ireland* (Dublin, 2013).

65

Wedding presents in modern Ireland

Orla Fitzpatrick

In the decades following the Second World War, there was a change in the way wedding presents were selected and displayed in Ireland. This reflected an increasingly consumerist society and shows the central role played by money, economics and status in the institution of marriage. The attitudes around wedding gifts are very much intertwined with notions of respectability and class.

Custom had previously placed an emphasis on the dowry that a bride brought to her new family. This was particularly important in rural economies and was partially responsible for the late age of marriage. This age had lowered by the 1960s and post-war women's magazines demonstrate a more consumer-driven attitude. A modest rise in disposable income was paralleled by a greater expectation that wedding guests would buy gifts.

Wedding presents are an example of domestic consumption centred around a particular event and life stage, i.e. the establishment of a home. Naturally, the most prevalent gifts were items associated with the setting up of this household. This is reflected in advertisements; for example, a notice in the *Connacht Tribune* in June 1962, placed by Corbett & Sons, William Street, Galway, suggested the following as suitable wedding presents: Waterford crystal, Royal Tara china teasets, table mats, coffee sets, teasets, companion sets, mantel sets and table lamps. The adventurous could purchase modern conveniences such as electric kettles, Pyrex ware and electric irons. Gifts could be divided into those for daily household activities and those kept for 'good' use, such as Waterford crystal and china teasets.

Several brands and ranges held particular appeal for newly married couples and we can trace the popularity and novelty of consumer goods through those that were pushed as wedding presents. For example, a notice in the *Irish Press* from the late 1950s mentions a brand that was considered the height of fashion: 'Royal DRU Holland—Oven to Table Ware. In beautiful pastel colours and hand painted. All have ground flat bottoms and are suitable for Aga, Esse, Rayburn, Jubilee Cookers or electric or gas cookers.' These cast-iron enamelled dishes, manufactured between the 1930s and the 1960s, were produced in pastel colours and decorated with floral borders or graphic designs. They combined a continental European cachet with utilitarianism and a design that matched the vogue for pastel interiors. Pyrex was another popular present between the end of the war and the mid-1970s. Its plain unadorned design epitomised modernity, and advertisements emphasised the notion that certain domestic tasks required specific equipment and goods.

There was, of course, a gendered aspect to these gifts. Several pieces of legislation were introduced in the 1930s that emphasised women's role within the home. In addition to the 1937 Constitution, the 1932 Marriage Bar and the 1935 Conditions of Employment Bill meant that female civil servants were obliged to give up their posts on marriage, and the private sector generally followed suit. The bulk of the presents associated with cooking and domestic duties were directed towards the bride. Her domestic role was idealised in the advertisements for the kind of goods she would receive as wedding presents. Few notices were directed specifically towards the groom. Adverts demonstrate that most gifts were either intended to be used solely by the wife or were for general household use.

Longer articles offered advice to the general public on what constituted a suitable wedding gift, showing that Irish people felt some social unease in this area. In 1963 Bernadette Plunkett devoted an entire instalment of her series *The Wedding Story* to the selection of wedding gifts. Appearing in the *Irish Press*, it emphasised the fact that the present should act as a lasting reminder of the special day. She warned against overly lavish as well as inadequate or thoughtless gifts.

This article also addressed the anxieties experienced by the couple with regard to how gifts should be acknowledged. Anxiety was particularly acute with regard to gifts of money. Plunkett suggested that the 'thank-you' letter or note should refer to the manner in which the money will be used and that ideally the note should include an invitation to visit. Her recommendations reflect an unease and reticence surrounding the monetary aspect of the marriage. Wedding presents connote a tacit approval of a couple's decision to marry and this is particularly true for gifts of money, which act as a validation of the union. The couple and their families are keen to acknowledge that relations and friends were supportive enough to bestow money on the couple. Nonetheless, there remains a sensitivity around appearing overly crude or mercenary.

The practice of displaying gifts is also mentioned. This trend, which originated with the aristocracy, was also taken up in Ireland. Maura Harris, in her 1960 wedding etiquette title *Planning your wedding*, includes a section on wedding presents, with particular reference to the display of presents in the bride's home.

Whilst evidence exists of the goods that were offered for sale as wedding presents, it is difficult to ascertain how these gifts were subsequently used within the home. Their reception is seldom mentioned in diaries or in letters, but glimpses of their afterlives can be traced in the way that contemporary writers used wedding gifts in their stories. The works of Maeve Brennan and Edna O'Brien, with their fine attention to domestic detail, are particularly valuable.

Wedding presents can form part of family rituals and routines for many decades. O'Brien's short story 'The favourite' tells the tale of Tess and her seemingly ideal marriage and life. In a passage referring to the early years of her marriage, we are shown how Tess and her husband fondly gaze upon their wedding gifts: 'Then they would admire the wallpaper, or the coal scuttle, or one of the many precious items in the china cabinet that had been wedding presents to her'. Interestingly, O'Brien has characterised the presents as having been given to the bride. This tallies with the etiquette manuals and articles directed towards the bride rather than the groom. It suggests that the female members of the household oversaw the purchase and receipt of gifts.

Several of Maeve Brennan's short stories mention wedding presents and they are used to illuminate certain aspects of married life and class considerations. In both 'A young girl can spoil her chances' and 'Stories of Africa', Brennan refers to a clock which was given as a wedding present. It occupies a spot on the mantelpiece of a middle-class Dublin suburban home. In the former story, which tells of the loveless marriage of the Derdons, the clock was given as a wedding gift by a friend of the groom, Frank Guiney, 33 years before:

> The clock was mahogany, and it had been a present from an old friend
> of Hubert's, Frank Guiney, and it had a place of honour in the centre of
> the mantelpiece.

Guiney has since emigrated and the Derdons have lost touch with him. The wedding present is used within the story to symbolise not only their friendship with Guiney but also a more hopeful period of their lives. In this example, the present has outlasted the friendship and, indeed, the love upon which the marriage was based.

In *The springs of affection*, Brennan refers to the lifelong impact of a marriage upon the maiden sister of the groom. Min Bagot views the marriage of her twin brother Martin as a betrayal of the family. Brennan uses Martin's rejection of their mother's wedding gift to illustrate his tactless and heartless attitude:

> He made his mother cry. For a wedding present, Bridget wanted to give Martin the good dining-table set that she had paid for penny by penny at a time when she couldn't afford it. A big round mahogany table and four matching chairs that must have had pride of place in some great house at one time … But Martin turned his nose up at it. No second-hand stuff for him and Delia, and the mahogany was too big and heavy anyway. He didn't want it. He and Delia went and ordered furniture made just for them.

This quotation shows the repercussions that acceptance or rejection of a gift could have in familial relations. It also hints at changing tastes and a consumerism that placed an emphasis on modernity rather than tradition.

The examples above pre-date the introduction of wedding lists specifying the items required by the couple. For most couples in 21st-century Ireland, the financial outlay on wedding receptions and associated events exceeds that of the preceding century. Most would hope to recoup these costs through presents and monetary gifts, and the approach to gift-giving demonstrates a practical approach and lack of sentimentality that may seem at odds with Plunkett's advice in 1963 to 'let the giving be an expression of affection, not a social obligation'.

Further reading

Maeve Brennan, 'A young girl can spoil her chances', in M. Brennan, *The springs of affection* (New York, 1997), 63–98.

Caitriona Clear, *Women's voices in Ireland: women's magazines in the 1950s and 60s* (London, 2016).

Edna O'Brien, *A scandalous woman and other stories* (London, 1974).

Louise Purbrick, *The wedding present: domestic life beyond consumption* (Aldershot, 2007).

66

The *Woman's Way* guide to successful marriage in 1960s Ireland

Ciara Meehan

oman's Way began to be published in 1963. Perpetuating the notion that marriage (and motherhood) was the primary vocation for women, the magazine provided emotional guidance on understanding and caring for husbands. Although replicating many of the themes of Catholic marriage manuals, the magazine also broached 'hidden' topics, such as physical intimacy, in the 1960s, thereby becoming a more modern version of the traditional manual.

As the twentieth century unfolded in Ireland, new wives typically bought or received marriage manuals as presents. The popularity of such publications is reflected in their longevity and the fact that they were reprinted multiple times. While some were still being published in the 1960s, it is difficult to find the same array of titles appearing by the end of that decade.

In comparison, by the middle of the 1960s *Woman's Way* claimed a spectacular readership of 280,000. In Eithne Ryan's regular column, readers received guidance on everything from the etiquette of getting engaged to planning a wedding and setting up a new home. Advice columns, feature articles and cautionary tales in the guise of short stories also instructed women on how to be perfect wives—or, at the very least, to maintain happy marriages.

Wives were advised to be patient and understanding of their husbands, and, above all, not to nag them! The good wife, according to Ryan, knew to take an interest in her husband's day—'welcome him home and make a fuss of him'—but not to expect the same in return. Women who wrote to *Woman's Way* complaining that their husbands did little to help around the house received a standard response: housework was not man's work, and asking him to 'do his share' was just another type of nagging. Maura Laverty believed that it was a husband's right to relax after a day at work. 'I consider it most unfair to expect the breadwinner to wash dishes', she wrote. She deemed women who expected such assistance 'lazy and selfish'. Echoing Laverty, Angela

MacNamara responded to a letter from a housewife complaining that she was overworked and received no help from her husband by asking whether the woman was as organised as she could be.

Mara Farrell considered it essential to trust husbands and to give them space. 'Every man hates a scene, and to avoid them he will become secretive, silent and eventually ... he will grow to hate her.' She praised a particular 'wise young wife' of 22 for encouraging her husband to go to the pub after work. Thankful that he was not 'tied to any apron strings', he looked forward to coming home to her within the hour.

Maintaining one's appearance was also essential to being a good wife. MacNamara told one reader, 'Don't forget to look as attractive and bright as possible for him ... no rollers in your hair!' As Eithne Ryan explained:

> Marriage is based upon more than perfect grooming, but personal care-lessness easily becomes disorder and if you have an orderly, tidy-minded husband, this can become an early cause of irritation.

The trick was not to permit a husband to see the preparation; he should only be given the opportunity to admire the final results. This could be difficult to achieve, as the married woman no longer had the privacy of her own room, and so she was encouraged to undertake her morning routine before her husband woke. The passage of time in a marriage was no excuse, Ryan reminded readers, for letting standards slip.

The above counsel bore a striking similarity to that found in traditional marriage manuals. The third edition of *The young wife*, published in 1938 by the Irish Messenger Office (Pl. 12), stipulated that 'your husband comes first in the house'. Likewise, *Woman's Way* attributed to the wife responsibility for maintaining her husband's happiness and well-being above all else. Whether in the marriage manuals or *Woman's Way* in the 1960s, the onus was clearly on the woman to create a harmonious living environment (Pl. 13). Nevertheless, amidst the familiarity of these themes, change was introduced.

Although covering topics with which readers were already familiar, *Woman's Way* also grappled with questions relating to the body or intimacy. Other than noting that intercourse was for the purpose of procreation, Catholic marriage manuals had not typically elaborated on the physical side of marriage. In February 1966 *Woman's Way* broached the issue of the 'first night' and enjoying physical intimacy. The word 'sex' appeared in the subtitle and 'climax' could be found in the main body of the article. These are hardly shocking words, but in February 1966 *The Late Late Show*, presented by Gay

Byrne, landed itself in trouble with the bishop of Clonfert. When audience member Eileen Fox was asked the colour of her nightdress on the first night of her honeymoon, she quipped that she hadn't worn one at all. The programme was denounced from the pulpit and Byrne subsequently found himself apologising for any embarrassment caused.

Woman's Way was clearly able to push the boundaries in a way that television could not. And while the page-length article did not provide any specific instructions about engaging in the physical act, it did offer reassurance to couples anxious about their first intimate encounter. As evidenced by *The Late Late* débâcle, sex—even when merely hinted at—was a taboo subject. The array of letters to *Woman's Way* from both teenagers and older women asking for basic advice about the facts of life points to a serious gap in knowledge. By covering the subject in this and other articles, the magazine was an important source of information for those in new and longer-established marriages alike.

Ireland was a country in transition in the 1960s, and women were trying to negotiate competing attitudes towards their position in society. That *Woman's Way* blended traditional guidance with a broader array of advice was not only appropriate but also made the magazine more appealing than the traditional marriage manual.

Further reading

Caitriona Clear, *Women's voices in Ireland: women's magazines in the 1950s and 60s* (Bloomsbury, 2015).

Ciara Meehan, *Publishing values? Advice literature, women's magazines and everyday life in 1960s Ireland* (forthcoming).

67

Desertion and 'divorce Irish-style' (1937–97)

Sarah-Anne Buckley

In 1937 an absolute ban on divorce was enshrined in the Irish constitution. As divorce law required a referendum to change the constitution,
two bitter campaigns were fought in 1986 and 1995. In 1996 divorce
was legalised and, contrary to the predictions of anti-divorce campaigners,
the floodgates of marital breakdown did not open. In fact, 'divorce Irish-style'
was a very common feature of Irish society from the foundation of the Irish
State. Many spouses chose to migrate (some with the consent of the other,
many without), to leave their marriages and set up in Britain primarily. The
women and men left behind became known as deserted wives and deserted
husbands—a term that one interviewee described as 'degrading' but one that
would become enshrined in social welfare from 1970 until 1991.

Previous research has demonstrated that the issue of desertion was a
complex and highly emotional one. It was a term that encompassed many
situations and feelings and could involve domestic violence, mental health,
trauma, economic dependence and, of course, love. While many cases in the
NSPCC files and in the press were ones of abandonment and anger, one
respondent told me that 'pride and depression must have gotten to a lot of
men', while another commented: 'when you think back to the war, and the
fellas coming back, they were not responsible for what they were doing.
And then, there wasn't an awful lot of work for them.' With regard to coping
skills, the same woman stated that 'a lot of women were able. And a lot of
women were not.' When I asked her about her children and their opinion of
their father, she said: 'I would never allow them to speak wrong about him.
I remember going to the school and I had to say to the teacher that we were
not living together. He said that makes sense because your boys never refer
to their father.'

The State and desertion

> Except for the Irish Society for the Prevention of Cruelty to Children (which, as its name implies, must be a last resort) nothing has been done to help these people. Governments anywhere are not concerned with human suffering unless the victims are organised and vocal.
>
> —'Deserted Wives' series, *Evening Press*, 1967.

> It would be an awful state of affairs if a man could clear off from his family and rear another family with another woman in another country just because his tea was not hot enough.
>
> —District Judge, Bunclody, Co. Wexford, 22 December 1936.

The first quote above is taken from a series of articles in the *Evening Press* on wife-beating and desertion. It is unlikely that the series would have appeared prior to the late 1960s in Ireland, as not only did it highlight emigration, desertion and domestic violence but also, and most importantly, it questioned the State's treatment of women and families since independence. Speaking about the violence that her father inflicted on her mother, her siblings and herself before deserting them, one woman observed that 'in some rural districts, a male's manliness is too often judged by the scorn he displays for women and how often he beats his wife'. In another case in the series, a woman whose husband had deserted her and her fourteen-month-old baby before Christmas in 1936 described how, after the child contracted meningitis and died, the NSPCC could no longer help her. As she could not trace her husband's death certificate over the years she could not receive a widow's pension, and as late as 1959 could not remarry, as the Church would not allow it.

Further demonstrating the economic and practical bind for women, in 1938 a wife and mother of two children made a complaint to the NSPCC inspector about her husband, who was working in London. The correspondence between the two is revealing:

> My darling, just got your lovely letter. I have only one fault to find with you that is you don't write often enough … I wouldn't like to rear children in this hole. I would like to give them a memory of Ireland until they reach about 12 so my dear when you are coming over, if you do, you'll have to leave one behind.

After receiving no money from her husband, the woman visited the NSPCC inspector. The following letter was sent by her husband after a visit from an English inspector:

> Received your threat which hasn't had any effect on me as you know yourself neither you nor the Cruelty man can do anything to me. I have offered you a home here and you have refused thereby putting yourself in a position that favours me in not maintaining you.

Not only does the second letter contrast starkly with the first but it also shows the arrogance of the man and his disregard for his wife. In the final letter, the husband's words were equally bitter: 'Better people than you have lived in one room'.

When we look at the State's role, it appears that its two primary concerns were cost and divorce. Divorce was not an option (although separations could be achieved with money or location), but the development of a welfare state was also rejected vehemently. If men could not or would not pay maintenance after a court order, a wife's only option was to go and ask for home assistance. A meagre sum, this was not always granted. In 1945, however, the Galway County Manager estimated that the budget for home assistance would need to be increased from £12,000 to £15,400 to deal with the demands 'occasioned by men who are working in England abandoning their wives and families', demonstrating that it was being given out.

Deserted husbands

The issue of deserted husbands came to the fore after the introduction of the deserted wives' allowance, which was not extended to husbands. One campaigner, Dennis Dennehy, argued that:

> the sympathy and financial benefits conferred on deserted wives are due largely to the incessant lobbying and agitation conducted by several exclusively women's groups. Deserted husbands have not banded together to campaign for equal treatment—and that is why their plight has been ignored up to now.

As late as 1998, one deserted husband was pursuing a case in the Supreme Court, the argument being that he had been discriminated against by the social welfare system when he was refused a deserted husbands' payment similar to the deserted wives' payment from 1984 to 1989. The Supreme Court concluded that the 1984 decision and a later 1993 High Court judgement be upheld. The court cited statistics from the 1970s and 1980s showing that married women were less likely to be in the workforce and therefore less able to support themselves compared to men at that time. It held that women, if deserted by their husbands, were more likely to require financial assistance. On the back of this case and other cases brought by deserted husbands, in 1989 the government introduced an allowance for widowers and deserted husbands similar to the non-contributory widows' pension and the deserted wives' allowance. In 1991 the payment was absorbed, along with a number of others, into the lone parents' allowance.

Conclusion

In 1970, when an allowance was finally introduced to help deserted wives, commentators such as Michael Viney and Nell McCafferty began addressing the connection between migration, separation, domestic violence and the lack of divorce in Ireland. Prior to the introduction of the allowances, Viney wrote an article entitled 'The broken marriage, desertion—who pays?' He began by quoting a passage from the British Committee on the Enforcement of Debts: 'Citizens in 1969 do not think of failure to discharge matrimonial obligations as criminal behaviour, and to treat it as such by imprisoning offenders'. He continued:

> We can only guess at what Irish citizens think, the point has so rarely arisen. As long as the husband can skip to England—if he's not there already—an Irish court maintenance order has been scarcely worth making, let alone pressing to the point of jailing the defaulting husband.

By 1986, when the first divorce referendum was defeated, there were 11,500 persons classed as 'deserted' in the census. Of these, 9,000 were women and 2,500 men. The deserted wives' allowance was hard-won, a result of years of campaigning, and was problematic for many involved in the early years. The fact that both Church and State were willing to ignore the plight of deserted wives for so long whilst facilitating annulments and separations demonstrates that marriage was as political and personal an issue as it could get.

Further reading

Sarah-Anne Buckley, *The Cruelty man: child welfare, the NSPCC and the State in Ireland* (Manchester, 2013).

Diane Urquhart, 'Irish divorce and domestic violence, 1857–1922', *Women's History Review* **22** (5) (2013), 820–37.

68

'Getting in Touch' (1961–98): the lonely-hearts column of the *Irish Farmers' Journal*

Miriam Moffitt

Although the *Irish Farmers' Journal* was published from 1950, it was only in November 1961 that it included a 'Getting in Touch' column, established to connect prospective marriage partners. Prior to that time the *Journal* published a small number of 'Matrimonial' notices, which had led to marriage on at least one occasion, although it was later noted that the lady in question would never admit how she met her husband (18 May 1957). 'Getting in Touch' was a runaway success, attracting letters from all over the country. Letters were published under a *nom-de-plume*; sealed replies were sent to the *Journal* and subsequently posted to contributors, although some persons preferred to collect replies from the *Journal*'s office, as they were sure that their post would be opened 'by mistake' at home (5 June 1965). Letters were initially published free of charge, but a fee of 5s. per letter (2s. 6d for teenagers) was introduced in 1966. By 1998, when the column was renamed and transformed into a more modern format, 'IFJ Voice Personals' (presently functioning as an on-line service), publication of a letter cost £5.

It is clear that the two factors which strongly impacted on Ireland's history also influenced a farmer's choice of marriage partner: religion and land. On both counts, letter-writers outlined their expectations in plain terms. A minority of letter-writers outlined specific and rather questionable requirements, which appear to have been considered acceptable. For instance, six weeks after 'Spanked' appealed for replies from girls who had been 'strictly brought up', the *Journal* asked the girl who had forwarded her photo to also send her name and address, as 'Spanked' was interested in getting in touch (28 August and 16 October 1965).

Contributors frequently revealed their religion and, by inference, the religion of expected respondents. The proportion of letters from members of the Church of Ireland far exceeded the denomination's size, comprising roughly one third of all letters throughout the 37-year lifespan of the column.

Of the eighteen letters published on 20 July 1963, five persons identified themselves as 'C. of I.', six as 'R.C.' and seven did not reveal their religion. 'Tall and Slim' was a '30-year-old C. of I. farmer's daughter from Offaly … refined and educated … of a very highly respected family'; 'Purchase Tax' was 'a very respectable, refined, well-to-do farmer's daughter from Co. Tipperary … R.C. and T.T. [teetotal] … excellent character background and health … [with] large capital', while 'T.D.', a 25-year-old Limerick man with his own farm, gave no indication of his denomination. Religion was often revealed indirectly: 'Willow Tree' was a pioneer (4 May 1963) and 'Country Boy' could provide a reference from a parish priest (5 August 1967).

Religion was important but so also was land, and landownership (or lack thereof) was a crucial determinant of marriage prospects. Some men shamelessly confined their interest to farm-owning women. 'Cork Man' was looking for a 'nice girl with her own farm or business' (20 July 1963); 'Lucky Day for Me' from Limerick wanted to make contact with 'nice' Protestant girls 'who have their own large farms' (22 July 1967), and 'Creso' was interested in finding a 'respectable farmer's daughter or businesswoman … provided she has her own business or farm' (28 August 1965). Property-owning women were not shy about publicising their wealth: 'Roaring Twenties' had 'large capital and her own farm' (1 April 1967) and 'Mursheen Durkin' boasted of her holding in Kerry (1 July 1967). Owning a farm meant that women were not confined to farming husbands: 'Try Again', a 37-year-old Galway woman with two farms, was interested in a relationship with an army officer, a teacher or a guard (16 October 1965).

Dowries, like farms, were worthy of great consideration. A girl without a dowry might not be considered, and female contributors often provided details of wealth. 'On the Spot', a university-educated Meath woman, had a dowry worth £3,000 (9 July 1966) and Cavan-based 'Miss Nan' had a 'large dowry' (13 April 1968), but 41-year-old 'S.O.S.', 'a disillusioned woman', had suffered several jiltings 'for lack of dowry' (2 May 1970). Some men believed that a dowry was essential ('Sea Breeze', 2 November 1968) while others merely stated that they would welcome one ('Blackwater Country', 22 April 1967), but the absence of a dowry wasn't a deal-breaker for some men ('Blue Bird', 24 February 1968). Dowries, it seems, could also travel from the man to the woman. 'Up Tipp', the female owner of a well-stocked 100-acre farm, included the phrase 'Dowry expected' in her letter (12 February 1977). Another worthwhile attribute in a woman was the ability to generate an off-farm income. Tipperary farmer 'Mr Right' appealed for 'a nurse or a girl with her own farm' (20 July 1963), 'Fed up with Dancing' sought 'attractive teachers or professional girls' (14 February 1970), and 'Pat' from the midlands hoped for a 'nurse, teacher, bank clerk or secretary' (17 April 1971).

Letters reveal changes in living conditions and in women's expectations. 'Home Sweet Home' from Kilkenny boasted that electricity and running water were 'laid on' (27 April 1968). 'Corkman' gave the same assurances and, lest any prospective wife be worried about long-term interference, he added 'parents in their seventies' (15 May 1976). A further sign of societal change is reflected in the inclusion of statements that replies from unmarried mothers would be welcome. This was first mentioned in the letter by 'Irish County Life' on 5 July 1975 and the first letter from an unmarried mother was published a month later ('Lonely', 8 August 1975). Shortly after this, a letter from 'Be Mine' specifically stated 'unmarried mother welcome' (14 February 1976), and 'Tender Heart', a 43-year-old Limerick farmer, wanted to hear from a 'nice unmarried mother' who 'like myself may be very alone in the world' (28 August 1976). It must be noted, however, that the number of letters appealing to or written by unmarried mothers was small and, in this respect, Protestant letter-writers were very significantly under-represented. Although 'Rex', a 50-year-old Protestant, invited replies from widows and unmarried mothers (12 February 1977), very few of his coreligionists followed suit and it was another twenty years before the first letter from a Protestant unmarried mother was published ('Southeast Girl', 13 September 1997).

The trends noted above relating to religion, land and wealth persisted throughout the decades. Protestant letter-writers continued to contribute in significant numbers; four letters were printed on 22 March 1969, two from Catholics and two from Protestants. Of the ten published on 31 October 1998, shortly before 'Getting in Touch' came to an end, four were from Protestants, one from a Catholic and the religion of five letter-writers cannot be identified. Income-generating wives—the proverbial 'laying hens' of rural Ireland—remained popular. 'Leinster Bachelor', Church of Ireland (24 May 1997), and 'East Waterford', Catholic (28 June 1997), hoped to attract a nurse or a teacher. Women continued to emphasise their own property or income: 'Liz', a self-employed professional with her own house, and 'Midland Lady', who owned a house and farm, were each looking for a 'sincere professional person, or a farmer' (both 12 September 1998). References to dowries declined with the passage of time but notions of the practice persisted, if only to be rebuffed; it was last mentioned in the letter from a 47-year-old Church of Ireland farmer who considered the payment 'not important' ('Lonely for Love', 2 October 1993). Just two years earlier, however, the owner of a 100-acre Munster farm explained that a dowry or means would be 'an asset' for a prospective partner ('Sean', 28 December 1991). Letters by or appealing to unmarried mothers continued until the column ceased in 1998. The last letter from a single mother ('Kate') and the last appealing to single mothers ('Leinster Guy') were both published on 13 June 1998.

There is no way of estimating the actual success of the 'Getting in Touch' column, and we must consider that people may have been reluctant to acknowledge availing of its services. The continued stream of letters confirms its popularity among the *Journal*'s readership and, occasionally, letters to the column told of resultant marriages (written under *noms-de-plume*). Despite the lack of concrete evidence of success, the column has provided another function. It has captured the mind-set of the Irish farming community over a 40-year period and provides a window on past attitudes to marriage and relationships which suggests that societal change might not have been as immense or as swift as we now believe, until the turn of the millennium at least.

69

Knock Marriage Introductions

Stephen Farragher

In 1991 I was asked by the then archbishop of Tuam, Joseph Cassidy, to take up an appointment as Pastoral and Youth Director at Knock Shrine, Co. Mayo. I commenced my appointment in early August of that year just prior to the start of the Annual Novena to Our Lady of Knock. One day, as I made my way from the presbytery to the basilica, I was approached by a man who had an eager look of anticipation on his face as he asked me, 'Father, can you tell me where I can find the Marriage Brewery?' Having a fair idea that he was looking for the Knock Marriage Bureau, I asked in reply, 'Is it a wife or a drink you're looking for?' I don't know whether it was as a result of such confusion that the name was later changed to Knock Marriage Introductions, but little did I think on that occasion that one day I would be the director of what may well be Ireland's first Catholic dating agency.

A recent programme in RTÉ's *Reeling in the Years* series featured some news clips in black and white from the 1960s. In one of them Fr Michael Keane, the founder of the Knock Marriage Bureau, explained the reasons behind his decision to found the agency.

Towards the end of the 1960s emigration from Ireland was rife, especially in the west of Ireland, where there was little or no industry and where the farm holdings were small and incapable of supporting more than one family member. It was the era of the dance halls and the showbands. Many of the men were emigrating to England or to the USA, while many of the young women were migrating to Dublin to work in the civil service or to train as nurses or teachers. Fr Michael Keane was a man with a keen pastoral sensibility. He observed a lot of loneliness and isolation in the west of Ireland and felt the need to do something to address the situation. The era of the infamous matchmaker was coming to an end, so a new approach was needed. And so it was that in 1968 he founded the Knock Marriage Bureau. The fact that it was a priest who was the founder of the dating agency drew much media comment. One local newspaper ran the headline 'Young curate plays Cupid'.

Since its inception in 1968 Knock Marriage Introductions has been responsible for 925 marriages. Five marriages took place in 2016. The traditional image of the agency was one in which the majority of the male applicants were farmers in their forties and fifties in dire need of finding a wife who would provide them with offspring to inherit the family farm. For her part, the bride was expected to bring a dowry to complement the value of the groom's farm and stock. Today the picture is very different. Applicants come from a wide variety of professions and backgrounds, from teachers to nurses, radiographers, doctors, dentists, farmers, engineers, carpenters and so on.

The motivation for seeking a marriage partner can also vary greatly. One particular man wrote to the agency explaining that he was getting on in years, that he was '43 years old and his mother could do with a helper around the house'. He further explained that he could do with getting 'a nice girl for his mother'. Another instance was that of a woman who lived alone and was lonely for company. She wrote to the Bureau stating that she was not really interested in marriage but that she had the 'heating on 24/7' and it was no joke being on her own! No doubt she'd agree with Pope Francis's approach in his encyclical, *Laudato Si'*, in which he recommends practical ways in which we can protect the environment and limit the use of fossil fuels. Other applicants could be very exact in their requirements. One gentleman wrote to the agency and, having viewed the photo of a lady, agreed to meet with her. However, while in the photograph the lady had blonde hair, upon meeting her he found that she now had black hair and was convinced that he had been introduced to the wrong person.

The system by which the agency operates is still much the same as it was at the outset, except that nowadays it has a website and it is possible to make an application on-line. Applications are handled by a secretary, who takes care of arranging the introductions. An initial fee of €170 obtains a year's membership, which entitles the applicant to numerous introductions during the course of the year. Applicants come from all backgrounds and situations. They must, however, be free to marry within the Catholic Church.

The agency offers a service that is more personal than some others. Some couples mention that they have had some negative experiences of seeking a partner on-line but generally don't elaborate on the nature of their experience. Couples who meet and get married through the agency often write afterwards to say how happy they are and how they would not have met without the assistance of the agency, expressing their appreciation for the personal and confidential nature of the service. Five marriages have already taken place this year (2017) and four engagements.

What comes across from those who apply to Knock Marriage Introductions is that in Ireland today if a single person is looking for a person with similar values (e.g. faith or religious values), and if one is not into the pub or club scene, there are limited opportunities to meet a potentially suitable marriage partner. The fact that Knock Marriage Introductions continues to receive a steady stream of applicants says something significant about the isolation still felt by many today, even in this age of connectivity.

Further information

http://knockmarriageintroductions.com/

70

Marriage in the Travelling community[1]

Michael and Nell McDonagh

Preparing for marriage

Traditionally, courtship didn't exist. In our situation—we're 42 years married (married in 1976)—our marriage was arranged. We come from a very traditional Travelling family. Ours was an arranged marriage. That was the practice at the time. You didn't marry a man for looks or money or anything like that; it was more to do with compatibility of families. In our time—and in fairness, in today's world, in this generation of Travellers, it's no different in that sense—marriages were made on the basis of how families would get on. There was no such thing as courtship.

There were very good reasons for this practice. Large traditional families would usually marry into each other and you'd nearly know what names married into which families. If you go back through my family history, you'll see a pattern of names and they link into certain families. When a marriage was being arranged a number of things were taken into consideration. You must remember that Travellers were extremely nomadic; they moved around in family units and they worked certain areas. So, in a lot of cases, if a boy was marrying out of the family into another family there would normally be a boy from that family coming back into the family; so you had a crossover of arrangements, for want of a better word. And that was to keep the workforce in place. So it's not unusual to this present day for a number of Travellers to have what's known as a double first cousin, where you had a brother/sister marrying 'crossover' a brother/sister from another family.

---

1 This is a slightly abridged version of an interview that I conducted with Nell and Michael McDonagh in Navan on 16 May 2018. I have, for the most part, retained the text just as it was spoken and have made only some minor edits, for instance removing repetition in some places and clarifying meaning in others. Where a text is indented, it signifies that one of the speakers is recounting some information that specifically pertains to himself/herself. Otherwise, the text is a composite rendering of the observations of Nell and Michael regarding Traveller customs surrounding marriage—Salvador Ryan.

'Courtship' was a getting-to-know-you process, but not a dating process. It would be done under very strict rules and chaperones would be involved. And you would have a situation where you wouldn't be going to the cinema or to dances. Generally speaking, Travellers never socialised in that way, so they wouldn't be going to the local dance hall, regardless of what was happening, whether you were getting married or not. You know how the old song goes, 'going to a wedding was the makings of another'—that was very true for Travellers. The question was when would a very nomadic people get together? It was occasions like weddings, funerals, christenings. But also the fairs and markets were very big occasions. At these gatherings—fairs like the Puck Fair or Spancil Hill—joyful times like these were where marriages would be arranged. So your courtship as such didn't exist. But the getting-to-know existed to an extent. If you were getting to know your future marriage partner, it wasn't she herself you were getting to know as much as her family. When you visited, it was the family you were visiting rather than the person.

There were very good reasons for this too, for the moral identity of a Travelling woman and a Travelling family was—and still is—very important. Even today the moral reputation of a Travelling girl is so important that if the wedding didn't go ahead, and if there was any talk or suspicion of scandal, if there was any question about that girl's sexual morality, as in dating or courting and being alone with the fellow she was to marry, well then her reputation was destroyed. Young women walked an extremely thin line and if they stepped off that line it was very hard to step back on it. Because of these moral concerns, courtship was almost impossible. If the marriage didn't go ahead, the family had to be able to say 'My daughter'—and it was most often daughters—'is still fit for marriage; everything is okay here'. But if you allow dating to be part of it, and for them to be on their own, then the questions begin. And not only will it affect the young woman but it will have serious effects also on her younger sisters. If there's any slur on that girl's character in any shape or form—even by saying it, whether it's true or not—there's almost a paranoia attached to it. And it still exists in many families today in 2018. That girl's sisters, children and their future children will be affected.

One of the traditions that Travellers had was what was called a 'proven match'. And the proven match was very important. If there was a question, they had the right to prove it. And that was done with a priest. And there was normally a select number of priests around the country that Travellers had huge faith in. One of those select number were the friars of Multy [Multyfarnham]. It could only be proven—that the slur was untrue—in the presence of a priest. That priest would have to be someone that was recognised as a special priest, for example a healing priest. The Franciscan friars of Multy were famous for it.

Marriage and status

There were a huge number of positive aspects to Traveller marriage custom as well. Marriage gave you status, and if you didn't marry by the time you were a certain age there was deemed to be something wrong. Marriage played a major role in the Travelling community.

When we got married in the 1970s the normal age for Traveller marriage would have been around sixteen. If you were seventeen and a half you would have been considered quite old, and at eighteen you would have almost been past it. I know women who were married at fourteen or fifteen. In the '70s, if you weren't married by eighteen you were old.

The time between the match being made and the marriage itself would have been very quick; it wouldn't have been drawn out. At that time Travellers didn't have a huge amount of material goods, so getting a house and mortgage wasn't the highest thing on your agenda. Your priority at that time was getting transport—whether that be a horse or a car—and getting accommodation that was mobile, and that gave you your sense of security. Where today, if you listen to people speak—and it's always a strange one—where settled people look at being stable and being secure with a house and permanency, for Travellers security comes with being mobile. It's just a different way of looking at it.

The process

During the fifties, sixties and seventies, there was a lot of thought put into marriage; there was a process in place, and that process was very strict. And secrecy was very big around it. First of all, you would have had the parents—most likely, fathers—of the two children who were going to get married, talking about it; they more than likely would have known one another and could be relatives of one another. The young couple may not even know at this stage that the marriage is taking place. Then the young man would be approached and it would be discussed with him. Last, but by no means least, the young lady was approached. The girl could agree or disagree—everyone had the right to say 'no'; hence the need for privacy, so that it didn't leak out to the wider community of Travellers that this was even happening. If he or she said 'no', nobody would know what was taking place except a very small group of people. Nobody was any the wiser if it didn't happen. If a girl got a reputation of saying 'no' or breaking off a wedding, she would be known to be a very awkward and hard young one to live with and mightn't be asked any more. If that girl was constantly saying 'no', that she didn't think the other person good enough, it would be thought of her, 'Who does she think she is?' Then there could be a big ripple effect across families. Anyway, when a girl came to a certain age she knew she was getting married. If you are reared up in a society in which this is common practice and acceptable practice, it's not strange to you and you don't see any issues around it.

Nell and Michael recall how they first heard they were to be married

Nell:

> I remember I was told when I came home from school one day; I was told by my brother. My brother was itching to tell me something the whole journey home after we went to the shop. He said to me when Daddy got out of the car, 'You're getting married'. I asked 'To who?', and he said 'I don't know, but I know he's from Dundalk'. That was it. And I wouldn't dare ask my father what was happening until I went home and I was told.

Michael:

> We were slightly different from many other Travellers in that we lived in a house at that time and my father was a military policeman and in the army. And I remember being called in one Saturday. We were reared up in a housing estate and I used to hang out with a lot of country [settled] lads. And these were my best friends—we did everything together. I'll never forget it; we were standing out, underneath the street light, chatting as usual, and I remember being called into the house and being told 'Michael, you're getting married; she's a girl from the Midlands', and that was grand; we'll say this was around six or seven o'clock in the evening. Now I'd been hanging around with my friends all day. So I go back out to them and explain to them I was getting married. And I think that was the first time that I realised that these lads I was reared up with—I had never before seen us as any different in any shape or form from each other (we did everything together)—that was my first time to realise that there's a different mind-set here because they couldn't get their heads around it. To them the process should have been: you

went to the dance, you met somebody, you dated for a while, you got to know one another, then got engaged and about twelve months later got married. For me, I was hanging around with these lads one minute, went into the house the next, and ten minutes later I was getting married. How did that happen? And it was a funny enough experience because here you had seventeen- or eighteen-year-old young lads who thought they ruled the roost, and thought they knew the world, debating something they didn't really understand, myself included. And it clicked, then, for me, that they see things differently from how I would see them. So one of them asked me a question, which was a simple enough question: what did she look like? And it dawned on me that I hadn't seen her at this stage. So, lo and behold, my brother was there, who was eleven months older than me, but he had been there at the negotiations—not playing a role in them, but he was there. So I called him over and he explained what she looked like. And to them that was even stranger—how could you be getting married to someone that you'd never seen in your life? But that's what happened at that time, and I remember at the end of the discussion the two lads asked 'Can we go to the wedding?' and I said 'You can, no problem!' And they came, too.

Wedding customs

Nell:

At that time, when we got married, the day you got married you went back to your parents' house, and the day after you got married you still remained at your parents'. You were at least three days married before you moved in with your husband. My aunt tells the story that the day she got married she was sent home to mind the children in the camp and the older ones were let go to the wedding. That wouldn't have been unusual in that time. The bride would be sent home to mind the younger children for she was still only a young one, maybe fifteen or sixteen; so they let her go home and let the woman who was in her twenties go out to the pub with the family. So the bride wasn't at her own wedding. She was at the chapel all right, but then she was sent home. That was very common.

There were different customs among different families. As regards rings, it would have been quite unusual for men to wear wedding rings at that time. You only bought one ring (for the bride).

Even now, the young ones in our community are in an apprenticeship for marriage almost from about the age of thirteen or fourteen. From the day your children are born you are thinking of who they're going to marry. And if you're not thinking it, someone else is! The most important sacrament is marriage, so you're in preparation for it all your life—as a young girl particularly.

To this day even, Travellers don't have an adolescent life; you turn from children to adults very quickly. So from the age of twelve or thirteen young people begin to look around at what's happening. You'll see young girls making sure that their caravan or home is kept spotless clean and that everything is right; you'll see young lads at eleven, twelve and thirteen working with their dads or their uncles and making sure that they'll be ready to earn a good living. And people would be looking at these things and concluding 'he's a good capture' or 'she's a good capture'. So it's like an apprenticeship at that time to prove to people that you're a good match.

Traveller marriages are huge events and important events because they bring together all the different families that are linked into one another and it's a huge time for celebration. It's not a one-day event. Normally you would put aside three days for a wedding. And the big day for Traveller parents is the day after the wedding, because on the day of the wedding the role of the parents is to entertain and look after everybody. So they don't get a chance to sit down until the day after the wedding.

Also, coming up to a wedding you would always sell a horse or something else you would have, and that was to cover the cost of the wedding.

Interestingly enough, when a wedding was taking place, if you got an invitation to it, you more than likely wouldn't go. If you got an invitation, you'd be saying to yourself 'What's wrong with me? Why am I getting an invitation?' Because travellers never give invitations; your family was expected to show respect and attend the wedding. So by giving an invitation, which is starting to happen now, it causes unrest. Travellers would see it as an insult. This has become more of a problem since Travellers have moved from having their weddings in the open, outside, to nowadays using hotels. It makes it very difficult because of numbers. How many are coming? Well, it could be a hundred; but it could be two hundred, three hundred or four hundred—we're not sure!

Also, if an arrangement happened, travellers had a saying: 'Well, they're after jumping the budget'. We're familiar with the custom of 'jumping the broom' in a wedding ceremony, for instance, but, for Travellers, it was 'jumping the budget'. A 'budget' was your toolbox—often a leather bag. And Travellers would 'jump the budget' to signify that they were now going to get married.

If you go to a Traveller's wedding, there's a basic division: there's the men's side and the women's side. Women sit at their tables and men sit at their tables. With the exception of the top table, of course. You'd have the father and the mother up there, but, I guarantee you, he doesn't want to stay there; he wants to get back down. For generations, in the evening time, on the camp you would have the men's fire and the women's fire. And they would have discussions among themselves. It wasn't to isolate anyone. This is how it is until later on in the night, when everyone has a few drinks and the sing-song starts; then the tables mix. Children would customarily sit on the women's side.

Release from the pledge

Lots of Travellers for many generations have taken the pledge against alcohol. Now they might have the pledge for twelve months and a wedding comes up, and they're going to attend it. They will then go to the priest and they will get the pledge taken off for three days. And after the third day it had to be reinstated. You could get a release from the pledge for three days and your pledge would still remain unbroken. That happened on a regular basis. It's interesting in that they would plan that into the general preparations.

Elaborate weddings

Weddings are getting quite costly now and I think the image of Traveller weddings has changed a lot. I think television in particular has portrayed Traveller weddings in a certain way. And, in reality, the majority of Travellers don't do that. Having said that, most families—particularly the father of the bride—wants to give the daughter her special day. And families will go all out to ensure that everything is 100% right for them—and no cost is spared in relation to having fancy cars, horses and carriages, dresses, etc. At one time among the Travelling community you went to a wedding the way you were—you didn't have to have all the fine clothes, etc. Today that's changed a lot. If you're going to a wedding now there's a huge amount of planning in it—hairdos, tans, nails, etc. And it becomes quite costly. The father of the bride will go out of his way to make sure everything is right, but not to the ludicrous levels portrayed in the 'Big Fat Gypsy Weddings'—they're largely for television entertainment, half of which doesn't reflect reality.

When Travellers married country people

In the past it was quite rare, and if it did happen, everyone was in awe of it. How did this happen? This was particularly the case if it was a Traveller girl marrying a settled lad. How did that happen? How did they know one another? How did they meet one another? So there would be a load of questions. Even in Famine and pre-Famine times, there were cases in which these marriages took place, but in 99% of these cases it was settled women marrying Traveller men. The reasoning behind that was that Travellers, particularly during the time of the evictions, were well able to survive on the road. And there were people being evicted out of their houses who couldn't survive and so the women, in particular, married Travellers and the men, their brothers, may have emigrated to the States or whatever. But then suddenly that stopped completely. And you would have had a time when it was unbelievably rare to hear that a settled person married a Traveller. It would be under very unusual circumstances. Today it's not, though. And, funny enough, in more recent times, for many of the settled people who marry into Traveller families it's a status thing—a status up for them. Because a lot of these settled people who do so come from very poor backgrounds, maybe very dysfunctional families, so to marry into the Travelling community is to gain a strong, stable family. There's also a lot more mixing now than there would have been in the past. In our generation there was very little mixing. However, it was, and often still is, frowned upon. And it left a lot of children not knowing their identity. In most cases where a Travelling man married a settled woman, the children were very quickly identified as Travellers and would live that life. Whereas if a Travelling woman married a settled man, it would be the opposite way round. When a girl would marry a country [settled] boy, unless that country boy was reared among Travellers she would go off and become a country girl. But there were always the exceptions to the rule.

Marriage breakdown

When we were a nomadic people it was much easier to keep your identity as an extended family. Now what has happened to us is that we are being assimilated into the settled community and often it's a negative thing. You are now being assimilated and are adapting to a way of life that's not your way of life; your children are mixing with country people and are being educated with and as country people. Because up until today there is nothing in the curriculum about Travellers. More and more of their identity as Travellers is disappearing. This has resulted in breakdown of family structure and the respect for your role in the extended family, and now you have much more family breakdown. It's not that the couple broke down. The whole ripple effect of what's happening in their wider communities is a factor. We, as Travellers, have lost the support of our extended families.

In the past, women were expected to put up with whatever was given to them. That's why there was an awful amount of domestic violence. And a woman had to stay within the home. Your role was to put up with your lot. Then, as we move forward in time, men adapted in a positive way and didn't see the need to use domestic violence. So they began to play an equal role in taking care of children and providing for them. And then we move forward to today when there are more breakdowns in marriages and the reason being that young people don't see the role of aunts and uncles in the family in helping couples to sort problems out. It was usually a family discussion. Now the breakdown of respect leads to a lot of couples making their own decisions to separate.

When you live in an extended family, everything you do—whether it's down to cutting your daughter's hair—has to be a decision made by the family; you cannot cut your daughter's hair without explaining to your mother and your grandmother why you're doing so.

Remarriage

A woman who has children and her marriage breaks up will find it almost impossible to enter into another relationship. Also, if you are a widow, and you lose your husband when you're, say, 25 years of age, under no circumstances is it accepted for a widow to remarry. You stay with your parents. Although there are some rare exceptions to the rule.

When your partner dies, most often you do not remarry through choice. You'll get huge family support, of course. Whereas if you did go off and get remarried it would be frowned upon—'Sure they're not worth talking to at this stage'. It has happened, but it's not the common practice; nor is it accepted.

Pregnancy outside of marriage

Today it's still not accepted among the Travelling community. It's not as common as people think it is. Where it has happened, you would probably get more support today than you did in the past. People would be more accepting. If a girl got pregnant, some members of her family would still look after her. But it would not go down well among the community and would not be encouraged. And in the cases in which it did happen, that girl would still not have an easy time, but she would have an easier time today than she would have had in the past. Grandparents are very young in the Travelling community, so often her parents would rear the child. However, her chances of marrying afterwards would be very slim.

And yet, if you were a single man and your marriage had broken down and you had two or three children and you married a Traveller girl who's single, she would rear your children. But the likelihood of a single Travelling man marrying a woman with a couple of children, we don't know of any example of that.

Priorities

When you think of how country people map out the life of their daughter—for instance, they will think of primary school; secondary school; good results; college; good career; and then, if she gets married, so be it, once she does well in her career. The thoughts of Traveller parents, however, will be, first of all, that their daughter have a good marriage. While Travellers are very proud if their daughter goes to college, etc., their aim is that their daughter be happily married first. After that stage of their life, if they want to return to education, they can. If a Traveller girl goes to college for a four- or five-year period and will come out at 24 or 25 years of age, you would hear the parents or grandparents remark on how stupid that is, for she'll never get a man. Let her get a man first, and get married first, and then if she wants to go to college, she can.

There was a genuine fear of daughters who weren't married getting into some scandal, or of something being said about them. It wasn't simply for the sake of getting their daughter married. There were genuine reasons for this. There was also fear of influences from outside, from among the settled community; the fear of a daughter getting married to a country man. The main aim of a Traveller parent is, once they're in a stable, happy marriage, they're fine; so the priority was marriage, and still is marriage.

71

Marriage—a journey, not a destination: a reflection

Johnny Doherty, CSsR

Some years ago I travelled to Philadelphia to represent our family at the Golden Wedding anniversary of our uncle Joe and his wife Teresa. It was the first time that I went through the Immigration process at Dublin Airport. As we made our way along the winding aisles from the back to the front of the hall we had plenty of time to look at the Immigration officers. Some of them seemed very pleasant; others were obviously doing their job according to regulations. One man stood out because he seemed to be giving everyone a hard time. I'm sure we all had the same thought as we went forward: 'I hope I don't get that man!'

I got him. Having given him my name, where I was coming from and where I was going, he asked me what my reasons were for going to Philadelphia. I told him that I was going for the Golden Jubilee of my uncle and aunt's wedding. He looked at me sternly and asked what that meant. When I told him that they would be 50 years married on Saturday, he asked with amazement: 'Fifty years married to the same man, to the same woman? Gee, ain't that something!' He seemed so shocked that he waved me on!

For 40 years I have been working as a priest with couples preparing for marriage as well as at every stage of marriage, including, at times, the distressing situation of separation and divorce. Every couple that I have met had one thing in common—they wanted their marriage to last forever. The question has always been: how can this be accomplished?

There is nothing, of course, that can guarantee success in marriage. Nevertheless, from my experience of working with couples over the years, there are some things that promote health and happiness in a marriage relationship.

The vision for marriage

The title of this article is the vision that I like to present to couples preparing for marriage. At that time, with all the emphasis on the wedding day, a couple can see marriage as a destination at which they arrive on that day. The mentality can be that once they are married it's just about settling down and living out their lives together as best they can. When they look at their marriage as a journey, however, they can see their wedding day as the beginning of a new journey together. It's a different journey from when they were going out together, and even from their life if they have been living together for some time. The difference, of course, is that they have now, in the wedding, publicly made a commitment to love each other all the days of their lives. That is a wonderful and awesome commitment.

For any journey, two things need to be decided on: where do you want to go, and how do you propose to get there?

The destination of the marriage journey is unity with one another: it's a daily journey towards one another, knowing that there is no end to the possibilities of love. The way of travelling that journey is to build unity of mind, which means a common purpose; unity of heart, which means constantly being predisposed towards the goodness of the other person; and unity of affection, which means showering the other constantly with affection in word and action.

The reality of marriage

A successful marriage is that of a couple who enter into between fifteen and twenty different marriages with each other in the course of a lifetime. That is the reality of marriage! It keeps changing as things change around the couple's life. The secret of success is to enter fully into the present relationship and make it a relationship of love and life. How can this be done? There are a few important elements that need to be worked at as part of the relationship that will make it possible to live out the commitment of love for better, for worse, for richer, for poorer, in sickness and in health.

- Make sure to have regular, good, creative time together. It needs to be regular time because then good communication does not depend on crisis time only. It needs to be good time—time when you are good for one another and not just the time that is left over from everything else. And it needs to be creative time that you use to grow closer to each other in the ways that you need in the present.

- Make thanksgiving a feature of your relationship. One of the worst experiences in a marriage relationship is when one partner feels taken for granted. Unfortunately, this is a common experience.
- Practise affection in word. It is so important that the word of love is often spoken in order to be heard and also to be followed. And develop the ability for affection in action with touch, embrace, a kiss, and a good, vibrant sexual lifestyle.
- Make affirmation and praise a real part of your relationship with your husband or wife. Criticism is generally the beginning of growing apart. Affirmation is an important way of growing closer together.
- I generally deal with couples who are married in a faith community. I always encourage them to make prayer for each other and prayer with one another a part of their love relationship. This will certainly help them to rejoice in the good times and be strengthened in the difficult times. A committed married love is such a wonderful part of human life that it cannot depend only on the two people themselves. Even for people who don't have religious faith, I would recommend that they call on the help of a higher power to bring them into the fullness of life with one another.

There is no reason why almost every couple could not look forward to the celebration of their Golden Wedding anniversary. All it takes is to want that, and then to work for it together.

72

'Maybe I will, maybe I won't': making the transition from living together to marriage

Ashling Jackson

'The natural progression is marriage and family ... not necessarily in that order' (laughing)

—Joe, research respondent, cohabiting with no plans to marry[1]

Traditionally, relationship development went through very clear stages. Boyfriend/girlfriend was the first stage, followed by engagement, marriage, setting up home together and having children. That is still very often the case. Increasingly, however, couples live together before marriage, while some continue to live together without marrying. Multiple pathways now exist for relationship development. Premarital cohabitation, particularly in the early stages of a relationship, has become a normative behaviour in Ireland. Premarital cohabitation is defined here as living together as a couple, without being married, at a shared address. Nevertheless, marriage as a stage in relationship development still holds an intrinsic value in our society. This short article discusses some influences on the decision to make the transition from living together to marriage. Based on romantic ideas of 'being in love', 'finding a soul mate' and 'wanting to live happily ever after', it seems that this should be a very simple thing. In truth, however, the decision to marry for cohabiting couples is often much more complex, requiring serious deliberation.

This discussion is based on research conducted in Athlone in 2007 which explored why people live together in their relationships prior to their first marriage, and then why in those relationships they decided whether to marry or not. Forty-one in-depth interviews were conducted and an event history calendar was used to record events in people's lives to determine what was happening and how that affected relationship decision-making.

---

1 Research respondents have been assigned false names to protect anonymity.

The sample comprised cohabiting couples with plans to marry, cohabiting couples with no plans to marry, and couples who married without living together first. For the latter group, religion acted as a structural constraint. It strongly framed decisions made within relationships, including the decision not to live together, while positively influencing the decision to marry.

For cohabiting couples with no plans to marry, there was no objection to marriage. As Andrew stated, 'It is an option down the road'; Peter emphasised, 'I just think everything has been fine and it has worked OK, so, like, if it's not broken, don't fix it type thing'. For cohabiting couples planning to marry, there was no plan to marry at the start of a relationship. Nor was there a plan to marry when a couple decided to live together. That decision came about later in the relationship. Many chose to live together because, for example, it was a natural step in their relationship, they needed time to allow their relationship to develop, they wished to travel, achieve educational and/or career goals, have financial security and/or buy their own home. There was such personal and social importance attached to marriage by respondents that everything had to be 'just right'. 'Just right' meant that what was happening in other areas of life—such as finishing education, travelling, career, financial stability, having one's own home and the needs of children, if present in the relationship—was important, as well as ensuring that the emotional needs of the couple were met and would continue to be met within the relationship.

Marriage also emerged as being valued for its symbolic significance, i.e. for achieving emotional satisfaction in a relationship. Of course, emotional satisfaction in a relationship is not exclusive to marriage *per se*. It does mean, however, that marriage has moved from being a marker of conformity to being a marker of prestige (as noted by Julia Carter and Simon Duncan). Now marriage is something to work up to. It has a different personal and social meaning in terms of the emotional bond and commitment involved.

In 1988 Penny Mansfield and Jean Collard concluded from their research with 65 newly wed couples in London in the 1970s that marriage crystal-lises a sense of the future, as it is a commitment for life. This was also true for the couples in my study who decided to marry, whether they were living together or not. There was a difference, however, in the type of commitment for couples when they were at the living-together stage compared to when they decided to get married. Greta reflected that 'We just became a little bit more committed to each other'. Therefore commitment is a reflexive process that increases as the relationship develops. It also confirms a collectivist or communal ethic, through which couples are directed towards marriage to commit more fully to each other.

Children often triggered the decision to marry, but only once a relationship met the emotional needs of the couple. Couples with unplanned pregnancies were more likely to live together until they were sure of their relationship. Unplanned pregnancy or having children outside of marriage no longer means that a couple has to marry. We have moved from a normative position that, for example, valued staying in a marriage for the sake of the children towards one which values primarily looking after individual and couple emotional ties. Procreation is no longer considered a primary function of marriage. It is certainly often a desired function but not a primary function.

Lastly, living together provides a way of testing the strength and durability of the relationship, which might then act as a bulwark against divorce. In this way, premarital cohabitation is a way of minimising risk in the very fluid social environment in which we all live. Ciara stressed the importance of this, 'to make sure that surely the mistakes that happen during marriage could be picked up before marriage, and like alarm bells don't ring …'.

In this brief discussion, we can see that the decision to make the transition from living together to marriage is very complex. It is not something that is taken lightly by cohabiting couples. This means that the 'test' for marriage may now be higher—everything must be 'just right'. This augurs well for the future of marriage in Irish society.

Further reading

Julia Carter and Simon Duncan, 'UK wedding paradoxes: individualised conformity and the "perfect day"', *The Sociological Review* **65** (1) (2017), 3–20.

Ashling Jackson, 'Premarital cohabitation as a pathway into marriage. An investigation into how premarital cohabitation is transforming the institution of marriage in Ireland' (unpublished Ph.D thesis, Maynooth University, 2011).

Penny Mansfield and Jean Collard, *The beginning of the rest of your life: a portrait of newly-wed marriage* (London, 1988).

73

Facing the music: the work of a wedding singer in modern Ireland

Nicole Robinson

The music chosen for their wedding ceremony, be it civil or religious, is of great importance for the vast majority of couples. Well-chosen music can transform a wedding from an impersonal, run-of-the-mill ceremony to a moving and memorable occasion for all in attendance. The immense responsibility for this crucial aspect of a marriage ceremony lies on the shoulders of wedding singers and musicians, both amateur and professional, who must work in consultation with the couple and the celebrant to provide a programme of music that is appropriate to the occasion yet reflective of the musical tastes of the couple in question.

I began singing at weddings professionally at the age of fourteen and, before I knew it, what had started out as a way of earning some pocket money during the weekends and school holidays ended up as my sole form of income during my two-year hiatus between school and college. My experience as a wedding singer over the past decade or so has been varied to say the least, but, after being in attendance at what must be over a hundred weddings, I have found that nothing reflects the tastes and personalities of the couples getting married more than their choice of music. Even though I cannot admit to enjoying everything I am asked to sing at weddings, being a wedding singer requires a delicate balancing act between accommodating the bride and groom as much as possible and maintaining my integrity as a professional musician. To me, the wedding music chosen by a couple is a reflection of who they are, both as individuals and as a unit, and so it is of the utmost importance that they have a very real say in the music that is played on their special day. Nevertheless, it is up to me to guide them in their choices and to ensure that their musical programme is also tasteful and appropriate for the occasion.

As I was brought up in a traditional Church of Ireland home, the concept of a wedding singer was almost completely foreign to me as a child. I was born into a Church where the music for services, as a rule, consisted of the congregational singing of three or four hymns accompanied by an organ, and weddings were no exception. Despite the lack of a wedding section in our church hymnal (as exists for the likes of Baptism and the Eucharist), it would be fair to say that there are certain 'favourites' when it comes to the choice of wedding hymns. Chief among these are James Edmeston's *Lead us, heavenly Father, lead us*, Charles Wesley's *Love divine, all loves excelling*, Henry Francis Lyte's *Praise, my soul, the King of Heaven* and Thomas Kelly's *Saviour, send a blessing to us*. These hymns, and others like them, have for generations played an integral role in Church of Ireland wedding ceremonies, with many couples still able to recall the hymns that were sung on their 'big day' while memories of other details may have grown dim.

Having grown up as part of a tradition where the members of the congregation were active participants in the music-making of every liturgy, including weddings, the first Roman Catholic wedding at which I was employed to sing was certainly an eye-opener! While the worship of the early Catholic Church certainly included the communal singing of hymns and psalms, by the fourth century Church leaders had begun to impose restraints on congregational singing, both to guard against heresy and to exercise their power and authority over the laity. The Council of Laodicea in AD 367 declared that 'Besides the appropriate singers who mount the ambo and sing from the book, others shall not sing in the church', and with the evolution of the Mass most singing was delegated to trained choirs. While the Reformation returned music to the congregations of many Protestant churches, Roman Catholic congregations continued to have a passive rather than active role when it came to church music, with liturgical music performed by choirs rather than sung by all present. The legacy of this can still be seen today in many parish settings.

When I sang at my first Roman Catholic wedding as a member of a vocal trio, I was astounded at the sheer volume of music required of us. Unaccustomed as I was to anything other than congregational singing in church, Catholic weddings seemed to me to have more the makings of a concert than of a religious ceremony. Not only were the entrance and recessional pieces to be sung but we were also to sing during the lighting of the candles, the responsorial psalm, the Gospel acclamation, the offertory procession, the exchange of the sign of peace, the administration of communion and the signing of the register, in addition to the parts of the Mass, such as the *Sanctus* and *Agnus Dei*, and the post-communion reflection. Compared to what I was used to, this was a veritable musical marathon!

Over time, as I became more *au fait* with the world of Catholic wedding music and as my repertoire expanded to include seemingly innumerable versions of *Ave Maria* (including one by Beyonce!), I began to notice various patterns emerging regarding the music chosen by different couples. Firstly, there are those couples who are regular Mass-goers: these couples are, in my experience, generally few and far between. They know exactly what music they want to have included in their ceremony and it's usually relatively traditional and appropriate for a church wedding. Secondly, there are couples who probably went to Mass in their youth but have long since fallen out of the practice. These couples often request a mixture of simplistic children's songs that they learned in school (which have about as much melodic interest as John Cage's *4'33"*) and some unusual but perhaps not completely inappropriate songs from the charts, such as *How long will I love you* by Ellie Goulding or Kodaline's *The one*. In order to tick the 'religious' box they might also ask for some popular cross-over songs, which might appear on the surface to have some semblance of liturgical propriety attached to them but which, on closer inspection, are quite tasteless and unsuitable for singing in a church setting. This is best exemplified in the multitude of brides who ask for Leonard Cohen's *Hallelujah* to be sung. While the title of this particular piece of music might lead one to assume that it was spiritual, or perhaps even liturgical, in nature, a preliminary inspection of the lyrics would quickly disabuse you of this notion.

Finally—and, to my mind, most interestingly—there are those couples who have little or no experience of Mass whatsoever but who still want a church wedding, and these are certainly the most challenging weddings from the perspective of music choice! These couples often come to me with completely unrealistic expectations regarding my role as a classically trained wedding singer, and a great deal of compromise is often needed. Pieces I have sung for such couples (albeit somewhat reluctantly!) include *One day like this* by Elbow and Coldplay's *Viva la vida*. Often, when I suggest to these couples that perhaps they should incorporate some religious and classical music into their ceremony and leave the popular music for the signing of the register, they request absurdities such as the Andrew Lloyd Webber version of the funeral piece *Pie Jesu*, with one bride even asking for Sarah Brightman's *Time to say goodbye*!

No matter what the religious or musical background of any couple getting married, getting a bride, a groom, a singer and a priest all singing from the same hymn-sheet (so to speak!) regarding what is appropriate for a ceremony that is first and foremost a religious rite can be challenging. Nevertheless, I have found that a compromise can almost always be found and, while this might mean that I end up singing pieces that wouldn't necessarily be to my personal liking, the most important thing is obviously to provide music that reflects both the tastes of the couple getting married and the dignity and solemnity of the occasion. Well-chosen church music can transform a wedding and so it is important to get it right. After all, music is the food of love, and so, despite the frustrations, I'll play on!

74

Sesame Street, drag queens and religion: the introduction of marriage for same-sex couples in Ireland

Sonja Tiernan

A 'gay cake' row in Northern Ireland was the perfect recipe for a media sensation, with Bert and Ernie of Sesame Street fame taking centre stage in a court case that would run from 2014 into 2016. The cake row emerged during a dramatic series of events stemming from an RTÉ encounter dubbed 'Pantigate' in the Republic of Ireland. The flamboyant drag queen and prominent gay rights activist 'Panti Bliss', AKA Rory O'Neill, helped generate media frenzy across the island and beyond with sensational and often comical headlines. These events, however, signified something deeper and more disturbing about the question of extending full marriage rights to same-sex couples in Ireland. Both of these events stemmed from 'No' campaigners citing religious justification to oppose extending marriage rights to all. Religious leaders in Ireland expressed various responses to the marriage equality debate. Nevertheless, these two events show how organisations attempted to use a repressive historical overlap between Church and State in Ireland, most especially the Catholic Church in the Republic and Presbyterianism in Northern Ireland, to prevent the introduction of full civil marriage equality.

The Northern Ireland case centred on an evangelical Christian bakery which refused to bake a cake bearing a slogan supporting marriage for same-sex couples under a depiction of Bert and Ernie. In 2018 Northern Ireland remains the only part of the UK that does not afford same-sex couples the right to civil marriage. DUP leader Arlene Foster, First Minister of Northern Ireland, made a commitment in October 2016 that her party would continue to block the introduction of marriage for same-sex couples for the next five years. Many consider this an abuse of the powers granted to the party through what is termed a petition of concern, originally designed to protect minority rights in Stormont's power-sharing assembly. The party has close links with Presbyterianism; DUP founder Ian Paisley established the Free Presbyterian

Church of Ulster. Foster's announcement was made in the wake of the decision to uphold a legal finding that Ashers Bakery had discriminated against a customer on grounds of sexual orientation. Similarly, the 'Pantigate' drama emerged from a religious backlash when members of a Catholic lobby group, the Iona Institute, took a legal case against the national broadcaster and Rory O'Neill for comments he made on a national television chat show.

In the run-up to the marriage equality referendum, emotions ran high in Ireland as both sides of the campaign attempted to secure their favoured outcome. The Catholic Church had played a role in drafting the Irish Constitution in 1937, with de Valera often incorporating submissions from Fr John Charles McQuaid, the future archbishop of Dublin. In the 1980s a drive for social liberation led to a series of referenda in which the Catholic Church played a dominant role, with many priests directing citizens on the way to vote and often preaching to their congregations on the wrongs of pertinent issues such as divorce and abortion. Examining just a few incidents that occurred during the marriage equality referendum highlights how Church and State have now been successfully separated in Ireland.

In January 2015 Fr Martin Dolan mounted the pulpit of his church of St Nicholas of Myra, Francis Street, in the heart of inner-city Dublin, where he had served as the parish priest for fifteen years. He addressed the topic of marriage equality in his homily and announced that he was in support of the 'Yes' campaign. While it was an unusual move by a Catholic priest to express an opinion in opposition to Catholic teaching, what he did next was even more unexpected. Fr Dolan announced that he himself was in fact a gay man. In an instant his congregation reacted by overwhelmingly supporting him with a standing ovation.

Within months, another Catholic priest attempted to override this show of support for same-sex unions in a church. In March 2015 a Carmelite priest, Fr John Britto, launched into a homily opposing same-sex marriage at his Saturday evening Mass in the church of St Mary, Star of the Sea in Annagry, Co. Donegal. Fr Britto criticised Donegal GAA footballer Éamon McGee for openly supporting the 'Yes' campaign, insisting that such unions had been a 'problem' since the days of Sodom and Gomorrah. He went further by maintaining that even 'nature does not approve a same-sex union, [because] nature does not give them a child'. The priest could not have anticipated the reaction he would receive from his congregation. Many of those attending the Mass walked out of the church in protest.

The referendum on the 34th amendment of the Irish Constitution was held on 22 May 2015 and resulted in a clear victory for the 'Yes' campaign, with 62% voting to grant marriage to couples 'without distinction as to their sex'. Ireland became the first country in the world to extend marriage to same-sex couples through a public vote. The Catholic archbishop of Dublin, Diarmuid Martin, admitted that this represented a 'social revolution' in Ireland and that the Catholic Church needed to take 'a reality check right across the board'.

Fr Dolan welcomed this 'social revolution' by thanking his congregation at his Saturday evening homily following the referendum results. He said that the Irish people had heard the 'pleas of desperation of a minority' and had answered that call. He also responded to Archbishop Martin's comments that the Church needed a new language to speak to young people, stating that, 'with great respect, it is not a new language that we need but a new way of being and living'. The amendment to the constitution resulted in the passing of a Marriage Act which recognised the foreign marriage of same-sex couples from 16 November 2015, and the first marriages took place in Ireland the following day. By the end of that year, 91 same-sex couples had married in Ireland.

Further reading

Gráinne Healy, Brian Sheehan and Noel Whelan, *Ireland says yes: the inside story of how the vote for marriage equality was won* (Dublin, 2015).

Una Mullally, *In the name of love: the movement for marriage equality in Ireland* (Dublin, 2014).

75

Till death us do part: marriage, loss and enfranchised gay grief

Kevin Myers

Ann-Louise Gilligan and Katherine Zappone first met at Boston College in 1975 and were both admitted to the same religious theology doctoral programme that year. After a brief romance, Katherine and Ann-Louise knew that they wished to spend their lives together. In 2003 they married in British Colombia, Canada. On coming to Ireland, they contacted the Irish Revenue Commissioners and Ireland's State Registrar. Their correspondence was based on a somewhat simplistic tax-related issue: they wished to avail of the institutional benefits that are afforded married couples within the Irish State. Owing to the nature of their relationship, however, their engagement with these State bodies proved fruitless. Their marriage in British Columbia was not recognised by the administrative and legal framework of the Irish State. They took their grievance to the Irish High Court, a case which they eventually lost. This ruling worked both to seed and to advance a conversation, one also taking place throughout much of the world: the campaign to enable same-sex couples to marry and thereby obtain the same legal recognition as their heterosexual peers. Over a decade later, in mid-2014, the Irish government called for a public referendum to address the issue. After a heated debate, a significant majority of those who voted endorsed the constitutional change. Katherine and Ann's goal was realised; the deed was done. Shortly afterwards, they married each other with the full legal recognition of the Irish State.

What's love got to do with it?

Ann-Louise and Katherine's story is both simple and complex. Their understated Irish registry office service was conducted within the context of seismic cultural and social shifts in attitudes taking place in many countries. As a social institution, marriage has carried various meanings and functions for centuries. Over the past century, however, this rite seems to have taken on a more personalised and somewhat emotive role. It can be argued that understandings of marriage began to shift, moving it away from a practice which often reflected both religious and patriarchal connotations and towards the direction of individualistic satisfaction. This shift is undoubtedly a product of wider social changes, whereby processes of secularisation and individualism have altered traditional understandings of many aspects of life. For many today, as noted by Ann Swidler, marriage is viewed as a public declaration of private emotion.

Bonds and the ballot box

We Irish are bonded to the ballot box. The Irish constitution contains within its pages a clause, formally referred to as Article 46.2, which sets out the requirements for potential changes to the document. Essentially, proposed amendments are to be put to the populace, a process in which we can perhaps identify both strengths and weaknesses. The Irish public voicing their opinion on various matters (principally in relation to EU law) may appear rather enlightened, but we can also look at the article with a slightly critical eye. Essentially Article 46.2 enables a situation where the rights of minorities are left to the mercy of the often-changing attitudes found within popular public opinion. Other constitutional democracies, such as the United States, have established measures that safeguard the rights of minorities against the attitudes of the majority.

Marriage, divorce and death: emerging grief equality?

Marriage tends to end in two ways: through either divorce or death. (Nullity is another matter.) Ireland's 1995 and 2015 marriage-related referenda enabled people to divorce and marry respectively. Whereas the former explicitly addressed the ability of a married couple to end their legal relationship, the latter did so more implicitly. After all, if gay couples can marry, so too can they find space within the legal, social and cultural recognition of bereavement bound up in both separation and loss. The singer Ronan Keating was to separate from his wife, Yvonne Connolly, by means of divorce. Katherine Zappone was to be separated from her spouse by death. Both were endings of sorts and, importantly, both were constitutionally, and largely culturally, recognised as legitimate.

Returning to Katherine, we witness something quite new, particularly for a person who holds public office. On 29 July 2017, Katherine appeared on a popular RTÉ chat show. Talk of her political life, her duties and responsibilities as a government minister, was openly suspended, to be discussed at another time. This public appearance addressed a singular issue: Katherine's experience of the loss of her wife. When Katherine spoke of the death of Ann-Louise and her experiences of grief, she did so with unrestrained honesty and reflection. When asked about how she was coping with her loss,[1] she stated:

> 'My entire life has changed. I will never be the same. Not only was I deeply in love with Ann-Louise and we had 36 blissful years together and we supported each other and everything that we did … It was a great gift, we were very blessed … I know that she would want me to find a way to … allow this extraordinary heartbreak that I feel.'

As an evolving social institution, marriage typically signifies commitment. It is a social practice loaded with meanings and understandings, but it also reminds us and others of the pain frequently felt by the death of our spouses and kin. Katherine and Ann-Louise long advocated for 'marriage equality'. In doing so, they perhaps inadvertently went further, moving to enfranchise one group among many that are denied the social recognition of both their love and their loss. For Katherine and many others, this was true grief equality.

Further reading
Ann Swidler, *Talk of love: how culture matters* (Chicago, 2001).

---

1 Katherine Zappone interviewed by Miriam O'Callaghan for *Saturday Night with Miriam*. RTÉ Televison, 29 July 2017.

76

Navigating intimate relationships through yoga and meditation

Sophia Pallaro

Knowing that the other person is angry,
one who remains mindful and calm
acts for his own best interest
and for the other's interest, too

—Buddhist scripture (Saṃyutta Nikāya, 1:188)

Yoga is a practice that originated in India as a religious and spiritual discipline between 1700 and 500 BC. The popularisation of yoga in the West took place from the early 1900s but particularly from the 1960s, when it developed a strongly secular flavour. In Ireland in the past two decades yoga and its meditation techniques have become common ways of taking care of oneself and of dealing with life stresses. What appears to be appealing is the fact that yoga is a comprehensive discipline that aims at the harmonisation of the body, the mind and the emotional world of the individual. The number of yoga studios and meditation centres across Ireland, and the introduction of these practices into institutional contexts such as schools, hospitals and the workplace, are all indications of how popular they are becoming in the Irish cultural landscape. My research on yoga in Ireland suggests that one area in which practitioners report positive effects is that of their personal relationships. The benefits reported by practitioners in the context of marriage, and intimate relationships in general, include an increased ability to deal with conflict, greater empathy towards a partner and an enhanced relational quality.

Pauline's story can offer a sense of how these practices can work in the context of marriage. Pauline is in her mid-fifties and has had a traditionally Irish upbringing. She has been practising yoga and meditation regularly for about three years. She attends three classes a week and meditates every morning before going to work. When asked what these practices bring into her life, she explains that they have allowed her to shift the way she relates to herself and others. She has developed greater awareness of her body, of her emotions and of the activity of her mind. This has resulted in the ability to be with, rather than react to, difficult situations, and to respond in a better and mindful manner. In giving an example, she goes on to explain how learning to hold and stay in physically challenging poses while cultivating awareness, kindness and compassion for herself has meant that she is now better able to approach others with similar awareness and compassion. When challenged by a difficult dynamic with her husband, rather than reacting and getting annoyed or upset, the skills she has acquired through yoga and meditation allow her to respond in a richer way.

Mary's experience with yoga and mindfulness is another example of how engaging with these practices can lead to profound transformations of romantic relational dynamics. Mary has been practising regularly for a number of years. She used to be very jealous of her partner—'I used to be extremely possessive and have real trouble with possessiveness'—and this would create conflict in her marriage. She explains that practising yoga helped her to 'feel the feelings and the energy that would take [her] over'. She learned to notice and to be with 'all these imaginations' brought on by jealousy. She would feel them in her body while doing her yoga practice. Over time, this has allowed her to overcome her troubling feelings and behaviours. Key to this resolution, she says, was the bodily awareness brought by yoga and a mindful attitude.

Globalisation and secularisation have both contributed to institutional and cultural changes in Ireland. Irish culture and institutions have shifted from being heavily influenced by the moral teachings and cultural practices of the Catholic Church to being shaped by the manifold influences of a multicultural and globalised society. In this transition two things appear to have changed dramatically: on the one hand the relationship to new and different cultural practices, and on the other Irish people's sense of self and of their body, which had previously been so strongly associated with ideas of sin and penitence. Pauline and Mary's experiences of integration of the benefits of yoga into their marital life are examples of how many Irish people have opened up to and embraced practices that would have been perceived as exotic or even obscure not too long ago. These women's stories are not isolated cases of extraordinary enthusiasm. Rather, they represent a cultural shift in understanding of ways to relate to oneself, to a partner and to others in general.

What distinguishes yoga from other physical and mental practices is that it involves the cultivation of an *embodied* self-reflexivity. Yoga practitioners are encouraged to bring attention and presence to what they are experiencing in their body *and* their mind, while building self-compassion, kindness and acceptance towards themselves. Cultivating an integrated awareness of bodily sensations, thoughts and emotions is synonymous with being mindful: in the words of Jon Kabat-Zinn, 'paying attention in a particular way: on purpose, in the present moment, and non-judgmentally'. This attitude allows practitioners to enquire not just about how their body behaves and responds through the practice but also about their thinking pattern, their emotional state and how they are reacting to a situation: 'What am I feeling right now?', 'How am I being with myself?', 'How is my mind framing my experience?'. It is no surprise, then, that yoga practitioners report some deep changes in their sense of self and in the way in which they relate to others.

The extent to which yoga and meditation are practised in Ireland, and the fact that practitioners are acknowledging their benefits even in the context of marital life, is an indication of a cultural transformation. In Irish society for a long time the understanding and the regulation of the body were shaped by the notion of sin, and both the prevailing culture and the churches provided a strict moral code and limited support for the emotional challenges of sustained intimate relationships. It is interesting to see that now people in Ireland may be finding a tool for enhanced marital happiness in an embodied practice that originates from the Eastern spiritual tradition.

Further reading

Jon Kabat-Zinn, *Full catastrophe living: using the wisdom of your body and mind to face stress, pain, and illness* (New York, 1999).

K. Wachs and J. V. Cordova, 'Mindful relating: exploring mindfulness and emotion repertoires in intimate relationships', *Journal of Marital and Family Therapy* **33** (4) (2007), 464–81.

77

Humanist weddings in Ireland today

Joe Armstrong

'I interpret Humanism as a perfect example of what Krishnamurti called the power of negative thinking,' says County Cork-based Bill Chase, a Humanist celebrant accredited by the Humanist Association of Ireland (HAI) and a registered solemniser for legal weddings. 'There seems to me to be no Humanist belief system. I understand Humanism as ethical desiderata. Humanist thinking is defined by what it doesn't affirm or even posit, so what is left is a lovely neutral spot where we can (if we're so inclined) celebrate the more significant moments of our lives, and as hyper-social beings we seem to need to do that.'

'As young hippies,' continues Bill, 'we were actually quite good at tearing down institutions and practices that we saw as hypocritical because they had become irrelevant over the years as our collective knowledge increased. The problem was that we weren't very good at constructing new and more appropriate ones. Performing a Humanist wedding or funeral seems to address that problem. What I hope we are doing is offering an alternative and somewhat relevant way of marking these chapters in our lives. And, when it works, this feeling of openness and freshness permeates the ceremonies we conduct. And, at their very best, these rituals give a sense of possibility to everyone who shares in them. That all sounds a bit *wo wo*, but there's some truth in it all. The occasions that we mark can be an expression of enhanced consciousness for all concerned.'

Weddings conducted by HAI celebrants such as Bill Chase have been legal in the Republic since 2013, when the 2012 amendment of the Civil Registration Act 2004 came into force. As with the ban on smoking in public places, which was introduced in the Republic of Ireland before England followed suit, Ireland is ahead of its nearest neighbour in the legal recognition of Humanist weddings. In 2017 it was still not possible to have a legal Humanist marriage ceremony in England, although there have been legal Humanist marriages in Scotland since 2005.

Meanwhile, in Northern Ireland the first legal Humanist wedding was held on 22 June 2017 on foot of a temporary authorisation by a High Court judge, who ruled that withholding legal recognition of Humanist marriages was a breach of human rights, as it denied to Humanists a privilege enjoyed by religious believers. The Northern Ireland attorney general appealed the High Court ruling, however, and, while the marriage went ahead and was legal, at the time of going to press it was not clear whether it would constitute a precedent. Brian McClinton, editor of the *Irish Freethinker and Humanist*, said that if the decision goes the right way it would be a great step forward for Ulster society and for the Humanist outlook in Northern Ireland.

By April 2017—only four years after the first legal Humanist marriage in the Republic of Ireland in April 2013—there were 25 celebrants accredited by the Humanist Association of Ireland, with five more in training and expected to be accredited by the end of 2017. According to the Central Statistics Office, as many as 1,437 or 6.7% of all opposite-sex marriages in 2016 were conducted by the Humanist Association of Ireland, compared to 1,264 (5.7%) in 2015. In addition, in 2016 the HAI conducted 97 same-sex marriages, representing 9.2% of all same-sex marriages in Ireland. In total, the Humanist Association of Ireland conducted 1,534 marriages (6.8%) in 2016, continuing the upward trend from 895 in 2014 and 1,264 in 2015. This shows significant growth in just four years. In fact, by 2016 HAI weddings had become the third-largest category, after Roman Catholic and civil marriages, with almost three times as many Humanist marriages as Church of Ireland weddings (372, or 1.6%) and more than the Church of Ireland and the 'other religions' (1,104, or 4.9%) categories combined (1,476, or 6.5%). And with one in ten (468,421 people) ticking the 'No religion' box in the 2016 census—a 73.6% increase since 2011—further growth in Humanist weddings is anticipated.

What do people like about Humanist weddings? HAI member Lucie O'Sullivan, who loves working as a Humanist celebrant and being with people at special moments in their lives, says, 'Secular couples are delighted to be able to personalise their ceremonies and to say words and vows that are more reflective of who they are. Ritual and ceremony are hardwired into our DNA and it doesn't belong solely to any church or institution. It always amazes me how relieved couples are when they realise that I'm going to help them design a ceremony that honours who they are … a non-religious ceremony can be really meaningful, heartfelt and beautiful.'

As for myself, I was accredited as a Humanist celebrant in 2013. Personal feedback from couples whose weddings I conducted reveals what people like about Humanist weddings. Ceremonies are inclusive of all: no guest is excluded from any part of the ceremony. And the ceremony is personal—it's about the couple themselves and their loved ones, with the secular readings of poetry or prose chosen by the couple themselves on themes of love, commitment, friendship and marriage. The couple alone choose the rituals they want, such as lighting candles, involving their parents and their children if they wish, and perhaps also remembering absent or deceased loved ones. They decide whether they want to do sand ceremonies, ribbon-tying rituals—tying the knot!—or unity bowl rituals involving all their guests, and many couples choose to pass their wedding bands around their guests so that they can wish the couple well or, if guests are religious, pray silently for them. Couples may choose rose ceremonies, stone ceremonies, planting ceremonies, wine box and love letter ceremonies, wine-sharing ceremonies, the exchange of rings and, yes, some choose to jump a broom to the delight of all at the end of the wedding ceremony. And of course couples choose their own secular music, whether Mozart or punk rock!

Weddings are typified by smiles and laughter, tears and applause, solemnity and fun, conducted in a relaxed tone, ever personal, and—yes, that word again—inclusive. For, although we don't have prayers or hymns, I've often had priests, nuns, brothers and religious lay folk thank me for feeling included in a Humanist ceremony.

Further information
See the Humanist Association of Ireland: www.humanism.ie.

78

Love creates home: housing and marriage in Irish society

Kevin Hargaden

While in myth and legend marriage is often depicted as an inevitable consequence of star-crossed destiny, in reality marriage in Ireland is commonly a much more pragmatic affair. In his first collection, *Death of a naturalist*, Seamus Heaney makes explicit the connection between matrimony and the other great romantic 'M' of Irish life: the mortgage.

In 'Scaffolding', Heaney compares his imminent nuptials with Marie Devlin to the construction of a house. The early stages of building a lasting relationship is likened to the erection of a house:

> Masons, when they start upon a building,
> Are careful to test out the scaffolding.

The platform from which stonemasons and bricklayers can do their work is compared to the time and patience required to cultivate a long-lasting relationship. Heaney continues:

> And yet all this comes down when the job's done,
> Showing off walls of sure and solid stone.

The preparation for marriage may involve hard toil, skilled labour and progress hidden by scaffolding, but on the day of the wedding what has been achieved will finally be displayed for all to see. Even if towards the end of the project some planks of the scaffolding start to wear, Heaney reminds his bride-to-be that they are not the thing to be prized. The goal is a marriage that will endure across the years, through rain and shine:

Never fear. We may let the scaffolds fall,
Confident that we have built our wall.

Matters of love are thus directly compared to the task that takes up so central a place in Irish culture: finding a way onto 'the property ladder'. Marriage and buying a house seem perpetually bound together.

In more recent Irish literature, the ties between housing and marriage can again be found. The acclaimed novelist Anne Enright depicted the centrality of securing a mortgage and purchasing a home to the matrimonial agenda in her 2011 novel *The forgotten waltz*:

> The day we moved in, Conor was inside in among the boxes, sitting at his laptop like a demented organist, cursing the internet connection. I didn't complain. We needed the money. The next few months were all about work and there was something frantic and lonely about our love in that little house (don't get sentimental, I tell myself, the sockets moved in the wall every time you stuck in a plug). We clung to each other. Six months, nine—I don't know how long that phase lasted. Mortgage love. Shagging at 5.3 per cent.

The Irish academic Ashling Jackson has argued in her examination of changing attitudes to cohabitation ahead of marriage that 'marriage is all about setting up home'. This view is backed up by social analysis. The 2008 European Values Survey found that almost 90% of Irish respondents felt that good housing was important for a successful marriage. Jackson's research demonstrates that young Irish couples do not consider home ownership before they move in together, but buying a house is a critical aspect of the decision to marry.

How do we account for this unexpected intrusion of the responsibility of mortgages on the romance of marriage? For historical reasons, connected in a complicated way to the colonial past, home ownership carries a heavy significance in Irish culture. John B. Keane's *The field* is just the most famous of the many works of literature that rotate around the desire to own a patch of land. This aspiration persists in the contemporary era, when changes in the Irish economy have made home ownership a more remote possibility for many.

One of the factors at play in the continuing attraction of home ownership in Ireland is that owner-occupation is the surest way to establish secure housing. Renting leaves the tenant at the mercy of the vagaries of the market and the convenience of the landlord. Availability of public housing has not come close to keeping in step with demand—there are now more than 200,000 people on housing lists. In such a context, as a young person's thoughts turn towards the future, to potential marriage and to child-rearing, plans for a mortgage tend to follow close behind.

Even with a cataclysmic property crash in 2008, the average price of a house has trebled in the last generation. Concerns around security of housing are not abstract fears, as evidenced by the rise in homelessness. Over 10,000 people are officially without a home. To buy any house is out of the reach of most people on their own. Marriage and mortgage are thus tied together, not because of some romantic, patriotic echo from the era of Ascendancy landlords or because Irish people are convinced that there is something intrinsically sexy about discussions of Annual Percentage Rates and Early Repayment Charges. We find weddings and home ownership woven together in our cultural fabric because of very contingent political decisions. Marriage is a scaffolding that makes housing possible. Prioritising market-based solutions to housing provision and construing homes as commodities has meant that, for most people, the only way to be sure of the roof over their head is to have a ring on their finger.

Further reading

Anne Enright, *The forgotten waltz* (Toronto, 2011).

Seamus Heaney, *Death of a naturalist* (London, 2006).

Ashling Jackson, 'Premarital cohabitation as a pathway into marriage. An investigation into how premarital cohabitation is transforming the institution of marriage in Ireland' (unpublished Ph.D thesis, Maynooth University, 2011).

John B. Keane, *The field* (Cork, 1991).

79

A snapshot of marriage in Irish society, 2016[1]

Aoife McGrath

Marriage has always been a popular institution in Irish society. From the time of the first population census of the Irish Free State in 1926, the number of people getting married has steadily increased, even on those occasions when the total population decreased. Since 1977 the percentage of the overall population of the Republic who are married has remained stable at around 37%. In the last recorded census (2016) there were 1,702,289 private households in Ireland, in which 4,676,648 people live (the remaining people live in communal establishments). Of these 1.7 million households, married households make up 48.5%. The most numerous are those comprised of married couples with children, i.e. 529,687 households; 254,744 households contain married couples living alone, and a further 41,119 contain married couples living either with other people or with children and other people. This is the same proportion of households led by married couples as in the previous census of 2011. Thus, despite the growing diversity in types of family units in contemporary Ireland (such as single-parent families and families based on cohabiting couples), families centred on married couples are of definite, and continuing, importance.

Marriage also holds an honoured place in the law of Ireland. While the constitution of the Irish Free State in 1922 contained no provision relating to family and marriage, in 1937 the new constitution of Ireland, *Bunreacht na hÉireann*, made provision for protecting the place of marriage within Irish society. In it, '[t]he State pledges itself to guard with special care the institution of Marriage, on which the Family is founded, and to protect it against attack' (Article 41.3.1°). In fact, it considers the family founded on marriage 'as the necessary basis of social order and as indispensable to the welfare of the

---

1 All statistical data included in this article are based on information obtained from the Central Statistics Office's website. Any errors are my own.

Nation and the State' (Article 41.1.2°). These articles ensured that married parents and their children received constitutional recognition and protection.

While the text of the Irish constitution did not define marriage as being between persons of the opposite sex, for most of its history the judicial legal system interpreted the constitutional provisions for marriage in that way. In March 2004 there was a debate in Dáil Éireann regarding amendments to social welfare legislation which would restrict the benefits of welfare schemes to the 'spouses' of qualified people, thereby excluding same-sex (and other non-married) partners. Subsequently, the Civil Registration Act 2004 explicitly declared that there was an 'impediment to a marriage' if 'both parties are of the same sex' (Interpretation §2.2e). In December 2006 the Irish High Court held that marriage as defined in the Irish constitution was between persons of the opposite sex and that there was no breach of rights in the refusal of the Revenue Commissioners to recognise foreign same-sex marriages.

For many, however, the composition of the constitution with respect to marriage comprised a human rights issue. They argued that Irish domestic law denied the internationally recognised human right of adults, regardless of sexual orientation, to enter into consensual civil marriage (*Universal Declaration of Human Rights*, Article 16). Furthermore, they argued, excluding same-sex relationships from the institution of marriage prevents same-sex couples from accessing a range of other rights, including rights to housing, social security, inheritance and the guardianship of children. These human rights issues concerned the many same-sex couples in Ireland: in the 2011 national census there were 4,042 same-sex couples cohabiting in Ireland (2,321 male couples and 1,721 female couples); 230 were same-sex couples with children, with the vast majority of these being female couples. In addition, 166 same-sex couples indicated in the 2011 census that they were married. Such marriages presumably took place in foreign countries, and these only became recognised as Irish civil partnerships when the Civil Partnership and Certain Rights and Obligations of Cohabitants Act 2010 came into effect in January 2011.

This Civil Partnership Act granted same-sex couples rights and obligations towards each other that were comparable to (opposite-sex) married couples. The national census captured same-sex partnerships for the first time in 2016. In April of that year there were 1,539 couples in the 'registered same-sex civil partnership' category. The Civil Partnership Act could not grant these couples the same legal status as married couples, however: for instance, the act did not make provision for the adoption or guardianship of children parented by same-sex couples, or for custody, access or maintenance payments for those children.

In 2015 the Irish public voted in a referendum to amend the constitution to specify that '[m]arriage may be contracted in accordance with law by two persons without distinction as to their sex' (Article 41.4). This amendment granted equal opportunity to marry, and the equal rights and obligations which constitutional recognition and protection provides, to both same-sex and opposite-sex couples. Following this amendment, the 2016 census records that 706 same-sex couples indicated that they were married.

The desire for civil recognition of same-sex marriage illustrates the continued popularity of marriage in Ireland. Of course, trends in cohabitation and marital breakdown (i.e. separation and divorce) have an impact on the presumed appeal of this institution.

Cohabitation has been increasing in the Republic since the mid-1990s, but the rate of growth has slowed considerably in the inter-censal periods. In the period between 1996 and 2002, households led by cohabiting couples increased by nearly 148% (from 31,229 households to 77,411); this rate of increase slowed to 53.9% in 2006, to 18% in 2011 and to only 5.7% in 2016. The total number of households led by cohabiting couples currently stands at 148,998, according to 2016 census figures, which amounts to 8.75% of the 1.7 million households in Ireland. The majority of these cohabiting households contain couples with children but no other persons (68,979 households), which is an increase of 25.6% since the 2011 census. Cohabiting couples living on their own (of which there are 68,396 households) is the second most common category in cohabiting households. This is actually a decrease of 6% from the previous census.

While the overall growth of cohabitation has slowed considerably, within cohabiting households there is continued growth in the proportion that contain couples with children. This may indicate a growing minority of couples for whom cohabitation (even with children) is an alternative to marriage. Nevertheless, there is still sufficient evidence to suggest that for most people cohabitation remains a prelude to marriage.

To measure the rate of marital breakdown in Ireland one calculates the number of separated and divorced persons as a proportion of those who were 'ever married' (i.e. the total number of married, separated/divorced and widowed persons). It is evident that this rate has increased steadily since 1986. There was a sharp increase from 5.3% in 1996 to 7.5% in 2002, following the fifteenth amendment to the Constitution of Ireland (1995), which provided for the dissolution of marriage under certain conditions (Article 41.3.2°). By 2016 the number of divorced persons had increased by 196% since 2002 (the first census following the introduction of divorce in Ireland). The 2016 census records 118,178 people as being separated, with a further 103,895 divorced. In total, this number constitutes a 10% rate in marital breakdown, up from 9.7% in the 2011 census. It is noteworthy that different census results consistently record a higher proportion of women in both the separated and divorced categories. The Central Statistics Office (CSO) attributes this (at least partially) to the higher proportion of men recorded in the remarried category.

For the sake of comparison with the percentage of married and cohabiting households in Ireland, it is useful to cross-reference the number of households with the marital status of the Household Reference Person (HRP). (The concept of the HRP allows the CSO to characterise a whole household according to characteristics of the chosen reference person.) This process shows that the number of households characterised by divorce in 2016 was 75,611 (up from 62,803 in 2011), and the number characterised by separation was 93,524 (up from 93,393). In other words, marital breakdown now directly affects almost 10% of the 1.7 million households in Ireland.

Notes on contributors

Sharon Arbuthnot has worked as a researcher and editor of the electronic *Dictionary of the Irish language* (eDIL), based at Queen's University Belfast, since 2009.

Joe Armstrong is a Humanist chaplain and celebrant.

Linda-May Ballard worked for many years as a curator at the Ulster Folk and Transport Museum, and is a minister in the Non-Subscribing Presbyterian Church of Ireland.

Katie Barclay is Associate Professor in the ARC Centre for the History of Emotions and the Department of History, University of Adelaide.

Sparky Booker is a lecturer in Irish Medieval History at the School of History, Anthropology, Philosophy and Politics, Queen's University Belfast.

David Bracken is the Limerick diocesan archivist.

Liam Breatnach is a senior professor in the School of Celtic Studies, Dublin Institute for Advanced Studies.

Sarah-Anne Buckley is a lecturer in History at the National University of Ireland, Galway.

Jenny Butler is a lecturer in the Study of Religions at University College Cork, and her research areas include new religious movements and Irish folk religion.

Angela Byrne is Department of Foreign Affairs and Trade historian-in-residence at EPIC, the Irish Emigration Museum, and research associate at Ulster University.

Leanne Calvert is a research fellow in Intangible Cultural Heritage at the University of Hertfordshire.

Caitriona Clear lectures in History at the National University of Ireland, Galway.

Patrick Comerford is a priest in the (Church of Ireland) diocese of Limerick, precentor of St Mary's Cathedral, Limerick, a former lecturer at the Church of Ireland Theological Institute and a former adjunct assistant professor at Trinity College Dublin.

Art Cosgrove is an Irish historian and one of the board of editors of the nine-volume *A new history of Ireland*. He served as president of University College Dublin from 1994 to 2003.

Bernadette Cunningham is deputy librarian in the Royal Irish Academy.

Eamon Darcy is author of *The world of Thomas Ward: sex and scandal in late seventeenth-century Co. Antrim* and teaches at Maynooth University.

Kristina Katherine Decker is a Ph.D student in History at University College Cork.

Johnny Doherty, CSsR, is based at the Redemptorist Community, Clonard Monastery, Belfast. He is the originator of 'A Movement of Continuous Prayer for Marriage and Family Life'.

Terence Dooley is director of the Centre for the Study of Historic Irish Houses and Estates, Department of History, Maynooth University.

John Glynn Douglas was a historian of the Society of Friends in Ireland. He died in February 2018.

Charlene M. Eska is an associate professor in the Department of English at Virginia Tech, USA.

Stephen Farragher is a priest of the archdiocese of Tuam and director of Knock Marriage Introductions.

Orla Fitzpatrick is a photo historian with a Ph.D from Ulster University.

Raymond Gillespie teaches at the Department of History, Maynooth University.

Kevin Hargaden leads the Jesuit Centre for Faith and Justice, where he works as a social theologian. He is an elder in the Presbyterian Church in Ireland.

Janice Holmes is a Visiting Research Fellow in History at the Open University, UK.

Ashling Jackson is senior lecturer in the Department of Social Sciences, Athlone Institute of Technology.

James Kelly is professor of History and head of the School of History and Geography, Dublin City University.

Liam Kelly, who was born in County Leitrim, is a priest of the diocese of Kilmore.

Laurence Kirkpatrick is professor of Church History in the Institute of Theology, Queen's University Belfast.

Kiera Lindsey is a Senior Research Fellow at the University of Technology Sydney (UTS), where she is conducting an Australian Research Council Discovery Early Career Researcher Award. She has written and presented for Foxtel's History Channel and ABC Radio.

Maria Luddy is professor emerita of Modern Irish History, University of Warwick.

John McCafferty is a professor of History at UCD and chairman of the Irish Manuscripts Commission.

Lir Mac Cárthaigh is art director at Veritas Publications, Dublin.

Barbara McCormack is a Special Collections Librarian at Maynooth University and St Patrick's College, Maynooth.

Michael McDonagh is a graduate of Maynooth University and has a research interest in Traveller history and language.

Nell McDonagh holds a Master's degree from Dublin City University and has an interest in Traveller community and cultural issues and Traveller history.

Valerie McGowan-Doyle is professor of History at Lorain County Community College and adjunct associate professor of History at Kent State University.

Aoife McGrath is lecturer in Pastoral Theology and Academic & Pastoral Support Coordinator at the Pontifical University, St Patrick's College, Maynooth.

Ciarán Mac Murchaidh is Head of School in Fiontar & Scoil na Gaeilge at Dublin City University.

Bronagh Ann McShane is post-doctoral fellow in the Humanities, National University of Ireland, Galway.

Carol Maddock works on exhibitions at the National Library of Ireland.

Denis G. Marnane is a County Tipperary local historian and author. His latest work is *The 3rd Brigade: a history of the Volunteers/IRA in South Tipperary, 1913–1921*, published by Tipperary County Council Library Service.

Olivia Martin is in her fourth year of a Ph.D (History) programme at the National University of Ireland, Galway.

Ciara Meehan is reader in History and head of History at the University of Hertfordshire.

Miriam Moffitt lectures in Church History at St Patrick's College, Maynooth.

Gerard Moran is a researcher at the Social Science Research Centre at the National University of Ireland, Galway, and has lectured in the Department of History at NUIG and Maynooth University.

Kevin Myers is a writer and sociologist. He is currently working as a research associate with the School of Education at Hibernia College.

Shawn Nichols-Boyle is a senior lecturer in the Department of English, Indiana University, South Bend, Indiana.

Colmán Ó Clabaigh is a monk of Glenstal Abbey, Co. Limerick, and a medieval historian.

Thomas O'Connor is professor of History at Maynooth University, director of the Maynooth University Humanities Research Institute and editor of *Archivium Hibernicum*.

Thomas O'Loughlin is professor of Historical Theology at the University of Nottingham.

Pádraig Ó Macháin is professor of Modern Irish, University College Cork.

Maeve O'Riordan is lecturer in Women's and Cultural History at University College Cork.

Sophia Martina Pallaro is a Ph.D candidate in the School of Sociology at University College Dublin.

Oliver P. Rafferty, SJ, is professor of Modern Irish and Ecclesiastical History at Boston College.

Jennifer Redmond is a lecturer in Twentieth-Century Irish History and director of the MA in Irish History at Maynooth University.

Ciarán Reilly is a historian of nineteenth- and twentieth-century Ireland based at Maynooth University.

Nicole Robinson is a professional soprano currently studying for her Ph.D in Musicology at the DIT Conservatory of Music and Drama.

Brendan Scott is a historian of early modern Ireland and editor of the *Breifne* journal.

Anthony Shanahan holds a Master's in Theology (History of Christianity) from St Patrick's College, Maynooth, and is based in Thurles, Co. Tipperary.

Jonathan A. Smyth works at Johnston Central Library, Cavan. He is an author and writes a weekly history column in *The Anglo-Celt*.

Frank J. Sweeney is a native of Donegal. He has taught for many years and has a Ph.D in History from Maynooth University.

Catherine Swift is lecturer in Medieval and Irish Studies at Mary Immaculate College, University of Limerick.

Clodagh Tait is a lecturer in the Department of History, Mary Immaculate College, University of Limerick.

Sonja Tiernan is Eamon Cleary Chair of Irish Studies and Co-Director of the Centre for Irish and Scottish Studies at the University of Otago.

Gregory Toner is professor of Irish, Queen's University, Belfast.

Thomas M. Truxes is clinical professor of Irish Studies and History, Glucksman Ireland House, New York University.

Diane Urquhart is a reader in Modern Irish History at the Institute of Irish Studies of the University of Liverpool.

Freya Verstraten Veach is a Victoria County History research associate at the University of Hull.

Jean Walker is a historian specialising in gendered aspects of Irish social history and histories of health and medicine.

Fionnuala Walsh is a lecturer in the School of History, University College Dublin.

C.J. Woods retired in 2006 from the Royal Irish Academy, where he was employed on its *New history of Ireland* and *Dictionary of Irish biography* projects; he was also an occasional lecturer in History at Maynooth.

Penelope Woods was formerly in charge of early printed books and manuscripts at the Russell Library, Maynooth University, and St Patrick's College, Maynooth. She writes on book history.

Jonathan Jeffrey Wright lectures in the Department of History at Maynooth University.

Natalie Wynn is a post-doctoral researcher affiliated to the Herzog Centre for Jewish and Near Eastern Religions and Culture, Trinity College Dublin.